Debi Marshall is a freelance
Tasmania. She writes extensively
ing in crime, and is an experien
A qualified teacher (BA, Dip E
English at college and university.

Also by Debi Marshall

Her Father's Daughter: The Bonnie Henderson Story
Lang Hancock

JUSTICE
IN JEOPARDY

The Unsolved Murder of Baby Deidre Kennedy

DEBI MARSHALL

RANDOM HOUSE AUSTRALIA

Random House Australia Pty Ltd
20 Alfred Street, Milsons Point, NSW 2061
http://www.randomhouse.com.au

Sydney New York Toronto
London Auckland Johannesburg

First published by Random House Australia 2005

National Library of Australia
Cataloguing-in-Publication Entry

Marshall, Debi.
Justice in jeopardy.

ISBN 1 74051 338 X.

1. Carroll, Raymond John. 2. Kennedy, Deidre. 3. Murder –
Australia – Case studies. 4. Victims of crime – Australia.
5. Children – Crimes against – Australia. I. Title.

364.1523

Cover design by Darian Causby/highway51.com.au
Back cover photo courtesy Faye Kennedy
Typeset by Midland Typesetters, Maryborough, Victoria
Printed and bound by Griffin Press, Netley, South Australia

10 9 8 7 6 5 4 3 2 1

For two very special women:
my daughter, Louise, and mother, Monica

In memory of Deidre

'Delay of justice is injustice.'

Walter Landor 1775-1864

Preface

I first read the story of Deidre Kennedy in the *Australian* newspaper, in early 2003. Overwhelmingly moved by it, I contacted Deidre's mother, Faye Kennedy, with a view to writing a feature article. Tired and emotional, Faye politely declined and I agreed to wait 12 months before I contacted her again.

In February 2004, Faye agreed to an interview with me for a national magazine. On a sweltering 44-degree day in Ipswich, the Queensland city where her daughter had been murdered 31 years before, we met for the first time. Despite the intense heat, she was dignified and poised but also still raw with grief, shaken by events and determined that her daughter's death would not be in vain.

It was during this interview that Faye agreed to cooperate with me and tell her family's side of the story in a book. In doing so, she knew she would have to re-open all the wounds and re-visit a tragedy that was so traumatic it was a miracle she ever recovered.

Sometimes words fail you. Sometimes there is nothing that can be said to help cross the divide of a mother's agony. And so it was this day, and in the interviews that followed.

Hounded by the press for more than two decades and heeding legal advice to say nothing, neither Raymond John Carroll – the man accused of Deidre's murder but acquitted of all charges he has faced in relation to the Kennedy case – nor any member of his family would talk to the media. Here, for the first time, is their side of the story. The story of Raymond Carroll. His third wife, Marilyn. His sister Sandra and her former husband, Roger. His widowed mother, Ilma. Each has kept their silence for more than 20 years until now.

All recollections or thoughts from Raymond Carroll or a family member not written in quotations have been taken directly from the taped, face-to-face interview I had with them or from phone interviews.

All narrative is taken directly from taped interviews, court transcripts or press reports. The only exceptions to this are when I have recreated scenes using information gained from interviews with police, lawyers and/or journalists who covered the court cases and dealt with the Kennedy or Carroll families. These recreations are a faithful word portrait of what was told to me and include a recreation of the killer's movements before and after Deidre's abduction. They also include events, emotions and atmosphere during the trials and appeals. All psychological profiling and sections including sexual fetishism and psychopathic make-up are the results of interviews with both a forensic psychiatrist and criminologist. Some interviews, of necessity, have been edited for length or repetition, but all use the vernacular of the person speaking.

Given the harrowing subject matter, this was a sad, difficult and sometimes bewildering book to write. For reasons that still remain a mystery, some senior bureaucrats and other agencies did not cooperate with my search for material.

This story seemed relatively straightforward, at first. But beneath the tragedy of a baby's murder, the trials and the acquittals, lurked a murky swamp that I had not anticipated. Human nature, bastardry, ego and ambition often collided with my search for truth. I should have been prepared for this. But I was not.

As a journalist for the past 20 years, covering countless crime stories, including the 'bodies in the barrel' serial murders in South Australia, the Port Arthur massacre and interviews with parents of scores of missing children around Australia, I thought I was prepared for what I would encounter. Again, I was not. Professionally, I kept building a brick wall as a fortress against the terrible details, but on a personal level – as a mother – I found it impossible to keep an emotional distance. This story strikes at the heart of every parent's fear – an innocent child the victim of a depraved paedophile, abducted, sexually abused and murdered. Every time I looked at photographs of a smiling Deidre taken before her murder, or of the savagery inflicted on her after her abduction, I cried. This was a story that seeped into my soul, and, by its conclusion, I could understand the obsession of the Kennedy family, police, lawyers, forensic experts and politicians to find out who killed baby Deidre. It had become an obsession for me, too.

I was often asked what compelled me to write such a gruesome story. How I could immerse myself, for months, in researching the intimate details of such a terrible crime. My answer was that I believe this is a story that must be told. Time will not erase the facts – that a child was murdered and that her killer has not been brought to justice. *Someone* knows who is responsible for Deidre's death. Perhaps the story will trigger a memory, stir a conscience, even a death-bed confession. Perhaps the laws of double jeopardy, so long under legal scrutiny, will change in line with modern technology. And perhaps, one day, the question 'Who killed Deidre Kennedy?' will finally, definitively, be answered.

PART ONE
Abduction and Murder: 1973–1984

'Closure is bullshit . . . the ramifications of murder go on and on and on.'

James Ellroy, 'Feast of Death'

Prologue

'Did you kill Deidre Kennedy?'
   'I did not.'

1

'**R**ight. Now it's my turn to ask *you* a question.' Raymond John Carroll has moved closer toward me. Close enough so that I can smell his cigarette breath and notice the tendrils of grey hairs that snake through the moustache covering his lips and teeth. Those teeth: Exhibit A in two Supreme Court trials, two appeals and a High Court hearing. He has fixed me with a penetrating stare. 'Well? *Now* do you think I did it?'

The question has caught me off-guard and a sudden, awkward silence follows.

'Answer me, please.' Raymond Carroll's voice has taken on a steely edge, more a demand than a request. He crunches the word under his tongue. *Please.* 'First impressions.'

This interview has been conducted in secret, and no one but Carroll and his family know where I am. It is warm on this October 2004 late afternoon, but a sudden chill has entered the room. For the first time all day, I feel slightly uneasy. Carroll's sister, Sandra, and his wife, Marilyn, are watching, alert as desert dingoes for my reply. I find my voice and peer up at Carroll, who is significantly taller than myself. 'I'm not here to make a judgment.'

'I'm not asking you to make a judgment.'

'Yes, you are.' My voice sounds wavery, thin as broth, and my laugh, designed to diffuse the tension, is tinny.

He will not give up. 'I'm asking you for your *impression*, please. Do you think I did it?'

I shuffle self-consciously. 'Raymond, the basis of you agreeing to talk to me was that you could terminate this interview at any time if you felt I was putting you on trial again. That was our agreement. It would be wrong of me to voice an opinion, so please don't ask me for one. I'm not here to make a judgment.'

It is time to take my leave.

2

Overnight showers drape the city in a damp overcoat and a light squall torments autumn leaves, bullying them into sodden pockets. A McCafferty's bus rumbles along Ipswich's wide streets on this April 1973 morning. Past the famous limestone hills of Queensland's oldest provincial city, poised at the crossroads to the Darling Downs and Upper Brisbane Valley; past Limestone Park and along the banks of the Bremer River. Soon, dawn will humour the sky into betraying its first crimson blush and the tired whoosh of air brakes will herald the Ipswich bus station for the passengers aboard.

Faye Kennedy rubs her eyes and rouses her two sleeping daughters, gently tousling their hair. 'Wake up, girls. We're here.' After waving goodbye to Grandma on Thursday morning, five-year-old Stephanie, always a sound sleeper, had happily snuggled down for most of the 17-hour bus trip from Longreach, in the state's parched west. But her chubby 17-month-old sister, Deidre, had been restless, climbing onto her mother's lap, wriggling and squirming throughout the long night. She had shyly buried her face in the crook of her elbow and burrowed her mop of blonde hair into her mother's chest when strangers had tried to amuse her in the night by playing peek-a-boo through their fingers. It had taken Faye hours to get her to sleep. Always superstitious, Faye's mother, Frieda, had warned her daughter to be off the highway and back home in Ipswich by Friday the 13th. Faye is grateful they have finally made it home.

She gathers her belongings and peers out the window to see if her husband, Barry, is waiting for them. It's an ungodly hour of the morning to haul him out of bed – 5.30 – and there is a definite nip in the air. He has been in and out of hospital for knee surgery and is now on crutches, but he's there as promised. At 26, he is two years older than his wife, and has the quiet affability of a bloke raised in the bush. Tall, with a hint of strawberry in his fair hair and Queensland-bronzed, he and Faye have been separated for six weeks, far too long for childhood sweethearts married six years who hate being apart. Faye taps on the window to get his attention, nudges the girls, *Look, there's Daddy.* They press their faces to the glass and Barry grins back, waving.

It's good to be home.

3

The shadows hide him. Crouching beneath the windowsill, his back ramrod straight and breath shallow. Breathing through his nose: in, out, in, out, and barely a rise in his heartbeat. No sounds in this suburban neighbourhood on the southern fringe of Ipswich city, save for canned laugher resonating from a television inside the house and an occasional car crawling along nearby kerbs. Young lovers cruising to find a place to park. Married men trawling for a quick liaison with a gay stranger.

He had passed no one as he noiselessly prowled the area, glancing up at windows shuttered against the chill of this Friday night. Friday the 13th. It had warmed to 21 degrees during the day, but the soles of his shoes are wet from the intermittent after-noon showers and his face flushed from walking – up around the empty park, cutting through backyards, dawdling the perimeters of vacant blocks. Police would later estimate the late-night excur-sion as somewhere between 10 and midnight. Prowling aimlessly, wandering around for hours. And now he has ended up here, loitering outside this old Queenslander with ladies' underwear hanging on the wide veranda.

Inside the house, in his bedroom off the veranda, Cecil – known for years by his nickname 'Nugget' – shifts his frame around the bed and grunts. His fever has broken but he still feels crook, the after-math of a throat infection that has lasted a week. He hawks into a grubby hanky and feels the rattle of a nasty cough deep in his chest. He has been on a Totally and Permanently Incapacitated pension since 1956 and the doctor has told him to give up the fags but, at 73, he figures it's not worth it. 'They'll kill you, Nugget,' the doctor had warned. 'That's if the grog doesn't get you first.' Nugget's teeth are the colour of mustard and dirty water and his receding hairline erupts into a shock of white hair that crowns a craggy face. He'll be dead within a year.

Nugget hauls himself up on one elbow and feels around the bedcover for his smokes. Pushes himself up to the side of his bed, sitting in the dark, rolling a twirly. He can hear Arthur Borchert's missus, Kathleen, and kids in the next room. It's always noisy: if it's not two-month-old Archie, the youngest of the brood of six, bawling for his bottle, it's the TV blaring through his bedroom wall. Bloody thing is never turned off: 'Hey Hey it's Saturday' to kick off the weekend, American soapies on weekdays and some wacky comedy at night – Graham Kennedy or Paul Hogan clowning around with his sidekick, Strop. Nugget has been boarding with the family at 14 Short Street for months. Sometimes he joins them to watch their favourite crime series, 'Homicide', but he mostly stays in his room, away from the racket. The family never turns on a light in the lounge: only the flickering of the television illuminates the room.

Arthur would now be in the kitchen with his mate, drinking and playing records. Forty years old, short and plump, his beatnik hairstyle straggles to his shoulders. Nugget would normally join Arthur for a drink, but he feels too crook tonight. He had heard them come in around 7.30, crossing the front veranda that extended along both sides of the dilapidated Queenslander, clanking through the front door with their dozen takeaways of Fourex beer after a session at their local watering hole, the City View Hotel – a euphemistic name; the only view from the front bar was a greasy window discoloured with cigarette smoke.

It can get a bit noisy at this end of the house; Nugget has more than once thrown up the sash window and snarled at the kids to piss off when they played outside his bedroom, darting in and out of the washing strung up on a makeshift line on the veranda. Nappies. Shirts. Nylon stockings. Ladies' brassieres and underwear in varying sizes, flapping in the breeze, colourful as a Chinese laundry. The house would once have been magnificent, with high ceilings, an impressively wide hallway and ornate features, but years of neglect from grungy tenants in this grungy side of town has bowed the old girl in defeat. The weatherboard needs painting and broken windowpanes fixing; cracks in the wall scream for plaster and the backyard is hidden by debris. Such a mess and a noisy household, with the TV and the kids and a constant stream of visitors, that tenants in the block of four units next door at 12 Short Street, a low-level grey cement block owned by the RAAF, sometimes complain. But nothing is ever done about it. The servicemen and women who work at Amberley RAAF base just out of Ipswich either post out to other bases or quickly move into more permanent housing. Only the bushes and overgrown shrubs that divide the boundary between the Queenslander and the units offer some semblance of privacy.

Tonight, on top of feeling unwell, Nugget's head is still sore from when he tumbled over and gouged out a chunk of his temple after a monumental binge on the rum. Now, distracted by a slight movement outside his window, he rubs his temples and readjusts his gaze to peer through the curtain. The light is on in his bedroom and it is dark on the veranda, but he has no doubt what he can see. The dim outline of a person, crouching underneath his windowsill. Someone is lurking outside.

He thinks it is Arthur Borcherts' 12-year-old son, Paul. Nugget looks again: whoever is outside appears to be between 18 to 20 years old, 172–174cm tall and about 10 stone. Slender build, broad shouldered. Nugget would be specific about the hair colour and length in depositions he would later make to police. The person he saw on the veranda had hair that was 'brown to fairish and about collar length'.

Nugget knows it is pointless to call out. No one in the house can hear him over the din of the music and TV. He grumbles as he hauls himself out of bed and rummages in the suitcase that doubles as his wardrobe, putting on his scuffs and adjusting the elastic of his pyjama pants before he shuffles up the hallway to the kitchen.

'There's a bloke hangin' around on the veranda.'

Arthur has had his fair share of grog, drains his beer glass and stares up at Nugget through blood-shot eyes. 'What? Whaddya mean?'

'There's someone outside me window,' Nugget repeats. 'Snow-dropping stuff off of the fucking veranda.'

Arthur and his mate weave slightly as they scrape back their kitchen chairs and walk outside with Nugget. They thread their way through the washing on the right side of the veranda, opposite the RAAF flats, and walk across the front landing onto the left side of the veranda. Peering over the railing into the darkness for a few seconds, they then head back to the kitchen.

'There's no one there, Nug,' Arthur shrugs, picking up his beer bottle and refilling his glass. 'No one.'

The beer has now run out and it is getting late. Arthur's mate has left, Nugget has gone back to bed and it's time to turn in for the night. Arthur would later recall, when talking to police, that his son from a previous relationship, Paul, had just returned home from a barbecue and had headed straight in to watch TV. He would be adamant: he wasn't that drunk that he couldn't remember small details.

Arthur pulls the kitchen window shut and idly watches a fellow walk down the cement path of the RAAF units opposite his house, toward the end unit furthest secluded from the road. He only just gets a glimpse of him: about 170cm or something, maybe 18, 19 years old. It is dark, except for a light on outside one flat. The bloke is heading down that way and appears to know where he is going. Either toward Unit 3 or 4. It's hard to say.

He tumbles into bed and is asleep within minutes. Arthur Borchert won't hear another sound all night.

4

Stephanie and Deidre, freshly bathed and hair neatly slicked down, giggle as they dance around in the new pyjamas Grandma bought them in Longreach the day before. Stephanie leads the way, and Deidre copies her. It is usually a floorshow: doilies on their heads and tea towels over their shoulders, but tonight, after their long bus trip, they are too tired for a performance.

The family had spent most of the day at their unit, 3/12 Short Street, apart from when they went grocery shopping and looked at the new house assigned to them by the RAAF. Deidre, eager to show that she could walk, tottered around a while with Faye as she hung the washing on the line outside the unit.

Faye is glad that they will soon be moving into their new home and is grateful that the dishevelled family who live in the shabby house near the units haven't yet appeared today to notice that they are back. More than 30 years later, she still remembers them as peculiar. 'They were the oddest people. The woman who lived there used to really bother me; she would just stand and stare at us. Not doing anything but standing there. I'd acknowledge she was there but that was all; kept my back door shut as often as I could so she couldn't see us. The kids used to come to the fence and it was difficult for me to explain to Stephanie why I didn't want her to play with them, without me sounding snobby. One of the girls was starry-eyed with dirty, dark, long hair, and she always wanted to play with Steph. But they were an unsavoury lot. The kids ran around the streets at all hours and they always had grubby noses. The little boy, who was about seven years old, would wander around in a dress any old time and the youngest would drink water or milk out of a beer stubby. It was just awful. As soon as we drove in, over they'd come. They were all ages and there was always someone sitting outside having a beer.' The police, regularly called to the household to sort out domestics, were well acquainted with the family. They reckoned that if they lived in Alabama, they would be called hillbillies.

Deidre wriggles wildly as Faye puts on her night nappy and pilchers under her pyjama pants. 'Keep still, you rascal,' Faye chides. It doesn't take much persuasion: exhausted from the trip back from Longreach, she is almost asleep by the time she is carried up the passage and put into bed around 7.30. Stephanie follows an hour later, tucked up in her bed under the window.

Soon after nine, Faye switches off the lounge-room light. Barry finds moving around on his crutches awkward, and swings up the short passage and straight into bed while Faye checks the unit. There is no need to lock the back door: Ipswich, no more than a big country town despite being called a city, is as safe as it is in Longreach where she and Barry had both grown up.

An hour later, Faye makes a final check of the children. Reaching over Stephanie's bed, she pulls the window shut and slides the curtain before gently tucking the blankets around the shoulders of both sleeping girls. Deidre is in a makeshift bed, on a mattress inside a playpen, closest to the door.

From his vantage point on the veranda of the old Queenslander, hidden by shadows and clothes on the line, he peeps through the chink in the curtain and watches as Faye tenderly kisses her sleeping daughters. He caresses the panties, women's step-ins and a silk half-slip he has just stolen from the line, feels the familiar arousal that always follows his pilfering of underwear. It's not just the risk of stealing without being caught, though that heightens the thrill; it's also naughty, forbidden, which makes it irresistible. A woman's crotch, warm and moist, has actually been inside these panties. They bring back erotic memories.

He had to have it. Had to steal the underwear, had to take it. No matter how great the risk, it is an overwhelming compulsion. He has to. Has to. Has to.

He closes his eyes and shivers, giving in to the sensuous rush that flows through his body as his fantasies take over. He is a naughty boy with stolen underwear. It is his little secret.

Suddenly on high alert, shaken from his fantasies by a noise in the bedroom behind him, he knows he can't afford to hang around here any longer. It seems someone inside the house may have spotted him. He's got to go. Now.

He jumps over the railing, landing softly as a cat in the garden of the RAAF units. Crouching, still before making his move. If the parents don't wake and if the girls don't make a sound, nothing should go wrong. He figures he can be in and out in less than 50 seconds.

He has banked on the unit not being locked, on being able to move stealthily, silently, to where the children are sleeping. The toilet light is on, the only illumination in the darkness. Fifty seconds. That is all he should need to get in and out of there.

There is no sound from the parents' bedroom opposite the passage where the girls are sleeping. He is in the girls' room now, his breath labouring with fear and excitement. Stephanie is deep in dreams, her hair splashing over the pillow. Deidre is at his feet, on the mattress inside the playpen.

Not a sound in the room but the children's gentle breathing. He hovers above Deidre's makeshift cot, swooping down and lifting her out of the blankets and into his arms in one seamless movement. She doesn't stir, her blonde hair falling over his shoulder as he sharply inhales, listening intently to check he has not disturbed the parents. Exiting the same way he came in, he skulks out into the night.

He needs to go somewhere private, where they will be undisturbed. Just him, and his precious possession. Somewhere private.

Only he would know where he took her. It would be his secret. When the pandemonium started, he would quietly gloat at the chaos and grief. The police could wonder all they like about how he entered the unit. Whether he quietly turned the handle of the unlocked back door and crept along the passage with his back to the wall, moving sideways with soft tread, careful not to trip in the darkness. Entering the girls' bedroom and exiting the same way, this time with Deidre in his arms. Or whether he climbed into the girls' bedroom after noiselessly sliding the aluminum window on its tracks, loping in one long stride over Stephanie's bed and picking up her sleeping sister from her cot. Let them wonder if he carried her away on foot, bundled her into a car, defiled her in a caravan or took her straight to the park. Let them ponder. It would be his special secret.

Lurking now at the park's entrance, he glances furtively behind to make sure no one has seen them. It is dark and late and Limestone Park appears deserted. Perfectly deserted. In the distance he can make out the silhouette of the toilet block, used during the day for sporting groups and families enjoying the sunshine and open air. He shifts Deidre higher on his shoulder and plunges into the park, half running under the canopy of trees that sprinkles them both with a wet confetti of leaves. Huddling deeper into his jacket to avoid the shower, he looks at the ground as he quickens his pace into a sprint. He will leave no tracks, no footprints, their absence leading police to the inexorable conclusion – but one they would never be able to prove – that this person seemed to know where he was going.

Stephanie opens her eyes as the first light of day filters into her bedroom, and looks across to her sister's cot. Slipping out of bed, she patters in bare feet across the passage to her parent's room, her small forehead puckered in a frown. 'Mummy, wake up,' she says, tugging urgently at Faye's shoulder. 'Dee Dee's not in her bed.'

5

The lines are blurring between night and day, dawn nudging out the moon, and light peeking through the trees in Limestone Park. The quiet call of migratory birds echoes through the crisp Saturday morning air. It is Westy Mill's routine to exercise his horse early, but the trotter is frisky this morning, trying to shake off his harness.

Something has caught Westy's eye. He turns the reins to manoeuvre his skittish trotter closer to the toilet block, trying to get him to keep still. 'Whoa, boy,' he says, peering up at the roof. 'Whoa.' A right shoulder, arm and head are hanging limply over the guttering. It is a rag doll, identical to those that Westy's three young daughters own. He moves closer, unsteady in the back of the gig.

It is as though she was arranged there, like an obscene Harlequin. Arranged as casually as a pornographic piece of art. Westy's stomach heaves. This is no rag doll. He turns in the gig to see who else is in the park. A man jogging alone on the far side of the oval. Two men training a greyhound less than 6 metres away. And suddenly they are standing next to him, answering his panicked cry that has reverberated through the park. *There's a baby here! A baby! Come over and help!*

Westy is trying to scale up onto the roof, unable to get a grip on the guttering and slipping back down with the dew and damp from yesterday's rain. Climbing the lattice, he straddles it precariously as he leans over and touches the baby. Her head is partly lying on a lady's silk half-slip. Westy has recently completed a first-aid course and feels her tiny wrist for a pulse. Nothing. He wrestles with what he should do. It doesn't appear that rigor mortis has yet set in; the tiny girl may still be alive. But, if he moves her, he could make it worse. He has to do something. Westy turns the baby over, lifts her into his arms, and gently lowers her to the people standing around below.

It would always unsettle them, this memory. Numb with shock, shaking and shuffling from foot to foot. The baby's damp hair clinging to the side of her cheeks, her face a tapestry of bruises where a large hand had run from her forehead to her chin. Diffused marks on one creamy dimpled thigh. Pink pyjama coat with bunny motifs covering the top of her little body, and her nappy, still inside her matching pyjama pants, hastily discarded on the ground outside the toilet. But it is what she is wearing that makes Westy lose all composure, makes him want to heave. Below the waist, her body is grotesquely arranged in women's step-ins and blue panties that come halfway to her chubby knees.

'Oh my God,' Westy blurts, his face ashen. 'Get a doctor, fast!'

'What's up, darling?' Faye is half-asleep, reaching out to Stephanie to snuggle in with her under the blanket. 'What's wrong?'

Stephanie repeated what she has just told her mother. 'Dee Dee is not in her bed.'

Stephanie can't be right. Deidre has only just started walking, tottering uncertainly on her little legs and reaching out her arms for Faye to pick her up when she falls down. It is not possible that she has climbed out of the playpen on her own. 'She has to be there, darling,' Faye says. She is startled, now wide-awake. Deidre is too little to open doors on her own. 'Of course she's there.'

Faye crosses the passage and switches the light on in the girls' bedroom. The cot is empty; Deidre's bottle of milk lies abandoned on the floor. Barry is standing behind his wife now, leaning on his crutches and gently quizzing Stephanie. 'You sure Dee Dee wasn't in bed when you woke up, Steph?' Deidre's blanket is pulled back, but everything else is as it had been the night before.

The little girl shakes her head, looks solemnly at her sister's cot. 'No, Daddy,' she says, her bottom lip starting to tremble. 'She wasn't there.'

Barry opens wardrobe doors while Faye searches under the beds. Bile is rising in her throat and she is struggling to control her panic. 'Deidre,' she calls, her voice shaky. 'Bubby, answer me. Where are you?'

Opening and closing cupboards, searching behind the couch,

frantically pulling back the blankets on their bed in case she is somehow hiding in there. Around and around the small unit, up and down the pathways outside. Stephanie is crying now, scared her little sister hasn't been found and shaken by her parents' panic. A cry catches in Faye's voice. 'You stay here with Daddy, Steph, and I'll go and talk to the man next door.' She looks at Barry, his face parchment white and he nods in agreement. They don't have a phone and Faye can move much faster than he can on crutches.

Banging on their neighbour Ian Lay's door with the balls of her fists. Hyperventilating, her breath steamy against the early-morning chill. Frantic now, begging him to please hurry up and open the door. He is tying the belt on his dressing-gown as he groggily answers her knock. 'What's up, Faye?'

Ian works with Barry at the RAAF base, but he doesn't know the family that well. The Kennedys haven't been in Ipswich very long. 'Deidre's missing. Deidre's gone. We've looked everywhere for her.' Faye's voice sounds disconnected, hollow, rattling in staccato sentences. 'Deidre's missing. We need some help to look for her.'

Ian stares dumbly at her for a brief moment, as though she has gone mad. 'What?'

'Deidre's missing.'

He has finally absorbed what she is telling him. 'Oh God, Faye. How long has she been gone?'

'I don't know. She wasn't in her cot this morning.'

Ian throws on some clothes and retraces Faye and Barry's steps in and outside the unit. It doesn't take him long to realise they are wasting valuable time. 'I'll be as quick as I can,' he tells them. 'I'm going to get the police.'

Barry and Faye stay behind. Opening kitchen cupboards, looking under the beds, calling out their daughter's name. Deidre has to be somewhere.

Detective-Sergeant John Reynolds yawns and looks up at the clock. It has been relatively quiet for a Friday-night graveyard shift: the usual drunks spoiling for a stoush after they have pissed their week's wages up against the wall, and the odd domestic, nothing too serious. Just under two hours to go and he can clock off at 8 o'clock, go home to his family for a leisurely Saturday-morning breakfast.

He snaps his head up from his paperwork as a bloke charges through the front door, planting the palms of his hands on the front counter to steady himself. He is babbling incoherently. 'Take it easy, mate,' Reynolds says. 'Slow down and tell me what's happened. First of all, what's your name?'

'Linklater. Ian Linklater.'

Reynolds leans in closer. The bloke obviously hasn't been drinking but something has badly unnerved him.

He takes a shaky breath before he continues. 'There's a dead baby in Limestone Park. All bruised and dressed up in ladies' underwear. A bloke found her and yelled out to us to help. She was on top of the toilet block. You'd better get down there, quick.'

Reynolds, who had joined the force six years before, in 1967, passes the information through the chain of command before he heads to the park. Detectives from Brisbane are immediately mobilised to Ipswich, a 40-minute drive away. Senior-sergeants from Reynolds's station had gone straight down after they received his report and a few bystanders are craning their necks to see what has happened. Reynolds moves in to join his colleagues, bowing his head, shocked and sickened when he sees her. Through all his years in the force and long after he leaves it, it is an image that will haunt him. She is only a baby, an innocent, defenceless child about the same age as his own daughter. Just like a little doll with blonde hair. So very tiny. Dressed in a pink pyjama top with rabbit motifs. Bashed, judging by the bruises on her face. Marks on her leg that look like human bites. No lacerations or indentations, just bruising. But the way she is dressed, the sick, sad way she is dressed below the waist, makes him recoil. Women's panties, a half-slip and step-ins that reach down toward her knee. Reynolds has no doubt that the poor tot has been the sexual plaything of an extremely deranged individual. He silently prays that she was suffocated before she was interfered with.

Police officer Robert Burns takes photographs of the dead child in situ. He places the camera on a tripod to keep it steady and to get clear photographs of the bite marks that are at randomly different angles and distances from her knee. He attaches a graph – known as a 'G scale' – to the picture, a standard reference that enables police photographers to reproduce a negative to the same size as the original object.

Reynolds looks at his colleagues, who are also fighting back tears. No amount of police training can prepare an officer for this. 'Oh my God,' he says, half to himself. 'Who would do this? What sort of sick monster would do this?'

Reynolds returns to the station. It's 7.35 and he can knock off shortly. But someone out there has lost a child.

His thoughts are interrupted as a man runs through the door, heading straight to him at the counter. It is the Kennedys' neighbour, Ian Lay. He is perspiring, beads of sweat shining above his top lip. 'There's a baby missing from the RAAF units at 12 Short Street,' he blurts. 'About 17 months old. We don't know how long she's been gone. She wasn't in her cot this morning.'

Policemen are walking toward Faye's unit. She knows, with a mother's instinct, that something is wrong. Knows by the look on their faces, the hunch in their shoulders, that it is bad news. The policeman's name is Kennedy, a small coincidence that she will always remember. A kindly older man with two younger officers.

She stamps her feet, stumbling backward and cowering from them as though they will physically hurt her. Covering her ears and face with her forearms, she now lurches forward, pummelling her fists into the older policeman's chest. She feels she is at the edge of the planet, stepping off into a dark void, an alien, terrifying darkness from which she will never return. The world is spinning, metallic sky meeting ground, and she feels she will fall. 'No, no, no!' she screams, a tortured, primeval wail that escapes from deep within her. 'No! Oh, please God, no!' The policemen look to Barry, Faye now crumpled limp in his arms. 'We're so sorry, Mr Kennedy. We think we have found your daughter.'

6

Dr William Josephson, called to urgently attend at Limestone Park, also initially thinks that this is a doll lying on the ground, somebody's idea of a perverse joke. He blanches when he sees it is a child, her temples, head and neck covered in extensive bruising and with abrasions over her left eye and upper lip. He notices that haemorrhaging is evident in the tissue under her skin and that she has obviously been strangled, though the small bones in her larynx are not broken. The doctor's eyes are drawn to the baby's upper left leg, covered in bluish marks between the knee and hip. He runs his ungloved hand over the marks to see if he can feel any indentation. Heavy bite marks would indent the skin, but a lighter bite would leave only bruising. Josephson is satisfied that there appears to be no indentation.

Josephson is shattered by what he sees. He has been a doctor for many years, and has been called to attend at numerous scenes: murders, suicides, a plane crash. But he is staggered by the murder of this tiny girl, colour draining from his face as he looks at her.

There is no question in Dr Josephson's mind that the marks, clear against the baby's soft flesh, are bites but he is not absolutely certain as to when they were inflicted. He would later surmise they were inflicted at or around the time of death, but it may have been earlier. What he did know was that Deidre had died several hours before he saw her. Hypostasis – the medical term for when fluid and blood accumulates in the lower parts of the body – had already set in. That only happens hours after death.

Barry Kennedy has to identify the child found in the park. Deidre is now re-dressed in her pyjamas, her small body lying on a tray and covered in plastic in the back of the undertaker's vehicle at the police station. Senior police gird themselves for his reaction, turning away in silent respect when they fold the plastic back.

Barry stumbles, his knees faltering beneath him, before he nods. *That's our baby. That's Deidre.* They momentarily leave him with his daughter and his grief, his desolate cries shattering the quiet of this secluded area of the station. A detective gently takes his arm and leads him away.

Deidre is taken to the Brisbane morgue, a 40-minute drive from Ipswich. The State Health Laboratory's deputy director, Dr Justin O'Reilly, has already started the post-mortem when Dr Josephson arrives from Ipswich. But, even with his years of experience, Dr O'Reilly is visibly shaken by the examination that spells out the extent of the child's injuries. Whoever was responsible for her injuries definitely tried to rape her and perhaps succeeded. With the evidence before him, O'Reilly has no way of being sure either way.

In his post-mortem report, death, O'Reilly surmises, occurred about 12 hours before he saw the body. He checks police notes and begins to write:

> The lower part of the body was dressed in a pair of blue panties and a pair of elastic step-ins. On the genital region of the body and on the crutch region of the panties and step-ins I found a few hair-like fibres and what appeared to be a grass seed. One of these hair-like fibres was found between the lips of the vulva. I collected these and handed them to Detective Senior-Constable John Morris.
>
> Just inside the vagina the lining was superficially torn and it appeared that this region of the vagina had been forcibly dilated. There appeared to be some irregular bruising of the skin in the region of the anus. The dilation of the vagina and bruising around the anus could have been caused by fingers or by an erect penis. It would not have required great force to produce these injuries. The vagina contained a small amount of pink fluid which I examined but could find no spermatozoa. I also took smears from the vagina which were subsequently examined in the State Health Laboratory and no spermatozoa was found.

O'Reilly continues to detail the injuries. Two curved lines of bruising that resemble a bite mark, each 1.5cm long and about 2.5cm apart, on the front of the left thigh just above the knee. The skin is not broken and the bruising not clearly defined. His impression, he notes, is that these marks were inflicted about the same time as the other bruises seen on the body, but they could have been inflicted some hours previously. There is a bruise on Deidre's forehead about one centimetre in diameter, several poorly defined areas of bruising near the left temple, and bruising, also, on the right temple. The bruises appear consistent with pressure applied by objects similar to the tips of fingers.

The litany of injuries continues. A tiny abrasion just above Deidre's left eyebrow and some bruising of the left lower eyelid. A superficial scratch on the right cheek and small abrasions of the upper and lower lip. A small haemorrhage on the right side of the neck. A line of bruising on the left side of the neck extending from just below the jaw to the back of the neck.

O'Reilly pauses before he continues detailing his results of the internal examination. Haemorrhage into the scalp and in the soft tissues of the neck, both under the line of bruising seen on external examination. Small haemorrhages in the lining of the upper air passages, indicating that pressure had been applied to the neck with enough force to cause obstruction but not enough force to cause any significant injuries to this area. Numerous haemorrhages into the lungs and over the surface of the heart. Deidre's stomach contained a small amount of partly digested vegetable material and some milk curd. 'In my opinion,' he writes, 'death was due to asphyxia from strangulation.'

The doctor puts down his pen and rubs his eyes, now strained with fatigue. Some days he wonders at the savagery of human beings.

Senior Lecturer in Oral Biology at the University of Queensland, Dr Kornel Romaniuk – known to all as Kon – responded immediately to his colleague O'Reilly's call. 'I've got a small girl here,' O'Reilly had told him. 'Very nasty business. Not yet two years old.

She has been murdered, and there are bruises on her left leg. I think they are very possibly bite marks. Can you help?'

Using dental impressions, Romaniuk had helped identify three murder victims in outback Queensland in 1965. Seven years later, he had been called to help in the identification of a skeleton found near Charters Towers. The 18-year-old woman would earn an ignominious place in Queensland's criminal history as one of the state's first hitchhiking murder victims. But this was Romaniuk's first bite mark case and he needed to follow particular steps to match the bite mark on Deidre Kennedy with the offender. First, photograph the bite mark and the suspect dentition – the arrangement of teeth in the mouth – and then compare the two. Second, note and explain similarities and dissimilarities. Third, rule out a suspect if any dissimilarities could not be explained.

Romaniuk bent to the task. He noticed small bruises in the connective tissue. As he examined the body, he spoke to O'Reilly. 'The marks are caused by human teeth, but they are not the result of a heavy bite. How can I tell this? Because there are no depressions in the skin. A definite type of dentition has produced this mark. Whoever did this has peculiar-shaped teeth.'

When Romaniuk finished his examination, O'Reilly handed him a copy of the black–and–white photographs taken of Deidre's body at the post-mortem. In death, she looked even smaller than she had been in life.

It all feels so surreal. Falling into a dark hole, a bottomless pit, watching people's mouths move but unable to absorb what they are saying. Sliding into a black emptiness, separated from the world. Stumbling around the unit, staring into space and washing Deidre's nappies in the middle of the night. They had found her in the park only that morning and a friend is guiding Faye away from the laundry and back into the lounge room, trying to find words to comfort her. 'It's OK, darling, sit down. You don't need to do this. Deidre is safe now. She doesn't need her nappies any more.'

It all feels so surreal.

7

Limestone. Captain Patrick Logan, commandant of the convict settlement at Brisbane, recognised it immediately as he navigated and explored the Bremer River in 1826. Five convicts and an overseer were dispatched to quarry the mineable rock and build a lime-burning kiln, signalling the start of the convict era that lasted fifteen years. Conditions were harsh: stinking hot in summer, with no sea breeze to cool the air, and extremely cold in winter, the area was open to drought and flood. Named 'Limestone', the small outpost 40 kilometres west of Brisbane existed for little else than provision of a convict base camp for quarrying lime and farming sheep.

Opened to free settlers in 1842, the area was renamed Ipswich the following year and declared a city in 1904. Her fortunes waxed and waned; the region was severely affected by shocking drought, the Great Depression and then World War II. But the war brought its own particular needs: a military airbase was built at Amberley with air-raid shelters and other installations, operating on a skeletal staff from June 1940. Today, Amberley is Australia's largest operational airbase, employing more than 3500 people and expected to double in size by 2012.

Head south, hit Brisbane; head north, Toowoomba. On quiet weeknights, Ipswich streets, wide enough to turn a tandem semi-trailer in, are used by hoons doing wheelies in front of the sombre heritage buildings. On Sundays, the streets are virtually empty, apart from the odd churchgoer and tourists who wander about, in search of a coffee.

It is a city cut in half by an invisible demarcation line, between the militarised, staid conservatism of the RAAF serving personnel in their air-force blues and the raffish, disorganised civvies. Caught at the crossroads between the growing sophistication of Brisbane and the rural charm of Toowoomba, Ipswich is perched in between, straddling yesterday and tomorrow. Changes in the Queensland economy have eroded her traditional mining, industrial and agricultural base.

In 1973, Ipswich was no more than a big country town that proudly called itself a city. Apart from the transient military population, neighbours knew each other, families stayed close together and kids played on the streets. The brutal murder of a defenceless baby was inconceivable.

On 14 April 1973, the afternoon edition of the Ipswich newspaper heralded the news: 'BABY GIRL HORROR IN IPSWICH PARK: Manhunt for Sex Maniac'. Ipswich District Chief Inspector McNeil, who was heading the investigation, described it by dint of its circumstances as the most brutal murder he had worked on in his career. Whoever had done this, he told the press, was a deranged pervert. The police would do everything possible to catch him. Someone, McNeill suggested grimly, possibly knew who the killer was. He appealed to the public to think, where does my son, or my brother go when he is out all night? Based on the information supplied to them by Nugget, who police interviewed the day Deidre was found, they had pieced together a description of a youth wanted for questioning. About 17 or 18 years old. Long blond hair. Slim build. Arthur Borchert's 12-year-old son, Paul, volunteered information to police when he was interviewed. He was returning home from a barbecue, he said, when he saw a youth in his late teens carrying a baby over his shoulder. The infant, Paul said, had something white on its head. Police investigations later ruled out his information. Paul Borchert had not told the truth. He had seen no one. Why had he lied? Police would never know.

The Queensland Premier, Joh Bjelke-Petersen, waded in with his opinion, adding weight to the story on prime-time television. 'We must apprehend the person responsible. It is hard to credit that anyone could do a thing like this.'

What was immediately clear to police was that whoever had murdered Deidre was a psychopath compelled toward deviant behaviour. They did not need the latest technology in forensic-crime profiling to tell them what they could see from the stark photographs: that biting, sexually assaulting and dressing a baby in women's underwear was the handiwork of a perverse, sick man. But if police were looking for a psychopath, they first needed to understand psychopathic behaviour. What sort of person would behave like this?

Until the 1940s, psychiatrists defined psychopathy as 'insanity without delirium'. But as research advanced, so too did psychiatrists' understanding of a psychopath's behaviour. Overwhelmingly, the psychopath – now referred to amongst psychiatrists as 'personality disorder, anti-social type' – lacks empathy for other human beings and has a callous disregard for their pain or anxiety. The cries of victims, or their family's pleas for mercy, do not move them. They not only don't care; they quietly salivate at the attention.

Self-centred, shallow and predatory, the psychopath finds it easy to manipulate others into their way of thinking. They lie effortlessly and are irresponsible, like a child who tries to shift blame. *It wasn't me, it wasn't me.* Their ability to deceive is so fine-tuned that they easily hoodwink people into believing they are normal. A nice person. The boy next door. Their range of crimes, wider than other criminals, is usually more violent, and their response to treatment frequently unresponsive. Of most concern for police in the Deidre Kennedy case, the violent psychopath is often a recidivist. If the person who murdered Deidre did not kill again, it was very possible he would do something of a violent nature. But when, and what, they did not know.

What they did know was that her killer was a paedophile psychopath with tendencies to fetishism. This did not help narrow the possibilities; the most common form of fetishism is dressing people up, and, of that, 58 per cent involves underwear. The range of paedophiles is also wide, commonly falling into three distinct age groups: males over 50, the mid-to-late thirties, and teens. Most paedophiles are heterosexual and many are married fathers. Typically, the frequency of paedophiliac behaviour often fluctuates with psychosocial stress. Emotional stress can trigger unconscious conflicts; people are more likely to behave differently when they are aroused or frightened. Frequently, they do not experience any self-loathing or distress at fantasising about children, or acting out their urges. The act is predominantly about dominance: the adult has the power and there is always an element of sadism. And whilst only a small percentage of paedophiliac encounters result in injury or death to the victim, aggression and sadism by the perpetrator are always inherent.

Paedophiles don't usually change their behaviour: the majority re-offend. The paedophile's physical superiority over a child fosters the erotically tinged aggression that is linked to arousal. The aggression may be under control, or subconscious, but it is never far away. Where the victim is a vulnerable child, injury may be inflicted in perverted passion, panic or cold blood.

The stealing of women's underwear for sexual gratification – 'paraphilia' – typically becomes more defined during adolescence and early adulthood. The paraphile is usually male, has more than one fetish and has multiple victims based on each perversion. Frequently, the shy male who has difficulty forming person-to-person relationships is pre-disposed to paraphilia. If they have partners, their sex lives are mundane, dull. The object is needed, or preferred, for sexual arousal; without it, erectile dysfunction is common.

Diagnosis of fetishism involves a determination that the patient has fantasised, over a period of at least six months, about the use of non-living objects. It is a compulsion. These recurrent and intense fantasies interfere with a person's ability to function and are not limited to cross-dressing or stimulation using sex aids. Subconsciously, the fetish is associated with people of importance in childhood, whether they are remembered in a negative or a positive light.

What psychiatrists don't know is the exact cause of the disorders. Perhaps memory of a disturbed childhood experience, replayed? One psychiatrist recorded that he had seen patients who, during their sexual stage of development, had watched their sister put on underwear and then developed a bizarre connection with pants and bras. Another had a patient who, in early adolescence, repeatedly broke into neighbours' homes and stole underwear and lingerie. He would then sneak home, dress up in the stolen booty and masturbate. Raised in a foster home, as a toddler he had been dressed in female clothing and treated as a girl. He could not remember his past, but it stayed in his subconscious, re-surfacing years later. Fetishists often go to extremes, including theft, to add to their collection. But many don't seek treatment because they want to; often, their partner forces them to get help, they collide with the law, or are caught going through a girl's underwear drawer.

Harmless on the surface, a fetish can often be the signal of much darker tendencies. As a teenager, American Jerome Brudos started stealing lingerie from neighbours' yards and within a few years had developed a foot fetish. He eventually became a serial killer, choosing his victims by their footwear. On occasions, he would cut the feet off his victims and keep them in a freezer. When the mood seized him, he would take the foot out of the freezer and dress it in different shoes for sexual excitement.

The indications were strong that whoever had killed Deidre Kennedy had delayed psychosexual development. What had *caused* that delay would not be so clear, but psychiatrists know that once conflict and fear has filtered through the child's mind into memory, these are not easily erased. In their search to understand a mind unbalanced by fetish, many psychiatrists turned to Freud for answers.

Soft and sensuous, with more nerve endings than any other part of the body, the mouth remains very important to our psychosexual development and sexual expression. The first stage of a child's development is sucking, the oral phase; people who do not mature beyond this are fairly common. The sucking reflex is required for survival, but people with derailed psychosexual development do not move beyond this stage. But why inflict bite marks? In a playful manner, biting is normal in lovemaking. But in the mind of a person with disordered development, anger and aggression frequently simmers over into acts of sado-masochism.

Psychiatrists knew that the person who bit Deidre wasn't consciously thinking about doing it; instead, he was highly aroused and following uncontrollable urges to gratify his deviant sexual expression. And, while there may have been some ejaculation or climax involved (masturbation during, or at the end of the sexual act) that was by no means necessarily what drove the compulsion to bite the baby.

Strangling is often another step in the sadistic ritual – not an act to silence the victim, but a further element of gratification. It is the ultimate dominance, like snuff movies where girls or boys are murdered on video. Psychiatrists theorised it was quite likely that Deidre's killer may well have spontaneously ejaculated as he strangled her. Because no ejaculate was found, it didn't mean it didn't happen.

Was the abduction and murder planned or opportunistic? Predators plan their activities. Paedophiles may take months to insinuate themselves into a family to gain access to children, but that does not mean they would look a gift horse in the mouth. If something tantalising is offered to them by chance, they will accept it.

Having achieved his goal to abduct Deidre, the killer's next step would have been to immediately examine her clothing. The pilchers – the plastic pants that cover the nappy to stop urine soaking through to the baby's clothing – first would have had to be removed. Vulnerability is a key element of the excitement and the pilchers were an unwanted barrier against that. He would have removed the pilchers but would not have thrown the pyjamas away, because they were a symbol of the child's defencelessness. And then he re-dressed her. Panties first. Then step-ins. And finally the half slip.

She is ready now, dressed for the taking. All his. A vulnerable child with skin as smooth as a woman. A sensuous, sexual woman who can't say no.

How could an adult male defile and then murder such a small baby? What sort of sex drive would the killer have? Very possibly high, but not for a mature adult on an equal footing. The preference of paedophiles is for children; paedophiles often have a low sex drive with adults, failing to maintain mature heterosexual adult-to-adult interest or performance. They dominate children because adults threaten them and they don't like that. *They* like to do the threatening. But it is only in the realm of sexual expression that people with psychosexual problems need display anything abnormal at all. With people such as family and friends, they are normal.

Whether planned or opportunistic, the murder of baby Deidre Kennedy was a gross, predatory act carried out without emotion. This was *not* a crime of passion: the goal was the cold-blooded taking of a vulnerable baby. There was virtually no chance that this killer would come forward with a confession. Apart from the fear of detailing his crime to police and the fall-out that would follow from confessing, the murder had not made him feel guilty. On the contrary: it had energised and excited him.

Psychiatrists now understand that adult-child sexual contact is far more common than it was known to be 30 years ago. But, in 1973, psychological profiling was still in its infancy and it would take years for therapists to work out diagnostic criteria for the perpetrator's profile. Right now, with the killer at large and a hysterical public demanding justice, the police had to figure a way to beat the murderer at his own game. And they had to do it fast.

8

Calls are issued for the driver of four cars, seen in Limestone Park on the night of the murder, to come forward. A van seen around 11pm, close to where Deidre's body was found. A Ford Zephyr in the same area around midnight. A 1958 Station Sedan seen parking at approximately 12.30 and leaving again 10 minutes later. A small Japanese car parked on the west side of the park and sighted earlier near the Kennedys' block of units.

Time is of the essence. Every hour of an early investigation is critical. They have now lost four days.

Mobilising 17 detectives, six uniformed police, and scientific and fingerprint experts, police begin the most intensive search ever undertaken in Ipswich. They face, one wryly notes, a 'long, tough slog'. Most police do double shifts in an attempt to sift through the avalanche of information pouring in from the public. They access the database of known child molesters in Queensland and inter-state but, without the technology of computers, it is a laborious and often thankless task, linking up with their national counter-parts and checking the whereabouts of strong possible suspects over the weekend of Friday the 13th and Saturday 14th. Patients at local mental institutions are checked for fingerprints, and as many leads as possible are followed up. Nugget is shown photographs of different male persons, but he can identify none of them as being the prowler he saw on the veranda. 'Nup. Nup. Nope.' He shakes his head as each photograph follows the last. Police do not publish an identikit picture of the person Nugget has described seeing on the veranda and give no explanation why. Instead, an artist draws a sketch of a prowler who has plagued a woman some distance away from the scene and publishes the image in the local paper. Police are interested in all prowlers, but this one proves elusive.

In the week following the crime, John Howard, the officer in charge of the Fingerprint Bureau in Brisbane, has examined the

Kennedy flat and the scene for fingerprints. All males in Ipswich and surrounding areas are asked to volunteer prints, and more than 3500 people come forward.

They all return a negative result.

Swamped by calls from the public but with no worthwhile fresh leads, police issue a call for people to be vigilant. Inspector McNeil clears his throat and adjusts his tie before staring down the lens of a television camera to ask that people consider their conscience if they are protecting a sadistic killer who could strike again. 'Whoever abducted and killed Deidre must have shown some reaction later, either at home or with friends,' he intones. 'Do you remember anyone who acted strangely the next day? Last Saturday? Was that person out alone on Friday night, probably well into Saturday morning? If so, he is worth considering as a possible suspect. And if he has some background of sexual mis-behaviour, then he becomes a real prospect for suspicion.'

Police also face another pressing problem. While the public bray for the killer to be found and the media keeps the story on the boil by giving it daily front-page coverage, the police have more questions than answers. And they know that each day the crime remains unsolved, the more difficult the investigation becomes. If a strong lead is going to break, it very often happens in the first 72 hours.

In the engine room of the police station, they hug coffee cups and fill ashtrays to overflowing as they work through the long nights grappling with their queries. Aerial shots of Ipswich are laid out on the table and maps covered in arrows point to all entrances and exits to Limestone Park and its proximity to Short Street.

For the third time in as many days, they run through the questions again. Does the killer have local knowledge of the area? The general consensus is that he does. The toilet block in the middle of the park seems to have been chosen as a specific target. How likely is it that a stranger from out of town would know where that is? The sexual assault and murder: were they planned or opportunis-tic? If planned, had the killer known that Barry Kennedy had been in and out of hospital, was incapacitated on crutches and that his family had returned to Ipswich around dawn on the morning his daughter was abducted? If not planned, did the killer, perhaps frustrated by an unsatisfactory visit to a house of ill repute close to where the Kennedys lived, instead impulsively seize the opportunity to abduct the sleeping baby? Both scenarios seem equally possible, and the police keep a question mark next to these.

'Any chance that there was more than one person involved? Maybe even a woman, which might explain how the baby was kept so quiet?' The question, asked by a young cop, hangs in the air before it is answered. The idea has been mooted before but while there seems little reason to believe this is the case, the sheer audacity of the crime means the possibility can't be ignored.

'In some ways we want to hope that there *were* two people,' a senior sergeant replies. 'At least that way there's always the chance that one person may break, split on the other. But, for my money, this bloke acted alone.'

The questions continue. Where was Deidre taken immediately after she was picked up from her cot? Was she sexually assaulted and murdered either in a private home or caravan and later dumped on the toilet block? With no eyewitness or information coming from the public to support this theory, they have no way of knowing. Did the killer get into a vehicle parked away from the unit after he abducted her, or leave on foot? The balance of probabilities is that he walked away from Short Street, but again, there is no proof.

An officer wearily checks his watch. It's 2am and he has put in only a brief appearance with his family in the past week since the murder. 'Anyone want another coffee?' he asks, and a heap of hands rise in unison. He wishes he hadn't asked. At this rate, they will definitely see the sun come up again today.

A detective has now hijacked the questions. What about the foreign seed found on Deidre's body? It didn't come from the park, so what was its origin? There are two possible explanations: either the killer unwittingly passed the seed on to her at some stage during the night, or she had picked it up from another place outside the park after she was taken from her bedroom. 'And what happened to the pilchers? Why weren't they with the rest of her clothes? Any clues?' The detective looks around the room, and silence answers that question.

How did Deidre get on the toilet block roof? Had her killer suddenly panicked after he killed her and thrown her up there, hoping she would not be found, or did he drive his vehicle to the block, stand on the seat for added height and deliberately place her there where she *would* be found? Or a third scenario: was she dragged up by someone who had first climbed on the roof? This last seems highly unlikely, judging by the sceptical looks on the coppers' faces, but the question has to be asked.

'OK,' the detective says, recognising the officers are showing signs of extreme fatigue, 'last question. If Deidre was not strangled at the same time she was abducted, why didn't her cries wake her sleeping family?'

'Because whoever did it was hardly going to announce his arrival and make a racket getting in and out of the unit,' an older officer responded, with some exasperation. 'And look at the facts. The father had been in hospital having an operation, the mother was exhausted from looking after two kids on a bloody long bus trip back from Longreach and Deidre's sister, only five years old, was fast asleep. I reckon that might explain that question.'

They will run through all their questions again tomorrow night. And the night after. More than 30 years later, there will still not be any answers.

Starting with houses around the streets closest to Limestone Park and then fanning further out, the doorknocks take weeks. Knocking, waiting, showing ID. *How many people live in this house? Are there any males in the house over the age of 12? Would all males in this household voluntarily supply fingerprints? Where were they on the night and morning of April 13 and 14? Were there any visitors to the household on those days who have since left Ipswich?* By the time the doorknocks are complete, police have spoken to thousands of people. But, if anyone has lied, or has been coolly protecting a friend or relative, it is very difficult to check. Police can only rely on fingerprint evidence and the theory that innocent people usually tell the truth. Usually, but by no means always.

Stymied by a lack of leads, Kennedy investigators look to an

English case solved 25 years earlier, charting the comparisons and bizarre coincidences of both crimes.

In November 1948, sullen 22-year-old ex-guardsman Peter Griffiths was hanged in England for the rape and murder of four-year-old June Devaney earlier that year. Just after midnight, the small girl was abducted from her cot at Queen's Park Hospital, Blackburn. Three hours later, her savagely mutilated body was found in a hay barn, less than half a kilometre from where she had slept. The girl had been raped in the hospital grounds, swung by one leg and killed by smashing her head against a stone wall. Police had few clues to work with: blood, hairs and clothing fibres found in the hospital grounds; fingerprints on a water bottle; a footprint on the freshly washed ward floor; and foreign hairs on the victim's body. Against a backdrop of massive public hysteria, police were pressured as never before to find the killer.

All but one fingerprint on the water bottle was identified and Scotland Yard mobilised all their resources to find a match for the lone print. None was found in the police database of known criminals, nor from the 2000 people who had access to the hospital. The decision was made to fingerprint every man who lived at Blackburn, a city of some 25,000 people. But, by the third month following the murder, all 40,000 sets of prints – the largest ever taken in England – failed to yield a match.

But cross-referencing data showed that a few men in Blackburn had not yet provided their prints. One of those men was Peter Griffiths, who acted surprised when his footprints matched those found at the scene. Police had finally hit pay dirt: when his fingerprints also matched those found on the bottle, Griffiths confessed. He pleaded not guilty at his three-day trial but, with overwhelming forensic evidence against him, the jury took just 23 minutes to convict him.

The similarities between the June Devaney case and that of Deidre Kennedy are overwhelming. A small child, probably chosen opportunistically. Abduction from a cot, apparently witnessed by no one, despite adults being in the immediate vicinity. A stealthy entrance and exit by the perpetrator. Sexual interference followed by murder, probably close to where the kidnap had occurred. June Devaney had been found in the grounds of Queen's Park Hospital; Deidre Kennedy at Limestone Park, part of the larger Queen's Park in Ipswich.

Ipswich police also have little evidence to work from. Fingerprints found on the toilet door at the park. Foreign hairs located on Deidre's body. Their best bet, they decide, is to follow the English model and take fingerprints of every man in the Ipswich area.

Every man.

Police talk to likely suspects and Kon Romaniuk gives models of seven sets of their teeth to a panel of ten eminent dentists. He has considerable experience in forensic pathology, but human bite marks are outside his expertise. He wants other opinions.

They will test for the identification of teeth marks using acetate tracing, a delicate method that is complicated and slow. First, plaster casts of both the lower and upper jaw will be made to produce a model of the teeth. Next, the model will be traced onto a thin sheet of semi-transparent material with a small amount of stretch superimposed over the teeth. Tracings will then be drawn and overlaid on the photograph of the bruise patterns.

The government botanist analyses the plant fragments found on Deidre's clothing, in the hope they might offer a clue to where the killer came from. Was Deidre taken miles from her home by car, murdered where this particular plant grew, and later dumped in the park? It is not beyond reason the plant material might help: in 1960, the kidnap and murder mystery of eight-year-old Bondi schoolboy Graham Thorne was solved in Sydney by analysis of the relatively rare plant material that was found on his body. Postmen were asked to be vigilant on their mail runs to see if the plant was growing in gardens on their rounds. It paid off: a postman found the plant in a suburb near Bondi and the killer, by then halfway to London, was returned to Australia, convicted and sentenced to life imprisonment.

But there would be no such breakthrough with the Kennedy case.

Senior scientific police officer Neil Raward's duties have involved the examination of the scene and collection and examination of exhibits. He has made a thorough examination of the grandstand area at the park and the area around the toilet block. Raward has also noticed that one of the pins in the nappy was in a closed position, but that the other nappy pin was open and placed into the nappy itself. Whoever had done this must have been in such a rush that he had only taken the time to open one side of the nappy before removing it. It was drenched with urine, but Deidre's pyjama pants were dry, consistent with her having worn pilchers. But Raward hasn't been able to find those pilchers.

Nine months later, pilchers would materialise on the roof of the RAAF units where the Kennedy family had lived. No one would ever be able to explain how they got there, or whether they belonged to Deidre.

The Department of Health's supervising bacteriologist, Neville Stallman, has been given the clothing and underwear Deidre was wearing to check for sperm, blood and saliva. He finds nothing, save for two saliva stains in the panties. There is little he can do with saliva: at that time, testing for its source is in its infancy. He also received from Raward two hairs in an envelope, labelled 'pyjama pants and nappy' and four hairs in a container labelled 'PM23433 Kennedy'. Using microscopic examination, he finds that one of the hairs in the envelope looks like a pubic hair.

A week after Stallman finishes with it, the hair is returned to Raward. He does not get the clothing back.

Reaction to the murder from local residents is overwhelming. Parents escort their children to and from school. Kids are barred from going outdoors and neighbours gossip about who may be responsible. Ipswich may be called a city, but country town parochialism and paranoia still prevail. Once a leafy recreational area widely used by locals, Limestone Park is now known as the Devil's Playground.

9

The first weeks after Deidre's death are a blurry haze for Faye and Barry. People coming and going, friends and relatives ferrying food and flowers, the press camped outside on the street and countless police in and out of the unit. Deidre's family is under suspicion, though they don't know it. Barry, Faye and Stephanie are fingerprinted and cleared and all accessible surfaces in the flat dusted for prints. Endless photographs of the unit are taken. Endless questions asked, always with the same polite preface. 'Sorry for the intrusion, but we need to know . . .' *How long has the family lived in Ipswich? Why had they gone to Longreach? Could they please retrace their steps from the moment they arrived home? Had they had any babysitters? Any recent visitors? Had they noticed any strangers loitering around?*

Answering by rote in a faltering voice, one word painfully following the other. *We chose that time to take the girls to Longreach because my mother was leaving the area and Barry was going into hospital to have knee surgery. I don't drive much and so it would have been difficult to visit him in hospital with the children. We returned to Ipswich by early Friday morning because Mum was superstitious about Black Friday. She had insisted we were all safely home by that date. We've only lived here a few months and we hardly know anyone. We have never used a babysitter. We don't go out at night. We don't drink or smoke. We haven't noticed any strangers loitering around. There is an odd household of people who live close to the units, but I didn't see them that day.*

Two days after Deidre's body is found, Barry speaks to the press. 'The brutal murder of our daughter is just something that my wife and I will have to overcome. No matter where we go or what we do, we will never forget what has happened. My wife and I are mature enough to overcome this as best we can. But how do you ever forget that one of your children has been murdered?'

Such a private family, such private people, they want to crawl away with their grief, cringe from the constant questions, the news reports, turn inward to mourn in peace. But it is impossible. The level of repulsion at the nature of the murder has opened a floodgate of letters to the newspaper editor and to the family. The public has taken Deidre Kennedy to its heart, and they want retribution.

Faye is asked to fold a nappy for the police exactly the way Deidre had worn it, and to hand over an identical singlet to the one she was wearing when they found her. Everything Faye says, everything she does, is an excruciating wrench. She cries and cries without end, feels as though she is on automatic pilot. 'The emptiness I felt was overwhelming. I couldn't stop crying. But Barry never did; he bottled it all up. We could so easily have lost two daughters that night. Barry just felt so guilty that he'd let us down by not protecting Deidre.'

They self-flagellate, consumed with guilt. The prowler had got in because the door was unlocked. What happened is their fault. They should have taken more care. They should have sensed someone was in the unit. They should have woken up. They should have got up.

Over and over, consumed with grief and guilt.

Their family arrives as soon as they hear the news. Faye's mother, Frieda, drives 15 hours non-stop from Longreach; by the time she arrives, the deep shock of her granddaughter's death has already taken a huge toll. 'I looked at her and thought, what have we done?' Faye recounts later. 'I had seen her only two days before, but the shock had put years on her life. She suddenly looked ancient. It took a shocking toll on all of us.'

Going over and over things in their heads, answering police questions, trying to remember the smallest detail. Is it possible that either Stephanie or Deidre had been the target? 'We'd only been in that flat such a short time,' Faye says. 'We kept to ourselves. Why would we be targeted? What would they want with us?'

Why would we be targeted? Why our family? Why our beautiful little daughter? Over and over, but never any answers.

A week has passed and the police have taken Barry aside, away from Faye, quietly quizzing him. Relentless and determined, investigators have now zeroed in on a particular family member as a possible suspect. Keith Kennedy, Barry's first cousin. Their fathers are brothers and Keith and Barry are the same age. Keith often visits Faye and Barry, driving or catching the train for a day trip from his home at Auchenflower, an inner-city suburb of Brisbane, where he lives with his sister and brother. Auchenflower, on the direct train line to Ipswich. The day before Faye and the girls had come home, Keith had picked up Barry from the hospital and taken him straight to the unit. And now police are telling Barry his cousin is a possible suspect.

'You've got it all wrong, Faye. Keith would never hurt our child.' Faye is cradled in Barry's arms, trying to take some comfort in his soothing words. But the thought is niggling.

Keith's actions had all been so hush-hush. Faye and Barry were still living in Longreach when it happened three years ago, but the family didn't discuss it. Keith's father, a decent and quiet man had been crushed, humiliated by his son's disgrace and the country community closed ranks to protect him. No one talked about it. And, until it came to trial, no one knew the extent of what Keith had done. Faye and Barry would hear only snippets of the story.

The jury had found Keith not guilty, on the grounds of insanity, of unlawfully and indecently dealing with a little girl at Gladstone, north Queensland, in April 1970. Exactly three years before Deidre's murder. Found him not guilty on the grounds of insanity for biting a three-and-a-half-year-old girl on the vagina.

'What does it mean?' Faye wants to know. 'What does it mean, not guilty on the grounds of insanity?'

'It means the jury found he did it, but he was insane and therefore not responsible for his actions,' Barry explains. 'You've got it all wrong, Faye. Keith would never hurt our child.'

Police look at a family photograph. Keith is blond, about 177cm tall. Not a bad-looking bloke, but his features are marred by slightly protruding front teeth with a wide gap between them, what dentists call a 'diastema'. They rake through descriptions taken immediately after the murder. Witnesses had said they had seen a blond man walking toward the unit. Someone who looked like he knew where he was going. Keith knew the family, and knew their movements. Most importantly, he had form.

More than 30 years after his daughter's murder, Barry Kennedy still fiercely defends his cousin, now deceased. 'Keith told me he'd been out partying and drinking the night he did that to that little girl,' Barry says. 'He'd just stumbled into the wrong place, and . . .' There is a pause and the flick of a cigarette lighter on the other end of the phone line. 'I never thought for a minute it was him. He knew that the cops would go hunting for him, because of what he'd done. As soon as he heard about Deidre, he knew they'd bang on his door. And, sure enough, they did.'

John Reynolds remembers the buzz around the police station when Keith Kennedy's form came to light. 'They jumped straight on to him; spoke to him very early in the piece. They worked out how he could have got from where he lived at Auchenflower to Ipswich and then back again in time to watch the television show he said he had watched with his family the day he picked up Barry from the hospital, the day before the family had arrived home. They gave him a cast-iron alibi.' Keith's hair, teeth and fingerprints did not match any found at the scene. He was exonerated. For now.

10

Faye and Barry were carefree country kids, born and raised in Longreach, a central western Queensland town in the parched outback, almost 1200 kilometres from Brisbane. Where the men say g'day in a lazy drawl and wear Akubra hats to ward off the savage midday sun, this is pioneering territory built by cattle kings. Harsh though rich country of verdant plains and Flinders grass, the town derived its name from the 'long reach' of the Thomson River that runs nearby. The streets are all named after land and water birds – eagles, jabirus – and the landscape dotted with coolibah trees. Only a few thousand residents live there permanently, the population bolstered when cow-cockies, drovers and tourists wander through for a taste of outback Australia.

When they were children, Faye and her siblings would grab a blanket and head out to the lawn, sleeping out under the stars and watching the moon glide across the sky. Faye's father worked with the Postmaster General's office after his return from the war in Egypt, a hard desert war where he served in the army. Faye, christened Lynette Faye, was a post-war baby, born 24 July 1949 before her father's war nerves got the better of him and shattered the household's former peace. The family lived free as a bird in a house in the scrub out of Longreach, Faye the second eldest child. Two sisters and a brother followed.

The family moved into town when she was 12, but Faye hated school. Her elder sister was the scholar; Faye only went for the sport. Landing her first job at 14 with the local jewellers, she was too shy to even ask to use the toilet. A tomboy, she also worked at night at the local pharmacy and eventually worked there full time. Travelling around the district, competing in basketball and tennis games, Faye and her friends toffed up once a year for the Longreach Show ball, a rural hootenanny where elders from the local Church of England diligently acted as unpaid moral chaperones lest the country lads got too frisky.

An edge had crept into Faye's household. Her father had started drinking heavily, talking incessantly about the war. Arguments between her parents were increasingly frequent and increasingly escalating into violence. Her sisters jumped out the window when the blues started but Faye, now in her mid-teens, stood up for her mother, many times copping what was meant for her. She had a stubborn streak that showed most at times like this.

Most nights her father was passed out, drunk as a lord, but Faye never took the chance that she may wake him, tip-toeing back into the house after a night out with her shoes in her hand and hopping into bed fully dressed. He never touched the kids apart from the odd strap, but it was a household on tenterhooks. Once, when her mother had ordered that she wait by the bedroom door, her father went rushing past Faye with a cutthroat razor in his hands. Faye still believes that if her mother hadn't locked herself in the bathroom that night, her father would have killed her.

Her dad, she reflects, was a decent man haunted, like many of his generation, by memories of war and dead mates. He was always sorry after his bitter, violent outbursts: sober and sorry; but the marriage couldn't survive. By the time Faye was 15, it was over.

From the moment they met on a basketball court in Longreach when Faye was 17, she and Barry were inseparable. Both quiet and private, they loved sport and the outdoors, particularly camping. Married 18 months after they met, on a balmy late October day in 1967, Faye was completely lacking in sophistication. 'I wouldn't say boo to a goose when I was younger. We shared a house for a short time with another couple and my eyes used to pop out of my head, some of the things the woman said. I thought she was so worldly.'

Locals waved to Faye as she stepped out in her white wedding gown, hanging over their front fences and calling out good wishes. Most had known her since she was a tiny girl. The newly-weds honeymooned on the Gold Coast for a week before returning to married life at Longreach.

Faye knew nothing of the sordid side of life. She and Barry

were innocents, country people who never locked their doors or windows and didn't even own a television set. Police, unsullied by allegations of corruption, verballing and bashings in custody, were still trusted and welcome in the community. The Church was a sanctuary, its priests and ministers God's holy messengers. Politicians didn't tell lies; courts punished the guilty and psychopaths, predators and paedophiles lived in another world, completely outside their understanding.

They had missed the idealism of the '60s, the revolutionary fervour of young anti-war protestors who had love-ins for peace, wore flowers in their hair and chanted on their stoned path to hypnotic grace. They did not know that around the world, the '70s heralded a shift in attitude, becoming a decade of disillusionment when the hopes and dreams of the hippy generation soured into the harsh reality of international terrorist threats, preventable third-world famine and wars that exploded like powder kegs in hotspots around the globe. Cocooned in outback Queensland where the sun appeared as a halo against the super-fine ochre dust, disasters were acts of nature and gossip was traded at the post office. Faye taught Sunday school and dreamed of starting a family. Barry, an air-conditioning mechanic, played footy and came straight home after the match.

A year after they were married, on 20 April 1968 their daughter Stephanie was born. By late 1970, looking for a career change, Barry joined the RAAF as an instrument fitter and the family moved to Wagga. Soon after, they were thrilled to discover Faye was again pregnant.

Deidre Maree was born at Longreach Base Hospital where Faye had returned to give birth close to her family, at 6.20 on the night of 22 November 1971. Admitted to hospital weeks earlier with alarmingly high blood pressure, Faye had been induced early that morning. At 5 o'clock, right on the nurses' teatime, she went into labour. 'I was so alone in that labour ward,' she remembers. 'The nurses said to me, "You'll be right," and off they went to tea. By the time they got back, there was no skin left on my elbows from hanging on through the contractions.' Drug-free, the birth was, at least, blessedly short.

Driving home that evening, Faye's brother Ken had passed the town doctor heading toward the hospital. In the laconic way of small communities, he became the town crier. 'I've just passed Dr Murphy on Eagle Street. I reckon he's on his way in to see Faye.' And he was. Everyone knew that if the doctor was heading to the hospital at teatime, it was a sure bet there was a baby on the way.

Thrilled at the birth of another healthy daughter Barry, unable to leave Wagga for another three weeks, sent a congratulatory telegram. They had already settled on the name of the new baby. If it was a girl, they would christen her Deidre. They liked its gentle sound, its old-fashioned, soft texture, like an autumn leaf fluttering in the breeze. *Dei-dre*. The name meant 'sorrowful', from a legendary heroine in medieval Irish literature. But, from the start, the family affectionately called her Dee Dee, a Hebrew word meaning 'cherished'.

A cherubic baby who inherited her mother's shy ways, Faye and Barry proudly announced her arrival in the local paper as 'a beautiful sister for Stephanie'. From the moment she was born, the girls were inseparable.

A contented, smiling baby, Deidre celebrated her first birthday in Wagga, where they lived permanently. When the family again returned to Longreach for Christmas, she was christened at the local church on Christmas Eve.

In December 1972, the family was posted to Amberley RAAF base at Ipswich. Deidre was 13 months old, Stephanie not yet five years old. It was the start of a new life.

Sixteen-year-old Raymond Carroll was looking for a new life, as well. He had been mooching around Ipswich, in and out of odd jobs since his family had returned from Darwin late in 1971. A loner who preferred his own company, he had to find something to do, soon. Perhaps he would follow in his old man's footsteps.

Raymond's father, John, had proudly worn the RAAF blues. At first glance, his parents were an odd couple: his mother, Ilma, was 189cm tall; John 162cm, struggling to reach her shoulders. Even Ilma found it a little strange at first, peering down from her lofty height at the man who would become her husband, but she soon got used to it. They were young and happy.

Married in the winter of 1951, their first child, Sandra, was born at Casino, northern New South Wales, in 1954. The following year they moved to Toowoomba, then a quiet backwater in country Queensland, where Ilma gave birth to Raymond on 17 August 1955. Raymond was bestowed with his father's name: Raymond John Carroll. The year of his birth heralded the worst natural disaster in Australian history, when catastrophic floods in northern New South Wales wreaked unprecedented havoc, killing 100 people and displacing 50,000 from their homes.

In 1956, John was posted to Malaya where the small family spent three idyllic years before returning to Ipswich where their second son, Peter, was born in 1962. Re-located to the tropical city of Darwin, Ilma gave birth to their second daughter, Debbie, in 1965, the same year they returned to Ipswich for a further three-year posting. By 1970, living in Richmond, New South Wales, their last child, Lee-Ann, was born. They were again posted to Darwin in 1971.

It was, Raymond and Sandra recall, an unremarkable childhood. Normal. Average. Nothing outstanding. They swap memories: sitting up a mango tree eating the fruit; gorging themselves on raspberries and gooseberries, their clothing stained with the juice. Just kids doing things normal kids do. But they are not all happy memories. Raymond grimaces at how often they moved, how often he changed schools. He counts them on his fingers and speaks out loud. 'Two, three, four.' He glances at Sandra. 'Four to six?'

'Try eight.' It is Sandra's prompt and he follows it. 'Oh, OK, eight. Both primary and high schools. Eight.'

Different schools and different classmates, who marked him out for special, unwelcome attention. It was his teeth that set him apart. Stained, protruding, he could not hide them. His classmates called out to him as he walked home from school. 'Hey, Carroll! Sabre-tooth!' Ribbed him, mercilessly, that he could eat an apple through a tennis racquet. Different states, different schools, different classmates, but the same old abuse. It never let up.

'Mum and Dad were poor as church mice, and they couldn't afford braces for Raymond,' Sandra explains. 'We've all got a slight overbite, but Raymond's is protruding. Mum desperately wanted to fix it for him, but she just didn't have the money.'

He was powerless to stop the taunts, his self-esteem shattered by the cruel jibes, the relentless, hurtful comments. He couldn't do anything to change himself. He couldn't run. Everywhere he went, the nagging taunts followed. 'Hey, Carroll! Sabre-tooth!' It happened so often, he found a way to deal with it.

He blocked it out.

The bottom dropped out of Ilma's world after John's sudden death in a freak accident four miles out of Katherine in the Northern Territory. Early morning in the stifling build-up to the wet season, clouds pregnant with pre-monsoonal rains, the air-force semi-trailer he was driving jack-knifed and hit the passenger door, springing open the driver's door and flinging him onto the bitumen. He had left for work in the early hours, in such a rush it was the only time in their married life that Ilma could recall he did not kiss her goodbye. Mid-morning, she was hanging the washing on the line when she heard him call out to her. 'Hey, Il,' he said, and she turned, smiling, expecting to see him. But he was not there. She pegged out the rest of the clothes – shirts, shorts, underwear – and then an RAAF Commanding Officer and padre were standing at her door. They didn't have to tell her something terrible had happened; she already knew by the look on their faces and the sound of her own voice, screaming. Backing away from them, in slow motion. 'No, no! Oh please, no!'

There was no reason to stay in Darwin now that John was dead. Ilma packed the family possessions and headed back down south, a middle-aged widow with five kids: the oldest 16, the youngest six. Three girls, two boys and a grieving mother settling into a new life at 13 Quarry Lane, Ipswich.

They would lead narrower lives from then on, Ilma's shock and sorrow enveloping her and dissipating her once fierce independence. She shrank from life; clothed in mourning, her laughter gone, she was not a neglectful mother but a sad one, a distracted one. Her keening would last six years, and the children would get away with more than she would normally have allowed. Sorrow took the edge off her discipline and Sandra, the eldest girl, stepped into the breach. She had always been old beyond her years – intense, responsible – and now she was catapulted by her father's sudden death into becoming her mother's confidante, the one Ilma relied on. The head of the family; the strong one. Raymond was the eldest boy, only a year younger than Sandra, but the responsibility did not fall to him. His mother withdrew and his older sister took over. 'Raymond didn't become the male head of the family; I did,' Sandra would later say, her voice tinged with a hint of defiance. 'I became Mum's partner. I was the one she leant on. I was the eldest.'

He doesn't remember a great deal about his father, except that they got on fairly well, despite the fact he annoyed the hell out of him. He remembers that, and his father's abrupt, tragic death. He was only 15 when he died, a traumatised young man without an older bloke to talk to. He does not hesitate when asked what stands out from his childhood. 'Dad's death,' he says, firmly.

Raymond had little choice but to leave behind his Darwin apprenticeship as an auto electrician. He left with a letter of recommendation from the Apprenticeship Board and an introductory letter from his former employer, but, after working for nine months in Ipswich, he failed to get his final indentures. There wasn't much work around in the provincial Queensland city: a few labouring jobs, bits and pieces. Not much work, and not much of a social life. Raymond stuck pretty much to himself; always has. He doesn't mind people, but he isn't comfortable in crowds. He won't have a conversation for conversation's sake.

He couldn't stop thinking about Desley Hill after he met her at a Christmas get-together at his Aunty Carol's house in Ipswich. He liked her innocent simplicity, the way she didn't try to dominate him. He reckoned she was around 17, though she may have been older; what he does remember is his mother was unimpressed with the age difference. Raymond was not yet 16. They spent their time together in long walks around Woodridge, her Brisbane suburb, and, afterward, Raymond would catch a train home, a lovesick teenager.

He would always remember Desley as his first love, but he was fed up with the lack of opportunities in Ipswich. He needed to make a decision: either to keep dragging himself around one job site to the next, or settle into some sort of a career. Raymond tossed the idea back and forth and finally made up his mind. He would follow in his father's footsteps, join the RAAF.

Dressed in his smartest bib and tucker, he headed down to the Brisbane Recruiting Centre and returned later for medical and psychiatric tests, which he proudly passed.

In the last days of January 1973, the world, weary with a war in which it had long ago lost heart, finally witnessed the signing of the Vietnam peace treaty in Paris. By the end of March, the last of the US troops straggled out of Vietnam. And, in between, on 5 February, 17-year-old Raymond John Carroll joined up. He would wear the air-force blues; make a career in the RAAF. Just like his old man.

He started recruit training at Edinburgh Air Base in South Australia, joining course 1203 on 9 February 1973. Boot camp: hard physical workouts, spit and polishing shoes, learning to salute and say *Sir*. Rise and shine. Half quick march. Halt.

Carroll's instructor, Corporal Raymond Martin, was impressed with Carroll's boots, holding them up for the rest of the recruits to see. 'I want them to shine so you can see your face in them,' he barked. 'Just like these boots.' Punctuality, obedience, service. That's what he expected from his boys.

Carroll lived up to dress expectations and appraised himself in the mirror. Peaked hat with RAAF badge and epaulettes on the shoulders of his pristine white shirt. Dark blue tie, mid-line crease in his trousers and wide studded belt circling small waist. Boots immaculately polished. He was perfectly turned out. His father would be proud.

His black hair was cut to regulation length – 'short back and sides' – and he was tall, over 184cm, and slightly built. His colouring hinted at a Mediterranean heritage: eyes dark as melted chocolate and hair that he wore swept back from his forehead. People were often surprised when they found he was Australian to the core, a born-and-bred Queenslander.

He moved closer to the mirror, preening. Generous mouth, that naturally turned down in a glum expression. Top lip raised to accommodate protruding upper teeth. Large ears and broad nose. Hollow-chested, his shoulders hunched slightly forward.

All recruits had to have their dentition checked and a chart recorded. Flight-Lieutenant Ross Dunn, attached to the dental section, noted that the corner of Carroll's front left tooth was chipped and that his right tooth was mottled. No work was done at the initial check and his fellow recruits, with whom he rarely mixed, would remember him for his teeth. 'He had very protruding front teeth with sections missing from it, and the inside sections of his front upper teeth were missing,' recruit Michael Sheean recalled. 'He was pigeon-chested and pigeon-toed.' Sheean also remembered Carroll was a fastidious dresser adept at spit-polishing his shoes and boots. Always immaculately turned out in his uniform. The RAAF was in his blood. He knew what was required.

From the start, Carroll was a loner, an odd-man-out who had little to do with other members on the course. It was in his nature to be quiet, and, if the other recruits didn't share his interest in mechanics or electronics, he happily stayed away from them. He didn't *want* to mix much; he was only interested in finishing his course and starting work. He knew that many of the other course members regarded him as somewhat aloof, but that neither surprised nor concerned him. All his life, he had been the target of bullies because of his teeth. *Hey, Carroll! Sabre-tooth!* Ribbed mercilessly. Get the course finished, get out and start work. That was his goal.

A quiet, unobtrusive bloke would always stand out amongst men in their late teens who bonded with backslapping, sport and drinking. They did not invite Carroll to share their sessions: he not only *looked* different, with deep brown eyes that could stare right through them, but some recalled he had unpleasant breath.

Michael Sheean recalled later that Carroll would sometimes materialise behind him, from out of nowhere. 'Once I was lying on my bed and I felt something move behind me. I turned around and there he was, quietly sitting on the end of my bed.'

Raymond got used to hearing it. 'Jesus, Carroll, you scared the shit out of me! Where did you come from?' They called him 'Fang' because of his buckteeth and laughed, cruel laughter that he did not join. But, if he was hurt by the attitude of some of the recruits, he never showed it. All his life he had endured taunts and ribbings. This was nothing new.

He admits he wasn't a typical rookie. 'As far as I was concerned, I'd been air force all me life. I was bottlefed it, ate it, slept it, dreamed it. Air force. Rookies was just a stepping-stone for me; no great hullabaloo. I just wanted to finish me course and start work.'

But Corporal Martin feared recruit Carroll had much to learn about diplomacy. A guest of honour at the RAAF graduation dinner, held well in advance of the final passing-out parade, Martin was seated next to a senior officer, Flight Commander Brady. Carroll took up a drink and placed it on the table. 'Thank you very much,' Brady beamed. Carroll looked surprised. 'The drink's not for you,' he replied. 'It's for Corporal Martin.'

The course had started on 9 February, and the passing-out parade was on 19 April 1973. He didn't have long to go now before he could get out of Edinburgh and start his real training for the job.

11

Faye is desperate to see her little girl. She has shed countless tears in the days following Deidre's murder, begging to be given the chance to say goodbye to her in private. 'I want to see her. When can I see her?' Incessantly pleading with Barry. 'I want to see her. When can I see her?'

'You will, mate. You will.' That is all she is ever told. Every time she asks, that's the response. 'You will, mate. You will.' Barry tries to protect her, tells her to remember Deidre how she was. But all she wants is to hold her. Give her a hug, say goodbye in private.

Grief-stricken at his daughter's murder, Barry hides Deidre's injuries from Faye. Years later, Faye recalls: 'I asked Barry if she had been hurt, beaten about or anything and he just told me she had a mark on her forehead and had been suffocated.' Faye's face creases in a frown before the tears start. 'It was so disgusting, how that man dressed her. I knew I put her to bed safe that night, tucked up happy. Then this animal came in to our home and did that to her.'

Stephanie keeps asking where Dee Dee has gone. They try to explain to her that she isn't coming home any more, that God needs her in Heaven. She finds it impossible to comprehend how her sister could have been there at night when she went to bed and not there in the morning.

From the moment Faye tells Steph, she will barely remember anything about Deidre. Hypnotherapy will fail to conjure an image of the intruder's face; she can dredge nothing from her memory. The shock of losing her sister is so traumatic, she completely blocks it out.

Hundreds of people attend Deidre's funeral service, held at Mount Thompson chapel. But of Faye's family, only her mother and grandmother are there. The rest of her family is a long way away, with their own personal commitments. She wishes they were there to support her through her traumatic loss.

It is less than a week since Deidre was murdered, but Faye feels pressured by those around her to have the service before Easter. A funeral, they believe, will help bring closure. It is the day preceding Good Friday. After that, over the Easter period, the church will be filled with believers mourning the death of Christ, celebrating His Resurrection. Christ died for our sins. He rose again and sat at the right hand of the Lord. The same Lord who Faye now desperately asks for answers. Why have you abandoned us? How could you allow this to have happened? Why our precious Deidre?

The funeral service is the day before Stephanie's fifth birthday. That morning, Barry undergoes a dental examination by Kon Romaniuk, who is satisfied that his teeth did not cause the bite marks found on his daughter.

Still on crutches, Barry is dignified in his RAAF uniform. His colleagues have pulled together, left nothing to chance. Everything is organised. The chapel is an ocean of flowers and Deidre's tiny white coffin is adorned with pink carnations in the shape of a pillow. Prayers and hymns resonate around the chapel, and the forlorn sound of inconsolable weeping. The padre who delivers the service lost his own son at the age of 16, and has enormous empathy with the family. He speaks quietly, gently of Deidre's short life, and of her loss. The media, staked outside with cameras and microphones, are asked to leave the family in peace. *You blokes have had your story; please, respect the family's privacy. Leave them alone today.*

There is a desolate hush at the crematorium. Nothing to disturb the silence save Faye's sobbing and the bleak, soft sound of the coffin gliding on rollers and disappearing through the curtains.

Barry will remember nothing of the service, just a blur of hands on his shoulders and quiet talk. *Sorry, mate. We're really sorry, mate. If there's anything we can do to help . . .*

Deidre's ashes are placed at the mortuary and a tiny plaque guards them. 'Deidre – in our hearts forever.'

It will take time for Faye to reflect on the haste of Deidre's funeral. To wonder if the police were diligent enough with what they did before Deidre was cremated. Whether they were too rushed. 'In those days,' she says, 'you went with what you were told. We had kept asking when we could have her funeral, and I still believe it was held when it was because it was Easter. Was it too rushed? There was no DNA, then; that came later. Apparently there was a hair, but, from what I can gather, it was destroyed. There was nothing left of it.'

There will be time for reflection and doubt, but today is not that time. Today, the family is absorbed in their grief, in going through the motions of saying goodbye. They had promised Stephanie a birthday party, and they hold it the day after the funeral, as arranged. Five candles on the cake and so much pain in the room Faye can almost taste it.

From the time of her murder, Barry can never again bring himself to utter Deidre's name.

John Reynolds works on the Kennedy murder for seven months, but, with a huge load of other work that needs attention, and frustrated at the lack of fresh leads, his work on the file dwindles off. In the time since the murder, there hasn't been one suspect strong enough to get within cooee of warranting being charged. A few red herrings that have only wasted police time, a few nutters ringing up with outlandish theories, but never anything concrete.

The file will remain open, but it is now becoming what the cops call a 'cold case'. Faye and Barry accept that with the same stoicism they have accepted everything else. The police have done their best. Reynolds often flashes back to the morning he saw Deidre in the park, and he wishes he could do more. But, like his colleagues who have all been deeply affected, his hands are tied. He will be allocated time to pick it up again only when strong information filters in.

Raymond Carroll doesn't know what to think when he goes to the doctor with his girlfriend, Joy Meyers, and they find out she is pregnant. He is only 17 and it has been the first sexual experience for them both. They had met in Wagga, where Carroll was posted in August 1973, and they hung out together, mostly at the local bowls club. He waved her goodbye in February '74 when he went back to Amberley for field training, staying with his family at Quarry Lane. Three months later, he got a hell of a shock when he returned to Wagga and she told him she thought she was expecting.

He doesn't want to marry, resentful at being forced into a shotgun wedding. But marry they do, on 28 June 1974. It isn't quite how Joy had imagined her wedding day would be, either: six months pregnant and her dress billowing out the front. It disconcerts her, too, that her new husband is always harping on about what he wants to call their child if it is a girl. Deidre. She thinks the suggestion odd and, besides, she doesn't like the name. When their daughter is born on 9 September 1974, Joy calls her Kerry-Ann Sherrie.

They move back to Ipswich when Kerry-Ann is a few months old, living with Ilma at Quarry Lane. Carroll is stationed at Amberley but when Cyclone Tracy rips through Darwin on Christmas Eve 1974, thousands of military personnel are posted to help in the clean-up. He is one of them.

But Joy isn't happy. She has joined Raymond in Darwin, living at the RAAF base with Kerry-Ann, who has recently had her first birthday. The marriage is in trouble, but she can't put her finger on what is wrong. Raymond had gone down to Amberley for a course and their relationship has been seriously strained since he returned. Joy had discovered a letter sent to her husband by his ex-girlfriend, Desley Hill, in a childish hand complete with spelling mistakes. This and other letters written by Desley would later be aired in court.

'Hi, tall dark and sexy,' she begins. Desley bombards him with anxious questions. Did he land safe in Darwin? Does he think of her? And did he mean what he said about buying her an engagement ring? If so, she writes, the size is A. What, she continues, did his mother have to say when he went home on Sunday afternoon? What are his intentions? 'Do you realy wont me to go up to Darwin with you or was it only talk because I would realy love to go up there and to be with you.' There is an underlying anxiety in the letter. Is he going to stay true? Desley closes with lots of love from herself and 'your adopted Natasha. Xxxxx OOOOO'.

Joy had also received a letter from Desley telling her she was having an affair with her husband, but Raymond denied it when Joy confronted him, a denial that would never change. But there is another reason why Joy is unhappy, something she *can* put her finger on. Something much worse that she would later report occurred about three, four times over the course of their marriage. Years later, she would tell her story with blunt simplicity, repeating it verbatim. Never any change in the details. Never missing a beat. In court, when Carroll's defence tried to rattle her, break her, dismiss her, *I put it to you . . . I suggest to you . . .*, she would never miss a beat. 'You may suggest it, but I don't agree with it. I know what I'm saying.'

Kerry-Ann is screaming again. Joy has asked Raymond to change her nappy and he is in the bedroom with her, with the door locked. Joy can't see into the room through the louvre shutters but she can hear her daughter crying out in distress. Pacing outside the bedroom, waiting for him to open the door, she snatches the baby from him when he comes out of the bedroom and demands to know what has happened. Kerry-Ann's face is blotchy with tears and Joy rocks her gently to soothe her. 'Why is she crying, Raymond?' she pleads with him. 'What's wrong with the baby?'

He doesn't answer, just stares at her in a strange way, what she would later call his 'bad look' and takes off outside. Saunters back in a while later, casually asking what has happened to the baby, why is she still crying?

There are bruises on Kerry-Ann's little legs. Sometimes on both thighs, but mostly just on one, toward her hip. Joy has no doubt what they are. Bluish bite marks that last a few days before they subside. Sometimes, she would later recall, there were bruises on different parts of her body, and once there was a cut above her eye. Bleeding a little, the blood would be smeared on Kerry-Ann's face from where she touched it to show her mother where it hurt. Too little to put proper sentences together, to say what had happened, her pain showed in her eyes that were red from crying and in her breath that caught in sobs.

It happened about three, four times by Joy's reckoning. Always the same: Raymond in the bedroom changing the nappy and the baby crying loudly. Joy pacing outside the room, waiting for him to unlock the door, asking 'What's wrong with Kerry-Ann? What's happened to make her cry?', and him sauntering past with that bad look.

Desley Hill has got the message. There is no engagement ring, no trip to Darwin. She writes another letter, this time sad and desperate, addressed to Raymond and family.

She got his letter the other day, she writes, with all of the things in it. She was surprised to hear from him again, and tries to analyse her feelings. She had wanted someone to want her, is not sorry for what she did but is very sorry for saying those things in that letter she wrote to Joy. Desley's fghting spirit surfaces, but only for a brief moment. She had copped nothing but people giving her lectures after Raymond went back to Darwin, she writes, and she was very mad. 'I'm glad that you still love Joy,' she concludes, forlornly. She would really like to be friends with them both. She understands the situation.

No kisses or hugs end this letter.

Joy doesn't tell anyone about what is happening to Kerry-Ann. She has ample opportunity to do so, but never does. Even when people occasionally query how her daughter has got the bruises, she remains silent. She would later say that she was only a young woman and that she had wanted to keep her marriage together. But it is impossible. By November 1975, just 17 months after their wedding and shortly after Raymond's return from his field training course at Amberley, Joy has returned to Wagga with Kerry-Ann to live with her mother.

Raymond stays in Darwin and moves into the single men's quarters. He rarely sees his daughter, Kerry-Ann, in the years that follow, and does not contest custody of her at his divorce hearing in 1977.

In a document written for his legal team in 2000, to dispute Joy's allegation that he had an affair with Desley Hill whilst they were married, Carroll adamantly expressed that she was wrong. When he returned from Amberley, he wrote, he gave Joy the option of staying or going. 'She decided to leave. It would have been late 1975 to early 1976 that I began to have contact with Desley again. I had no contact with Desley whilst I was married.'

What was certain was that Desley Hill was now, herself, a mother. In late July 1973, she had given birth to a daughter, Natasha. 'I did not know [Desley] was pregnant until after she had Natasha . . .' Carroll countered. 'I remember seeing her for the first time after she had had the baby.'

12

South-east Queensland is submerged in water, triggered by the backlash from Darwin's Cyclone Tracy and Cyclone Wanda, which crossed the Queensland coast late in January 1974. By Australia Day, the deluge in Ipswich has resulted in major flood levels, a treacherous rising tide that saturates building basements and sets objects afloat in main streets. The flood takes all before it, including the doorknock investigation records from the Deidre Kennedy case that were held in the basement of the Criminal Investigation Bureau. And it is at this time that the inquest into the death of Deidre Maree Kennedy is held.

The police file is 60 foolscap pages, presented on 30 January 1974 at Ipswich Court. A formality, a necessity, its details are raw, obscene. Sixty foolscap pages, hideous details of a baby's murder and the smaller, inconsequential memories of those called as witnesses. And when it is over, when the police go back to the station and Faye and Barry return home, the result leaves them with more than disquiet, more than heartache: a peculiar emptiness, just words hanging in the ether and no finality.

The floods have hijacked any other news coverage, reporters too busy covering the disaster to do courts. The inquest has not been covered. 'The result would be at the State Archives Office in Brisbane,' a librarian at the Ipswich Library tells me. 'Check there, but be warned that this sort of information has been restricted since 1964.' The State Archives Office notes the information I require, and calls back. 'Bad news, I'm afraid. The inquest file on Deidre Kennedy *was* here, but there is a notation to advise that it was removed many years ago by the Queensland Justice Department. It has not been returned. You will have to contact them.'

The Justice Department calls back. 'There is no records of the file here and we don't have any idea where it is. We have checked with the Coroner's Office and they don't have the information.

They only store these files for 30 years. You are out of time and will need to go through Freedom of Information to access what you need.'

'Why is it that so many files relating to this case can't be located?' I ask. 'Why *doesn't* Justice know where it is when the archives office has noted that that department has taken the file? All I need is the actual finding.'

Going FOI will take too long: it will be faster to contact a lawyer who was involved in the case. 'I don't know what the result was,' Barrister Peter Davis says. 'But under the Coroner's Act 1958, a coroner had to determine only a number of specific issues. Cause of death. Identity of the victim. Whether anyone should be charged. This one was straightforward. The cause of death was obviously murder. Identity of the baby was never in question. In January 1974, no one had been charged so it's a safe bet to assume that the finding was that Deidre Kennedy was murdered by a person or persons unknown.'

Barry goes out to check on the flood levels and returns with an old couple he has found huddling in a bus shelter, their home totally flooded. They stay with the Kennedys for a few days, the old man, an ex-boxer, devastated that his lifetime memorabilia has been lost in the flood. There is another reason Faye particularly remembers this time. Soon after the old couple leaves, she discovers she is pregnant again.

They pray it is a boy, so they will not compare the child with Deidre. The delivering doctor had treated Deidre for repeated bouts of tonsillitis; when Faye went into labour, he kept up a mantra to the nursing sister. 'This has got to be a little boy,' he repeated. 'We need this baby to be a boy.' It is. On 7 September 1974 they are blessed with their son, Derek, who would grow into the image of his father. Faye wants Derek christened in the same church as the girls, but the minister refuses because she doesn't belong to the diocese. 'I've led a Christian life,' Faye tells the minister. 'I've brought my children up that way. God knows me, he knows who I am. That's good enough for me.' Totally affronted, Faye does not have Derek christened and never returns to church again.

The Kennedys patch up their lives the best way they can, re-building the family unit, slowly filling the hollow void with happy moments together. They go camping again, pitching a tent under a canopy of sky the same way they had done when they were young lovers at Longreach. Faye, Barry, Stephanie and Derek, lying on their backs with a warm breeze stroking their face, quietly talking and counting the stars. Faye points out the brightest, and warms herself with a thought: Deidre was up there somewhere, polishing them like diamonds. Stephanie, now eight, looks out for her two-year-old brother and understands her mother's fears when either of them are out of her sight. Nothing will ever subdue the pain of losing Deidre, but Barry and Faye have to try for the sake of their other two children. And they try hard. They are good years; they are a good family. Everything would be all right.

Everything is not all right with Raymond Carroll. Now 21, and separated for almost a year, single life holds little appeal. Still a loner, he does not comfortably mix with his RAAF colleagues, who invariably leave him out of social invitations. And he needs dental work. In late September 1976, RAAF dental surgeon Brett Halliwell examines his teeth, an examination he does not readily forget: Carroll's breath is malodorous, protrusion of his top teeth – a condition dentists call an 'overjet' – extremely pronounced and some teeth discoloured as charcoal. Halliwell restores the outside corners of both upper teeth, building and repairing them so they will become square. He instructs his nurse to record what he had done on a dental chart and tells Carroll that further work is required.

Whilst in Darwin, Carroll meets Jennifer Russell, who will become his second wife. Jennifer likes a verbal stoush, and it is a volatile union from the moment she and Carroll meet. 'She liked fighting,' Raymond would later say. Married on 29 July 1977, exactly a month after Carroll's divorce from Joy, 13 months later they start a family. Jennifer announces the news to Raymond after a trip to the doctor. 'You're going to be a father again,' she grins. 'Twice. We're having twins.'

The girls, Raylene and Samantha, arrive in August 1979. Four years later, their son, Saun is born.

Raymond Carroll is now the father of three daughters and one boy.

John Rowley hails from Wolverhampton, in Britain's west midlands, one of four gritty, working-class boroughs known as the Black Country. Steeped in history from its Saxon settlement, locals drink ale in ancient pubs and speak in their local burr, thick with inflections. They boast of the county's industrial heritage, and of the days when the south-east of Wolverhampton had the world's largest coal output and the town's damp back lanes were filled with men trudging home from the pit, faces darkened with coal dust. Locals are footy mad, too, though their famous team, the 'Wolves' have lost their great form of the '50s and '60s. The young John had played for the Wolves as an amateur, but he had no interest in staying in the Black Country and following his father into the steel industry. Dark haired, athletic and with boundless energy, he had wanderlust. At 15, he joined the army.

In 1963, aged 20, Rowley married a lovely lass, Christina, whom he called Nuala – Gaelic for Christmas – because of her December birthday. Still in the army, he was away a lot for work, but homecomings were always good, and a baby always followed. Altogether they had six children, five daughters and a son. In 1970, the family emigrated to Australia.

With its working-class roots and small population, Rowley felt at home in Ipswich from the moment they arrived. It reminded him in some ways of the Wolverhampton he knew as a boy: no four-star restaurants or uppity pretensions, just a good working-class town, easy to live in. And warmer than England's west midlands, where winter's cold seeped into his bones. He still wants to kiss the ground whenever he returns to Queensland from a trip overseas.

In 1971 Rowley joined the civilian police, but he only lasted 15 months. He recalls the pay was lousy, and the conditions abominable. The area had a high crime rate, with around a dozen detectives and 30 cops for 40,000 people. After baling out of the civvies, Rowley worked at a factory until he joined the RAAF police in 1977. It was a career move that would change his life.

A prowler is stalking through the corridor of the Women's Quarters of the Amberley Air Force Base. He has stealthily climbed a tree, jumped over the WAAF fence, walked about 25 metres and then clambered up a drainpipe, his boot marks clearly visible on the wall. Now inside, he noiselessly zeroes in to where he wants to go.

WAAF Jackie Toigo is asleep. An attractive young woman, she had posed, scantily clad, for a photo shoot earlier in the week, and the photographs now adorn her bed head. The intruder looks down at her sleeping form, quietly removes the pictures and creeps up to the laundry.

He spreads the photos on the laundry ironing board, arranging them in an aesthetically pleasing fashion. He has also stolen women's underwear and WAAF uniforms from the laundry area, and feels the rush of adrenalin as he picks up a sharp instrument and slashes the crotch out of the panties, front to back, leaving the waistband intact. He slits the nipple area from the bras and the uniforms in the crotch and breast areas. When he has finished, he sneaks out the same way he crept in.

One of 97 corporal investigators in the RAAF, Corporal John Rowley isn't the first on the job on 4 February 1982, the night the Women's Quarters are broken into. Military police Ian Harold and Peter Parrott had been on patrol and, in the early hours of the morning, noticed a car parked suspiciously some distance off the road near the base. It was an odd place to park, they thought; there were no buildings on that side of the road. They took down the registration number and noted boots on the vehicle's rear seat.

Rowley becomes involved in the investigation the next day, and still remembers, years later, how furious the women were. Irate that a perverted prowler had done that to their private underwear.

The first step is to trace the owner of the vehicle. Rowley goes through RAAF records, and finds the car belongs to a 26-year-old electrical fitter who lives on the base. Married, with twin daughters. Name of Raymond John Carroll.

Carroll is unperturbed when confronted by Rowley. He had, he tells him, been to a function at the golf club earlier that evening and was home before midnight.

Rowley has details from the notes taken by Harold and Parrot and his vehicle registration, but Carroll is in total denial about the whole thing. He never once gets stroppy; he is calm, detached. Carroll signs a statement the day Rowley interviews him, denying any involvement. 'You did it, didn't you?' Rowley says to him, but he doesn't change expression. He just looks at him.

Rowley also speaks to Carroll's wife, Jennifer, about his movements that night. She is incensed, indignant at the suggestion that her husband had been out after midnight. He had, she says, returned home from the golf club around 11.30, and had not gone out again. She makes her feelings plain.

Carroll is not charged by RAAF police. They never get any feedback from people they speak with, and shortly afterward Rowley is posted to Brisbane. He doesn't know what the outcome was, just that it was a very serious offence.

After he interviews Carroll about the break-in, Rowley sits, drumming his fingers on the table, thinking. Of the 97 RAAF Corporals, he is the only one with a close knowledge of Deidre Kennedy's murder because he lived there at the time. He had left the civilian police force a year before it happened, but had occasionally asked colleagues if there were any developments. The hairs had gone up on the back of his neck when Carroll had sat in front of him, calmly, dispassionately telling him that before he had joined the RAAF in February 1973, he had lived with his mother at 13 Quarry Lane, Ipswich. Quarry Lane, about 500 metres from Limestone Park where the Kennedy baby had been found. Nine years afterwards, it is still an unsolved murder. Rowley vividly remembers the case: as a father of small children, he was shocked at the savagery of the toddler's death. It was a case that seemed frozen in time, going nowhere. The only hope that police had, they told Rowley, was identification of the person who had inflicted the bite marks on the child's left thigh, and a match of hair that was found on her vulva. There was nothing else.

Rowley decides to start his own quiet investigation, anything to do with Raymond Carroll. But the Ipswich police are less than enthusiastic about his hunches, telling him they are pretty sure they know who did it, and discount his suspicions. They virtually fob him off. They have tunnel vision; they think they know who it is, and it definitely is not Carroll. But who they think it is, they never tell him. A detective tells Rowley he is pretty sure they have the bloke who did it, but they are frustrated because they can't prove it.

Astonished at the lack of action, Rowley keeps digging in the background. He does not believe enough investigation has been done to eliminate Carroll, but, without the support of civilian police, it is an uphill task. The only strong thread is his belief, based on Carroll's fingerprints that had been found on the photographs of Jackie Toigo, that the serviceman is a sexual deviant with a penchant for women's underwear. That, and Carroll's teeth. He knows that police were told that, judging by the shape of the bruise marks found on Deidre's thigh, whoever had bitten her had deformed teeth. He just can't let go of his suspicions about Carroll.

In an attempt to piece together the leads, Rowley reads back through copies of stories recorded on microfiche at the *Queensland Times*. He sees the name 'Nugget' from very early in the investigation, and notices his last name is also Carroll. Cecil 'Nuggett' Carroll. He thinks there is perhaps a connection with Raymond Carroll, but 'Nugget' is no relation.

Working on his own time, Rowley starts an unobtrusive surveillance on Carroll's home. It is now an obsession.

13

Investigating a case in Toowoomba, six months after the break-in at the women's quarters, Rowley and another RAAF policeman, Flight Sergeant Bowes, meet John Reynolds, who had worked on the case from the start, for a counter lunch. Reynolds knows Rowley from the days when he worked with the civilian police. As a military policeman, Rowley's area is now south-east Queensland, liaising with local coppers in areas with RAAF communities.

Rowley gets straight down to business. 'I think I know who may have killed the Kennedy baby.'

Reynolds is surprised; it has been so long since the murder, the case is now gathering dust in police files. But he has carried the memory of Deidre's battered body for nine years and is extremely interested in what Rowley has to say. Any leads deserved investigation. He puts his glass down on the table and leans in closer. 'Yeah? Go on.' He says it casually, in the flat vowels of his native Queensland. 'What have you got?'

Rowley outlines his theories. 'This bloke's been done for breaking in at the WAAF women's quarters and slashing underwear. Sick stuff; pinched photographs of a half-dressed woman, went into the laundry and took to the nipple area of bras and slashed the crotch out of ladies' panties. He's obviously a pervert. And Deidre dressed up like she was; it made me wonder if there could be a connection. His wife has stuck up for him, said he was home that night, but there's no question at all that he did it. His prints were all over the photographs. He also lived in a street in Ipswich near Limestone Park in early 1973 before he joined the air force.'

'Has he got any other form?' Reynolds is now more than just interested; Rowley has his undivided attention. 'Anything on file about him?'

'Not that I know of. But I reckon he's managed to just slip under the radar all these years.' Rowley pre-empts Reynolds next question. 'Look, he was doing a rookies course in South Australia when Deidre was murdered. But I don't think he should be dismissed out of hand. The civvies keep telling me they've already got a suspect, but they say they haven't got enough evidence to pin anything on him. But who is this suspect? Surely they should at least have a *look* at Carroll. It can't hurt. They aren't taking this seriously at all.'

Reynolds isn't surprised. In his experience, the young cops coming through do everything by the book. The days of relying on gut feeling and old-fashioned hunches are long gone, but he trusts Rowley's judgment. 'Leave it with me,' he tells him, standing and shaking his hand. 'I'll get back to you.'

Reynolds taps the steering wheel on the drive back to Brisbane, where he now works, going over the details of what Rowley has told him. He recalls details of the geographical map he had drawn of Ipswich when Deidre was first abducted. Limestone Park is at the apex of a triangle between Short Street and Quarry Lane. Close. Very bloody close. By the time he pulls the squad car in to park, he is determined to look into it further.

He goes to his boss and says he wants to do something with this, but warns him it is going to be a huge job. 'Anyhow . . .' It is a word Reynolds uses frequently, while he gathers his thoughts. 'Anyhow, he told me to have a yarn with Horrie Robinson, the Superintendent of the CIB.' Robinson knows Reynolds from the days when he was a uniformed sergeant and Reynolds was a constable. He knows his capabilities and his flaws: short on the minutiae of administrative duties, but long on results if they were achievable.

Reynolds outlines Rowley's theories. 'Do you want me to hand this over to Homicide?'

'Just hang on a minute.' Leaning back in his chair and opening the door, Robinson yells over his shoulder for the homicide inspector to come into his office. 'This is Detective-Sergeant Reynolds,' he says. 'He's now attached to the Homicide Squad to head up the investigation into the 1973 murder of young Deidre Kennedy.'

Reynolds asks that a young officer with whom he has been working be assigned to the case. He gets him. He then calls John Rowley to ask if he would liaise directly with them.

Rowley is grateful that someone is finally listening. Just because a case is old, he thinks, it doesn't mean it needs to die on the vine.

Scared that the press might get to them first, Reynolds decides that Faye and Barry, who are now living at Richmond, need to be informed that the investigation is being re-opened and that police now have a strong suspect. Rowley goes with him after they call ahead first to make an appointment. Barry appears stoic when he hears the news, but Faye is stunned. She listens quietly and nods when John Reynolds finishes talking. Rowley finds her bravery astonishing, and reflects that informing the Kennedys of the developments in the investigation is the hardest thing he's ever had to do.

Barry wasn't as stoic as he had appeared. 'Deidre's murder was so traumatic, I thought, "surely we're not going to dredge all this up again." I thought we'd put it behind us, and I knew it would be so hard for Faye.'

Reynolds starts in the records area at the Homicide Squad in Brisbane to pull up the old files. Although there has been virtually no movement on the case since 1974, he can't find half of what he needs. Cops call it the 'dungeon' and the place is a shambles. There are stacks of files on people who have been interviewed in relation to Deidre Kennedy's murder – some here, some there – but Reynolds knows that something isn't right. He knows that in a murder case this size hundreds of people would have been interviewed. He doesn't know what has been lost, but he knows the files are incomplete. He just can't tell who has been interviewed and who has not.

Reynolds finds a file on a RAAF member who had gone into the Ipswich police station in 1980 and admitted to the murder. He would have to be re-interviewed. Reynolds knocks on his door and goes through the preliminaries, but it is soon apparent that something is very wrong.

'Prove to me that I didn't do it.' The bloke's eyes are glinting with more than a hint of madness and he is leaning belligerently forward, taunting Reynolds. 'Go on, prove to me that I didn't do it.' It is enough for Reynolds. 'People run a mile if they think they're going to be charged with something; coppers don't normally get that sort of reaction. He reckoned when he watched TV that Coke cans would suddenly come flying out and start telling him things.' Reynolds laughs at the memory. 'There weren't many things to laugh about with this case, but that was one of them. Police often get people coming into the station, putting their hand up for something they haven't done. Maybe they enjoy their five minutes of fame, or they might be delusional. But whatever; when you start investigating, you find out they're a kangaroo short in the top paddock. A screw loose.'

Knowing that Homicide always keeps a copy of an investigation's running sheets, Reynolds decides to go back to Ipswich. Thousands of fingerprints are still there from when they were filed in 1973, and even though a lot had been damaged in the 1974 floods, there is basically a complete file. What he can't find are the doorknocks or the exhibits such as the hair samples, ladies' underwear, Deidre's pyjamas and other evidence from the scene.

The key to the missing files has to be in the Homicide exhibit room. Horrie Robinson asks him if he has looked for the doorknock and exhibits himself. Reynolds hasn't had time, and asks the staff who work in that area to do it for him. They come back and say they have looked everywhere but can't find them. 'Anyhow, we walked through to the exhibit room ourselves, looked to the right shelf and there was a big brown parcel marked "Deidre Kennedy". You couldn't miss it. Didn't the Super go off! He said, "you're telling me that you've been looking for these for three weeks?" He put a bullet through the place.'

Reynolds never finds the doorknocks. *How many people live in this house? Are there any males in the house over the age of 12? Where were they on the night and morning of April 13 and 14?* Paperwork detailing the scores of people who were interviewed in the days and weeks following the murder have simply disappeared. Hundreds of interviews lost. They are losses that the Queensland Police Service will be asked to explain, and for which they will never provide an adequate answer. Perhaps they went in the floods of 1974, ruined by water seepage into the basement of the CIB? Perhaps they were moved around in a re-shuffle and were misplaced? Unsurprised that voluminous amounts of material have disappeared, Reynolds is determined that it was in no way deliberate. But, he concedes, it could be seen as sloppy police work.

Kon Romaniuk, who had done the original bite mark investigation on Deidre's body, was expecting Reynolds. 'I need to talk to you,' he had told the doctor on the phone. 'I'd like to get a clearer picture of what sort of bloke we should be looking for.'

Romaniuk spells it out for the Detective-Sergeant when they meet. 'The marks were made by both the upper and lower teeth. The small, irregular pattern of bruises that look like "point" marks was made by the upper teeth, but the lower marks are less obvious. The killer will have deformities to his two front teeth that made the "point" marks on the skin. The teeth on his bottom jaw will be straight but his top jaw will be V-shaped.' Romaniuk reminisces about the marks. 'The baby did not have deep bruises. There were no indentations to her skin and there was a width between the upper and lower marks. That indicates to me that the biter's top and bottom teeth cannot close together when his jaw is shut. He has what we call an "open bite" and a significant overjet where his teeth protrude.'

Romaniuk signed a police statement regarding the photograph of the bruise marks and models taken of other teeth, including those of Paul Borchert and Stephanie Kennedy. Different dentists from the 10-strong panel he had convened within a year of Deidre's murder to gauge different opinions had selected different people as suspects. 'Comparisons of these models against that of the bite mark on the dead child were inconclusive, because of the meagre detail in the bite mark on the thigh of the child,' he wrote. Romaniuk concluded in his police statement that: 'In the final analysis it was agreed between myself and these ten men that it would be impossible to establish with any degree of certainty as to who would be responsible for this bite mark to the dead child . . . I am of the opinion that the bite mark on the thigh of the child was inflicted by a young person up to the age of 15 years or an adult person with a small mouth . . . The individual bruises caused by the bite are not sufficiently defined to enable one to arrive at any definite conclusion.'

Romaniuk had given his professional opinion in 1973, but his statement – which would become known as Exhibit 41 – would dog him.

Shortly after, the Superintendent, Horrie Robinson, wants to know what Reynolds intends to do. Robinson knows his form only too well: Reynolds's nickname might be 'the Legend' for the way he looks out for his colleagues, but he's not a cop renowned for spending too much time on the fine print.

'What's your plan for Carroll?' he asks.

'I'll go and get his dental impressions and take it from there.'

Robinson raises a quizzical eyebrow. 'Yeah, but what are you going to do if he won't give them to you?'

Reynolds is already out the door. 'Let me worry about that.'

By 11 October 1983 – 14 months after he first spoke with Rowley about the case – Reynolds is ready to speak to Raymond Carroll. He had called ahead to RAAF police at Amberley and asked that they have Carroll waiting for him at the base.

Carroll sizes up Reynolds as he walks toward him. Shorter than himself, stocky build and hair already starting to thin on top. He fits him straight away as a bloke's bloke, who wouldn't suffer fools for long. Not the sort of man who would casually saunter into a conversation and take a long time getting to the point.

Carroll is right. Reynolds introduces himself, gets straight down to business. They are, he tells Carroll, investigating a serious matter that occurred in Ipswich several years ago in 1973. 'Can you tell me when you joined the RAAF?'

Carroll holds his gaze. 'I joined the RAAF on 5 February 1973. Then I went to Edinburgh and did my 10-week basic training.'

'What did you do after you completed your basic training?'

'I then left Edinburgh and went to Wagga where I did my basic training in electrical fitting.'

'Do you know when you left Edinburgh?'

Carroll lights a cigarette, flicking away the match with his thumb and middle finger. 'I think it was about the end of April. Can you tell me what this matter is that you are suggesting?'

Reynolds doesn't take his eyes from Carroll's face. 'We're investigating the murder of Deidre Maree Kennedy, which occurred in Ipswich on the night of 13 April, or the early hours of 14 April 1973. It would be appreciated if you would accompany us to Ipswich police station, where we can talk further.'

At the police station, Reynolds grills him, and Carroll holds his ground. He was at Edinburgh at the time of the murder, he says. After graduating, he travelled with almost all of the squad by service air to Richmond, New South Wales, then went on to Sydney and later Wagga by train. No, he answers, staring at Reynolds, he did not go to Ipswich on the weekend of the murder. Most definitely not.

And now Carroll suddenly remembers. He was not in the recruit passing-out. He and another bloke were on the sideline because there was too large a number to march, what they call in the RAAF a 'blank file' – a missing person in the parade that made it look untidy – and that is why he would have sat out. He can't remember the other bloke's name.

'Raymond, are you prepared to give us dental impressions of your teeth?' Detective Morris, a senior sergeant working with Reynolds, has now temporarily taken over the questioning. 'Plus fingerprints and hair samples from your head, chest and pubic hair?'

'Have I got to?'

Reynolds flicked a swift glance at Morris. That was an interesting response. *Have I got to?*

'No, you haven't. But are you prepared to supply them voluntarily?'

'I suppose so, yep.'

Carroll remains cool throughout. A bit balky at first, but Reynolds keeps on track. 'Look, if you haven't committed this murder, you've got nothin' to worry about, have you?' Carroll agrees to have his impressions taken and signs the forms. He is like a brick wall. He has, he insists, nothing to hide.

Dentist Desmond Hannan makes an examination of Carroll's mouth and finds that restoration work has been performed to the outside of his upper teeth. He then takes a cast of both his upper and lower teeth and gives them to dental technician Ronald Morley. From that cast, Morley prepares a model of the teeth.

Reynolds is sweating on the fingerprints coming back. *Shit,* he curses when he sees the results. There is no match with Carroll, either at the Kennedy flat, or at the scene. He now pins his hopes on the odontological findings.

'Have a look at these, Kon.' Reynolds hands him the dental impressions, waits quietly as he places the records on his laboratory bench. Fanatical about his work, Kon Romaniuk has admitted to an obsession with the Deidre Kennedy case. For years, he has tried to match the bite marks on the baby's legs with every person who has been through the dental school. He has never even got close. But now he starts shaking, talking rapidly in his thick mid-European accent. 'This is the closest I've ever been, this is the closest I've ever been! But . . .' Romaniuk's voice trails off.

'But what?'

'It's close, but not close enough. The similarities are uncanny, but there is a problem with the upper marks. There is nothing to show what has caused these pressure points on the dental records.'

Romaniuk has already advised Reynolds to access Carroll's RAAF dental records, taken when he was inducted into recruits in February 1973, aged 17, so the men have them here to discuss. The records show his front teeth were badly chipped, broken away at the outer edges. But they also show something else. 'This man had some teeth reconstruction work done when he was 21,' Romaniuk announces. 'Two front teeth capped, the outside tip of the front, left and right corners, a few fillings and one extraction. But there's something still not right.' He picks up the telephone. 'I am going to speak to the dentist who did the work.'

Reynolds waits while the doctor makes his call, and Romaniuk hangs up after a few minutes. 'You may not believe this, John,' he grins. 'The RAAF nurse who recorded the restoration work done by Halliwell, the dentist, made a mistake. What you might call a red herring.'

Reynolds knows Romaniuk is eccentric, but he has never seen him so animated.

'One of Carroll's teeth was marked wrong on the chart. It was recorded that the *inside* of his left front tooth was built up and repaired, when in fact it was the *outside* of his left front tooth.'

Reynolds now also breaks into a grin. 'You're kidding! Who'd bloody believe it?' He is staring at the dental impressions. 'What are these marks on the back of his teeth?'

Romaniuk bends over for a closer look. 'Hang on a minute.' Grinding down the cast of Carroll's teeth with a drill to reproduce how they had looked in 1973, he peers through a macroscope to compare the impression with the light bruise mark patterns left on Deidre's delicate skin.

Romaniuk looks at Reynolds, triumphant. 'You've found your killer.'

14

Rebuilding the complete running sheets from the day of the murder, within a couple of weeks Reynolds has located the exhibits, including Deidre's clothing. But he doesn't get everything he wants. He asks that Kenneth Cox, a forensic scientist attached to the Health Laboratory who has found similarities between the baby's hairs and those of Raymond Carroll, be sent to Hong Kong – then the world's leading authorities in hair samples – to analyse what they have. But the bosses decide they have plenty of evidence to take to court without going to that extreme. The department, they say, cannot warrant the expense of sending them both.

Reynolds needs a second opinion. Romaniuk has advised him to go and see Dr Kenneth Aylesbury Brown, Senior Lecturer in Forensic Odontology at Adelaide University and founding President of the Australian Society of Forensic Dentistry. As soon as he gets clearance to go to Adelaide, he is off.

Dr Ken Brown is no stranger to controversial cases. He worked on the sensational Chamberlain case, which pivoted on the central questions: was nine-week-old Azaria taken by a dingo at Ayers Rock or murdered by her mother? Brown, a fourth-generation Seventh-Day Adventist, had his evidence discounted during the first inquest on the basis that he was unqualified to examine bite marks in clothing. He would, ultimately, be savaged for the evidence he presented to the second Chamberlain inquest in late 1981. Based on 'persuasive new evidence', it led to the findings of the late Coroner Dennis Barritt – who sensationally found that Azaria Chamberlain was taken by a dingo and her remains disposed of by human intervention – being quashed.

The clothing worn by Azaria on the August 1980 night that she disappeared was taken by Dr Brown to the London Hospital Medical College. There, Brown saw his British colleagues, includ-

ing Forensic Odontologist Bernard Sims, one of the chief specialists to conduct tests involving ultra-violet photography on the
clothing and who, with Brown, would later give key evidence at
the Kennedy murder trial. The experts came to the same conclusions: that the bloodstains on the jumpsuit were consistent with a
child of Lindy and Michael Chamberlain, and that the cuts were
made by instruments such as scissors or a knife.

Bernard Sims told the inquest he believed Azaria's clothing
showed no evidence of teeth marks and saliva from any member
of the canine family, and that it would be highly unlikely that a
dingo could carry a baby any distance without it dragging along
the ground.

Aired at the sensational trial, the observations of the British
forensic team damned Lindy Chamberlain as the mother from
hell. But if they had no doubts as to her guilt, others did. Cleared
after serving four years in prison, Chamberlain's conviction was
eventually quashed.

Brown is a little wary of Reynolds's questions when he flies to
see him in Adelaide on 28 November 1983. 'I'm not doubting the
opinion of your colleague, Kon Romaniuk,' Reynolds assures
him. 'I would like to know what you think of some aspects of the
Kennedy case.'

Reynolds assesses the odontologist. One hundred and sixty
centimetres, at a pinch. Pale colouring, from a lifetime spent
working in laboratories. Strong voice etched with upper-class
inflections and strong opinions packaged in an affable personality.
Dr Brown is an expert in his field, taught and mentored by the
best in the world, and does not take kindly to having his opinions
questioned by laymen. Reynolds immediately judges how best to
elicit the information he needs without offending the eminent
doctor.

'Kon has advised me to come down and get your opinion.
Please, call him yourself to check. I'll leave the Carroll exhibits
with you while you do that. They are his upper and lower dental
casts.'

Reynolds waits a few hours before returning. Brown is now
visibly more relaxed. He has made transparencies, comparing the

photos of the marks on Deidre's thigh with the casts of the teeth. He gets straight to the point. 'There is no doubt in my mind that these marks were made by human teeth, the same teeth represented by those casts. You've got your man.'

Reynolds is at the whiteboard, thinking out loud and trying to devise a strategy. Carroll had told Rowley that he had been inducted into the RAAF through a training course at Edinburgh Air Base, South Australia, in 1973. Went into course number 1203 as a recruit, which started in February and concluded with a formal passing-out parade on 19 April. Six days after Deidre's murder, and the day of her funeral. Reynolds knows it doesn't take Einstein to work out that Carroll couldn't have been in two places at once.

'The RAAF course records show he was at his graduation.' Reynolds is talking to his colleague John Morris. 'Thousands of kilometres away from Queensland, which gives him a perfect alibi. If he was there, he couldn't have been at Ipswich. Unless . . .' Reynolds pauses, resting the tip of the whiteboard marker on his bottom lip, 'unless the RAAF records aren't accurate.' He sits on his desk. 'Faye Kennedy and the kids were travelling east from Longreach at the same time Carroll was travelling north from Edinburgh. They both converged on Ipswich. But who would know if Carroll left South Australia? This is what we're gunna have to do. Get a list of all the recruits from that course. Find out where they are now, and let's go and talk to them.'

Morris affects choking on his coffee. 'Christ, that's a massive task. It's been 10 years since they graduated. They could be anywhere. And how reliable are their memories likely to be after all this time?'

'Dunno,' Reynolds shrugs. 'But we're about to find out.'

The list takes weeks to collate. Morris was right: the recruits from Course 1203 are scattered all over Australia, and two are in Malaysia. Reynolds works closely with his team: Sergeant Bruce White, Detective Senior-Sergeant John Morris, Detective Constable Mark Paroz and Corporal John Rowley to gather the information they need. Assigned to speak to former recruits living in different states, Reynolds briefs them. 'OK, they're not to know what we're investigating. I don't want them making their own conclusions. If they ask, tell them we're investigating a serious matter, but that's all they are to know. No further details. We need to ask them if anyone was missing from the passing-out parade and if everyone graduated.'

Morris is still not quite convinced. He wonders how much he would remember if someone asked him to recall events from a decade earlier. A lot can happen in a bloke's life in 10 years.

He is right to have doubts. Most former recruits laugh outright when they are asked the questions. 'You've got to be bloody joking! What do you want to know? It was years ago!' They were only young men at the time, usually in their mid-teens, and, for most, it was the first time they had left home. They remember bits and pieces: who they shared rooms with, the times they got on the grog, the hard slog of being a recruit. It was no picnic, out of bed at the crack of dawn, constant military drill, and missing the comforts of home. But no one can really tell the investigators what they want to know.

Reynolds and his team show them the course photograph. That helps, but not a lot. 'Yeah,' most concede. 'Someone's missing from the photograph, but I don't remember who. What's this all about?'

They use their rehearsed line, now down pat. 'We're investigating a serious matter but we can't disclose any further details. If you remember who was missing, please phone this number.' They hand over their cards and leave. There are only a couple of recruits left to speak to. So far, it's been a futile exercise.

Reynolds is totally discouraged. It has taken weeks to find the recruits, and they haven't yet advanced very far at all. 'I need to track down the course instructor, Raymond Martin,' he tells Morris. 'He was older than the recruits, might remember more.'

Martin does turn out to be more forthcoming. 'You're testing the memory but, yeah, I can recall that course because it was the first time I had instructed. All but two blokes graduated. One was back-coursed because his grades weren't up to scratch.'

'Do you remember his name?'

'Yeah, I'd know it from the course records.'

'OK. And the other bloke?'

'Yeah, he went home because there was something wrong in the family.'

Reynolds tries to remain impassive. Now he's getting somewhere. 'Can you remember the name of the bloke who went home?'

'No.'

'Can you describe him?'

'Yeah,' Martin says. 'Quiet. Bad teeth. Not very popular with the other fellows.'

'Was his name Raymond Carroll?'

'Yeah, that's him!' Reynolds makes a mental note. *You beauty.*

'Have you spoken to Mick Sheean?' Martin adds. 'He was one of the recruits on that course, and I think he helped pack Carroll's gear the day he left.'

Sheean is the last on their list and Reynolds finds him at Richmond Air Base in New South Wales. 'I'll fly down to see you tomorrow morning,' Reynolds tells him on the phone. It is the last day of January 1984. The team has been working on the case since August.

'I'm investigating a serious matter. Do you remember if a bloke went home from course 1203?'

Sheean answers immediately 'Yeah. Bloke by the name of Raymond Carroll.'

Bingo. 'Can you describe him?'

'Tall. Quiet. Once, I was lying on my bed and got the shock of my life when I turned around and he was there. He had teeth that stuck out. I didn't have much to do with him. He wasn't my sort of bloke.'

Sheean recalls that the final shoot at the practice range before their graduation was completed just before lunch on 12 April. Cleaning their weapons after lunch in preparation for an inspection, the instructor called Carroll out of his room. Ten minutes later, Martin told the recruits that there was an illness in Carroll's family and that he was taking compassionate leave. Sheean was one of the recruits asked to pack up Carroll's weapons. 'Carroll came in, yelled out "Hooray!" and said goodbye to a few of the recruits. He got in a RAAF vehicle and drove away. That was the last time I seen him during the course.'

Reynolds realises Sheean is the linchpin in this investigation. Up until now, Carroll had had the perfect alibi, but suddenly the foundations of that alibi seem to be shaking. They are gathering enough evidence to charge him.

15

John Rowley wants to know the reason Carroll would have gone home on compassionate leave. 'Who was sick? And how are you going to prove it?'

'We'll try and talk to his mother,' Reynolds says. 'And get hold of the doctor's reports. Maybe his brothers or sisters were ill.'

Rowley knows how the military works. 'Look, they would have to be *really* sick. You don't get sent home from rookies just because someone in your family has got the sniffles. A Commanding Officer would definitely have checked that it was all above board. Otherwise they would have these young fellows running off to see their girlfriends or just because they want a break from the discipline for a few days.'

They start trawling through RAAF records that prove to be as barren as a desert. Nothing to show Carroll ever left Edinburgh on compassionate leave. No pay books. No records at all that prove or disprove their theory. They must have been either lost, destroyed or thrown out years before. Reynolds knows this is a two-edged sword. If this fact got to court, both prosecution and defence would use it to their advantage.

Reynolds has another problem. If Carroll *had* gone to Ipswich on 12 April, how the hell did he get there from South Australia in such a short time? He had to have travelled home by civil aircraft. That's the only way he could have made it by that date. Reynolds checks the flight records of Australia's domestic carriers, Ansett and TAA, but draws another blank. 'Sorry, Sir. Passenger records are thrown out after seven years.' There is no way of proving his movements.

Reynolds goes over what he knows about Carroll. He was only 17 years old when Deidre was murdered. Away from home for the first time in his life. Probably homesick, lonely, pissed off. Unpopular with the other recruits, who no doubt made that obvious. Bit of a loner. No crime in that, but difficult when he had been thrown amongst a heap of strange young blokes. He may have had a girlfriend that he badly missed. Raised in an air-force family. His father killed in a RAAF vehicle in 1971. *Father killed in a RAAF vehicle in 1971.*

Reynolds figures that has to be key. The old-boys' network, protecting their own. He thinks about how it may have happened. Someone rang Edinburgh, said Raymond was needed at home. Probably spoke to the padre, who is as well respected as the Air Vice-Marshal. The padre would know the family history, would want to do the right thing. *Father was killed in a RAAF vehicle near Darwin in late '71. The family need our support. Forget the paperwork. Get recruit Carroll on the next plane.* It happened all the time.

If his theory is correct, then someone in Carroll's family knew that he was going home. But Reynolds doesn't think they protected him. Perhaps he just didn't turn up at the house, instead simply went AWOL after he left the base. But they are all just theories. He has no way of knowing if he is right. No way of proving it.

Names and dates cover the whiteboard, but something is not adding up. Reynolds has been puzzling over it for days but he's damned if he can see what it is. Trying to piece together different threads from a decade-old murder is proving more problematic than he had anticipated. His colleagues know he's stressed when he lights a cigarette and forgets to smoke it, ash drooping into the ashtray. 'Whoa, hang on a minute,' he suddenly says. He makes a couple of phone calls to bases where Carroll had worked, hangs up with a grin. 'That's what we had wrong. Carroll has been married twice. Let's find his first wife.'

Joy Grinter – nee Meyers – is now living in Wagga with her second husband. Slow talking and intense, she strikes Reynolds as a guileless, naïve woman who couldn't lie if her life depended on it. Dark haired in a shapeless tracksuit, she invites him to sit at her kitchen table.

'Why did your marriage to Raymond Carroll split up?' It is a straight question, delivered deadpan.

Joy looks surprised. 'Because he was abusing our child, Kerry-Ann.'

'What was he doing?'

'Sometimes he would change her nappy in the bedroom and I would hear her screaming and crying. But he locked the door and I couldn't get in.'

Reynolds hands start to shake. 'Right. Why? What happened?'

Grinter's husband is sitting, listening impassively. He has obviously heard this story before. 'Well, he'd come out of the bedroom real quiet and walk out of the house. He wouldn't say a word, just turn up later and wouldn't talk about it. I would go in when he'd leave the bedroom and find bruises from bite marks on her legs.' She looks at her husband, and back at Reynolds. 'Look, it's about time you told me; why are you asking these questions?'

Reynolds tells her he is investigating the murder of a child and thanks her for her time. Outside the house, he sits in his car, trying to calm down. It takes him 15 minutes to regain his composure.

In Darwin, shortly after continuing his investigations on the case, Reynolds receives a call from Wagga police saying that a woman called Joy Grinter wants to talk to him. He returns to Wagga to see her.

'Look, I've been thinking about all that stuff you asked when you met me last time,' she says. 'Can you tell me the name of the child who was murdered?'

In the first interview, Reynolds had carefully avoided telling her what police were investigating, saying only that it involved a child. Now, he momentarily hesitates, quickly weighing up whether to tell her. She obviously has some information that could be useful, decides to come clean. 'The baby's name was Deidre. Deidre Kennedy.'

There is a pause, a protracted sigh. 'I wondered about that. You know, I've often wondered about that. Before our daughter, Kerry-Ann, was born, Raymond said that if it was a girl he wanted to name her Deidre.'

Reynolds has gone over the evidence ad infinitum with police prosecutor Pat Youngberry. Finally, Youngberry gives him the nod. 'You've got enough now.'

Once again, Reynolds calls the RAAF police at Amberley, asks them to have Carroll waiting for him at the base.

Carroll is unruffled, composed, stares hard at Reynolds as he walks toward him.

'Hello, Raymond. I wish to ask you some further questions in relation to the matter that we have previously discussed.'

'That shit about the baby?'

Reynolds has never forgotten how pitiful she looked, lying on the ground. Like a little doll with blonde hair, so tiny the step-ins came down to her knees. *That shit about the baby?* The statement offends him deeply, and his muscles automatically go taut. 'That's correct. Are you prepared to accompany me to the Ipswich police station?'

Ilma Carroll is interstate when her son Peter telephones to advise her she needs to return home urgently. 'Mum, you had better come back home. Raymond's been arrested for the murder of that baby in Ipswich.'

The memory of the shock will stay in her mind for years to come, through her children's marriages and the births of her grandchildren. It will stay with her until her grave. A friend drives her back the three hours to Queensland, and she feels numb, mute with fear; then begins to scream during the drive. Ilma vividly remembers the murder. The park was so close to where she lived and her daughter Debbie, who was only nine at the time, was terrified. As soon as it started to get dark she locked the house up like Fort Knox, told her mother she was scared of being killed herself. Ilma felt so sad for Faye Kennedy. As a mother, if she had known at the time who killed her baby, she would have killed the person herself.

It is the longest drive of Ilma's life back to Ipswich.

The interview starts just before 10am, in the oppressive heat of 27 February 1984. It will run all through the day, recorded on reel-to-reel tape and typewriter, and not finish until 7.30 that night. A 24-page record of interview with 214 questions and answers.

Detective Morris reads Carroll his rights. 'I must first warn you that you are not obliged to say anything and anything you do say will be taken down on a typewriter by Detective-Sergeant White and may be later given in evidence. Do you understand that?'

Carroll is steady in his answer. 'Yes.'

Does he agree that he is being spoken to with regard to the murder of Deidre Kennedy? 'Yep.' Carroll lights another cigarette, slowly exhales the smoke. 'But why are you speaking to me about it?'

They ignore his question.

Asked if his teeth can be examined for repairs, as the RAAF records are inconsistent with the work that had been done in 1976, Carroll explains his badly discoloured teeth had affected his appearance and his job chances. 'First impressions, like . . . So I went to a dental lab and had the work done.' He asks Reynolds whether because the dental work on his two front teeth is different to what the records showed, does that put him further *in,* or *out* of suspicion?

They ignore this question, too.

Kon Romaniuk is waiting at Ipswich CIB to do the dental examination. He looks inside Carroll's mouth, sees the old outline of his teeth, clearly visible. He notes what he had identified before: that Carroll's upper jaw advances further than his lower and that his front teeth cannot meet when his back teeth are closed. Taking plaster casts of Carroll's upper and lower teeth and then duplicating them, he makes an identical working model. With the RAAF records from 19 February 1973 next to him and notes on the later work done to Carroll's teeth, Romaniuk removes the fillings from the duplicates. It doesn't take him long to confirm his original opinion. 'It's him, John,' he tells Reynolds. 'It's definitely him.'

The interview resumes, questions and answers bouncing between Reynolds, Carroll and Morris, a tense game of verbal ping-pong. What does he say, Reynolds asks, about Carroll's former instructor telling them that he had left the course early on compassionate leave? Carroll returns the question with a question. 'What was the reason for the leave?' he asks Reynolds.

Carroll points out that the last entry on his dental assessments from Edinburgh was dated 18 April 1973 – the day before the passing-out parade. That, he retorts, would indicate to him that he was there on that date. It is normal practice for RAAF members to carry their own personal documents each time they move to another posting.

But the police don't agree with his assessment. If personnel had to take urgent compassionate leave, documents would be posted.

'Good point,' Carroll counters. 'That is, assuming I *went* on compassionate leave.'

Reynolds nails him about the reasons he had given them for not marching on graduation day. The first time they had interviewed him, in October the year before, he had said that if there were odd numbers of men to march, it created a 'blank file'. But Reynolds has done his homework, knows this is not right. Instructors at the RAAF base have told him it is irrelevant how many members march on a parade ground. Whether there's three, or three hundred, they all march. He presses his point. Even with odd numbers, every member marches.

Carroll appears unfazed. 'All I know is I was at the graduation march but I didn't participate in the march.' He can't recall suffering any injuries that would have stopped him marching. Now he is shown a graduation photograph that he peers at, studies hard. He stabs his finger over a face when asked to identify himself. 'Possibly third member from left middle rank.'

Reynolds looks at the photograph, now 10 years old. 'Are you saying that you are the third person from the right in the centre row of this photograph?'

Carroll hedges his bets, which does not go unnoticed. 'I am saying it is possibly me.' He is counting the number of people in the photograph, mouthing the numbers out loud. 'Twenty-seven,' he announces when he is finished. He agrees there appears to be one member missing, but he is adamant. He was at Edinburgh on 19 April 1973 at the time of the Deidre Kennedy murder, even though it does not appear he is in the graduation picture.

When he left the graduation, Reynolds asks, who else travelled with him to Wagga? Can he remember?

Carroll stares hard at his interrogator. If he could remember, he says, he wouldn't be here now.

What of his previous statement to police that when he left Edinburgh, he travelled by service air to his new posting at Richmond with the other graduates? Reynolds has since found out that recruits do not use service air to get to their next unit. 'What do you say about that?' he asks.

Carroll again answers with a question. 'Did the recruits say what method of transport they used?'

On and on. Never an admission, always an answer. He wasn't given leave for any purpose. There was no sickness in the family to warrant compassionate leave. The passing-out parade was not the highlight of his career; it was simply one more task a person had to complete to stay in the air force.

Carroll asks for the outcome of the tests done on his fingerprints, hair samples and dental impressions. Reynolds winces. He would prefer not to discuss this yet. Reynolds knows he is obliged to answer him, though he is deliberately vague. His fingerprints, he tells him, could not be identified as being any of the prints found in connection with this matter. However, he adds, the other prints they have need not necessarily be those of the offender, either.

Reynolds invites Carroll to make a comment and he takes the opportunity to make a statement and ask a question. 'In my mind, I am innocent and, in relation to fingerprints, you said that the prints on the body are not necessarily those of the offender. How do you come to that conclusion?'

'At no time have I stated or inferred that those fingerprints to which I have referred were from the body of Deidre Maree Kennedy,' Reynolds shoots back. Carroll has made a major slip-up and Reynolds has noticed. 'The fingerprints to which I have referred were found at the scene where the baby's body was disposed of . . . a public toilet situation in Limestone Park, and the fingerprints which were found there could belong to any person who has public access to that park.'

And has there, Carroll wants to know, been any other such comparisons in the course of this investigation? Stuff like hair samples, fingerprints, dental impressions?

Reynolds is tiring of answering Carroll's queries. They seem to be verbally chasing each other around the interview room. Yes, he admits. In excess of 3000 fingerprints and a number of dental comparisons have been made, and there are no similarities with either. 'Are you prepared to continue with this interview in connection with the murder of Deidre Maree Kennedy?'

Carroll shrugs, gives a cryptic reply. 'To continue with it is only going to prove me innocent or guilty or guilty and innocent, whichever.'

He asks whether his mother has been interviewed, and Reynolds shakes his head in response. 'Efforts have been made but she is unavailable at this stage.'

Reynolds starts the questioning about Carroll's former wife Joy's allegations that he had abused their daughter, Kerry-Ann. 'Suddenly, his demeanour changed,' Reynolds recalls. 'He had a tear in his eye. I thought, "here we go, he's gonna break." Instead, he coughed and said, "can I have a cigarette?"' He demands to know why Reynolds is questioning him about his first marriage and daughter. The cause of their split was incompatibility, Carroll says. He had married Joy because he had to, and it simply hadn't worked out.

'Do you want to make any comment re the allegations of abuse against your daughter?'

'Nothing you can put on that sheet.'

'Did you argue about calling the child Deidre?'

'Don't know, possibly, possibly not . . . If we did, she must have won her argument because she's not called Deidre, is she? The child is called Kerry-Ann.'

Reynolds wants to know whether Carroll wishes to comment on allegations that the reason for the separation in the marriage was because of the treatment of their daughter. Carroll certainly does. He glares at Reynolds. 'I am not a child molester nor a child basher, and I can stand neither of the two.'

Reynolds asks whether he can give any reason why his ex-wife would say those things if they were not true? Carroll lights another smoke. When is this going to end? 'I smacked Kerry-Ann, but nothing more than what I have disciplined my own children now and my present wife has no complaints how I discipline the children. Can I ask a question?'

'Yes.' Reynolds leans back in his chair. 'Yes, you may.'

'Am I going to be charged with anything? This is getting beyond a joke.'

Reynolds face muscles tighten. He would admit, later, that if he had met Carroll in other circumstances, he still wouldn't have liked him. He tries to contain his contempt. 'We're still trying to make inquiries into a very serious matter, and at no time have we ever treated it as a joke and nor do we intend to.'

'I'm prime suspect number one, eh?'

There is a shift of mood in the room. Reynolds checks his watch, and shuffles back into his seat. It's getting to be a long day.

Round and round, over and over, back and forth.

Grinding on. Did he travel to Ipswich the weekend of the murder? And if he was in Ipswich at the time of the murder of Deidre Kennedy, could he have been affected by liquor as to not remember what he had done?

No. He doesn't suffer from any illness. No, he's never blacked out before. Yes, he's been drunk, and sometimes not remembered going home from parties, but he has never been in blackout.

'How often have you been drunk?' Reynolds inquires.

'About once every twelve months or so.' Carroll can't be specific. He doesn't keep records, he adds. He is fighting hard now to keep the sarcasm from his tone. 'At the time of the murder in question, I was only 17 and had not really started to consume alcohol in such high quantities. I did not really start drinking until the year I was in Darwin and my wife and I had separated and I was single, living at the RAAF in Darwin . . .'

The interview has gone on for most of the day. Interrupted by a uniformed officer, Reynolds suspends the interview at 5.07pm. Carroll's wife, Jennifer, is at the front counter, shouting at Reynolds to tell her what the hell is going on with her husband. She's a fiery piece, likes a blue.

'Settle down,' he says. 'There's no easy way to tell you this. I'm shortly going to charge your husband with the murder of Deidre Maree Kennedy.'

She glares at him. 'Is that right? And I suppose you'll want to know about our sex life and everything else!'

Her response startles him. No obvious sadness, shock or tears, as he would have expected. And, as a matter of fact, he *would* like to talk to her about their sex life. Given the sexual deviancy of the murder, that is exactly what he would like to find out. Reynolds knows from hard experience that if you want to know something about a man, ask his sexual partner. He wants to know whether her husband has an underwear fetish; whether he had a high or a low sex drive with her; whether he liked to bite. The information is personal, but relevant: whoever killed Deidre was a paedophile, and he would most probably not display the same fetishes with an adult partner. Still, it's worth asking. What is he like with their children? How does he discipline them? But he does not get the opportunity to ask.

'Go and get fucked!' Jennifer screams. 'I want to see him.'

Knowing he was about to be charged, Carroll and his wife do not waste time on preliminaries, instead launching into a discussion about who will pay the rent if he is locked up.

16

Reynolds re-starts the interview 30 minutes later, and Carroll wants to make his position clear. 'I don't,' he says, glaring at Reynolds, 'make a habit of going around pinching female clothing off the line.' And he has another question. When police interviewed him, did his brother, Peter, state that he was at home on the night of the murder?

'I have not interviewed your brother and at no time have I stated that I did,' Reynolds replies. 'What is the reason for your questions?'

Carroll doesn't hesitate. He wants to prove his innocence, and he also believes his mother has previously stated he was not at home on the night of the murder. Is that correct?

'I am not aware as to what your mother has stated, as there is no record as to any member of your family being spoken to at the time of the murder or up until this present day.'

There is no record as to any member of your family being spoken to at the time of the murder or up until this present day. It is an admission Reynolds did not want to make.

Carroll has had enough. 'Can I make a phone call?' he asks.

'Who do you wish to ring?'

'My mother.'

An alibi, Reynolds thinks. Does he want an alibi?

All through the day, through the criss-crossing of questions, the hostilities, the cat-and-mouse game played between police and suspect, the shrugs, denials and sighs, Carroll has maintained his composure. He has never once wavered. Never once made any incriminating admissions. But that isn't about to stop John Reynolds.

Just after 7pm, Reynolds ends the interview. 'I am now going to arrest you with the murder of Deidre Kennedy,' he tells Carroll.

He pauses, waiting for a reaction. There is none; Carroll's face is closed, expressionless. Taken to the Ipswich watch-house where he is finally charged, Carroll – tall, reed thin and wearing overalls – is slightly hunched over as he leaves the station, a coat covering his head.

Faye Kennedy is watching the hands on the clock turn round. She frequently glances at Barry, who is trying to maintain a calm composure. How much longer until they hear from the police whether the suspect has been charged?

Someone had tipped off the media that there had been a breakthrough in the Deidre Kennedy case, and they are crawling all over the police station. Reynolds is thankful that he had the foresight to phone Faye and Barry a few minutes earlier, telling them that Raymond Carroll has been formally charged with their daughter's murder. They took it with the same stoicism and relief he had come to understand from Deidre's parents. He didn't want them hearing news second-hand through the press, but, with a story this big, he knew there was little hope of containing it. The next day's headlines spell it out. 'Man, 29, to face charge. Police made a major breakthrough in one of Queensland's most baffling murder cases last night.' The newspapers are snatched up in a buying frenzy.

Held over the weekend at the Ipswich watch-house, on Monday 27 February, Carroll appears in the local Magistrate's Court where he is formally remanded in custody until mid-March. Transferred by police van to Boggo Road Prison the same day and admitted at a time unknown, it is his first taste of prison life. The van climbs the rise to Boggo Road, the barred windows of its old fortress exterior winking a sly hello in the bright sunlight. Carroll's mouth is dry, his stomach roiling. Perched on the edge of the van's seat, all his senses are primed for danger. Boggo Road is known as one of the toughest jails in Australia, full of intractable hard-arsed bastards and recidivists who just can't stay on the right side of the ledger. Carroll reeks of his own fear, sweat now pouring from his armpits. He hears the clangour of the prison gates opening and his name announced in guttural tones. *Carroll! Raymond John!* Handcuffed at the front, he dips his head as he climbs out of the van, squinting to adjust his eyes from the gloom to sudden glare, sees the guards turning to greet him, bleak as grim reapers and hostility buzzing around them like blowflies. Tastes the sour rush of acid that floods his mouth and touches the ground on which thousands of men before him have walked. And Raymond John Carroll suddenly knows, with a knowledge he is never tempted to forget, that this is what 'shit-scared' means.

Prisons don't come much worse than this hellhole. Brutality, violence and extreme discipline are an accepted part of the system.

Carroll stays in Boggo Road for no more than 24 hours before he is bailed – too long for even the hardest crims who shudder at the thought of having to return there. Perched at the top of a gently sloping hill in south Brisbane, No 1 Division was originally opened in 1883 to provide accommodation for short-sentenced prisoners. They had snickered bitterly at a newspaper description, which waxed that it was like a 'country gentleman's mansion within its own grounds'. In reality, it was a nightmare of uncontained savagery and violence exacerbated by close confinement. No 2 Division, which housed female prisoners, opened in 1903 and would later come to be used by long-term male prisoners.

The jail was built on slimy swampland at Bolgo Road. But for the prisoners it was, and would always be, known as Boggo Road. Surrounded by a 6.6 metre-high brick wall the colour of henna faded by sunlight, it was iced in bird droppings. The only opening was the main gate and, by the 1970s, No 2 Division became the maximum-security prison where the tiny cells – little more than cages – housed the state's most violent offenders. Rioting and escape attempts spelled the death knell for Boggo Road: following a commission of review in 1989 – ironically named the Kennedy Commission – the prison with its head in the clouds and its ankles deep in swamp, was finally closed down. But, before it did, Raymond Carroll would be back.

Immaculately dressed in fawn trousers and a dark brown shirt, Carroll is impassive at his committal hearing, which starts five months after his arrest, on 9 July 1984, and ends four days later. He enters no plea to both the abduction and murder charge of Deidre Kennedy and to stealing clothes from the veranda. Seventeen charges of breaking and entering, stealing and wilful destruction of WAAF property are also read.

It is the first time that Faye and Barry have had to face the man accused of murdering their daughter. Faye averts her eyes, trembling violently as she gives her brief, heartbreaking evidence about tucking the children safely into bed. Barry, visibly uncomfortable with the attention, fiddles with a button on his shirt and grimaces when he admits he had not locked the unit.

Faye sees her immediately: Carroll's second wife, Jennifer, walking straight toward her in the court passage. She looks Faye straight in the eye and asks, 'And how are *you* today, Mrs Kennedy?' and keeps walking.

Over the course of the week the witnesses have differing recollections. Detective Morris testifies that one of the Kennedys' neighbours had told him he saw a 'clean-cut person, like a serviceman' walking down toward the flats. Police admit that prints of Carroll were not found in the flat where Deidre was abducted. Forensic scientist Kenneth Cox says some hairs found on Deidre's body are similar to Carroll's. He describes the texture and colour comparisons as quite a good match, and the hair diameter as similar. 'They could have come from Carroll and he could not be eliminated as a suspect.' But, he admits, 'that's as far as I can go.' Reynolds quietly curses under his breath. He is sure that if the hair samples had been sent to Hong Kong as he had requested, Cox may well have been able to make a more definitive identification. One way or the other.

Carroll's Quarry Lane neighbour, William Jordan, looks bewildered and bemused that he has been called as a witness. He doesn't know, he says, whether Carroll was in Ipswich at the time the baby was murdered. 'He used to come and go all the time,' he shrugs.

Many former RAAF recruits are called, the first occasion they have collectively been together in years and had the opportunity to share recollections. They bounce around memories of course 1203. Who had been there? Who had to repeat the course? Who was not in the passing-out parade? It is a get-together that makes

Carroll's defence particularly uncomfortable. Having the chance to trade memories could lead to people adding missing pieces together that perhaps do not exist.

As many other RAAF recruits testify, Trevor Kitson tells the hearing that Carroll was disliked by his colleagues. 'Virtually everyone had very little time for him,' he announces dismissively. 'It was just one of those physical things. If you don't like someone, you don't like someone.' Carroll's former Commanding Officer, Lesley Meacham, admits that orderly room staff may have caused an oversight in the paperwork, not recording that Carroll had gone on compassionate leave. It is good news for the defence.

Kon Romaniuk is clear in his evidence that comparisons between Carroll's dentition with photographs showing the bruise marks are almost a 'perfect fit' and were likely made by a person aged 17. It is, he tells the court, 'highly likely that the teeth could have produced such a bite or bruising pattern' and that the possibilities of another dentition existing like Carroll's would be astronomically low. But he admits to defence barrister Phil Hardcastle that he had had very little experience with bite marks in 1973 and could not be absolutely certain then that Carroll had made the marks.

Police prosecutor Senior-Sergeant Pat Youngberry hands up 51 exhibits, including the underwear found on Deidre's body. He tells the court that a recruit had gone on leave but that his departure had not been recorded. It is, he testifies, 'highly unlikely that anyone else other than the defendant caused the bite marks on the girl's body.'

The defence, funded by Legal Aid, is scathing. The case against his client is purely circumstantial, Hardcastle objects. 'There are no written records to show Mr Carroll was granted leave at the time of the murder. There is no evidence to suggest anyone can identify him or that he was even in the area at the time. And there is no evidence of an admission in the records of interview; in fact, Mr Carroll says quite categorically: "No, I didn't do it," in the police interview.'

But the defence argument does not sway Magistrate Bill Pullar. On 13 July 1984, the same day 17-year-old Boris Becker sensationally becomes the youngest tennis champion ever to win Wimbledon, Pullar holds over all charges against Carroll involving the theft and destruction of women's underwear at the women's quarters but hands down his decision on the counts of abduction and murder.

'I have taken into account the defence evidence and it has not, in my view, been sufficient to justify me acquitting the defendant. Accordingly, he will stand trial.'

John Reynolds steals a sharp look at Carroll. He notices that his face hasn't changed expression. He is emotionless, just as he had been on the day Reynolds had charged him with murder.

Reynolds had tried to find the original reel-to-reel interviews they did five months before with Carroll. They had disappeared into smoke. The officer who had done them, who worked under-cover for the Bureau of Criminal Intelligence, was killed in a head-on car accident and police couldn't check with him where they were. All the audio was simply gone. Whether they were lost when the police moved buildings, Reynolds does not know. But he has the typed up interviews to work from.

If Reynolds is struggling to find evidence, Carroll is also doing it tough. Bailed pending trial, he is treated as persona non grata when he returns to work and most of his colleagues snub him. In the lunch room, they skite that they intend to lock him inside the fuel storage area and not let him out. He would be dead within minutes. But privately, they admit they are just big-noting. No way are they going to go up on a murder charge. Not for Raymond Carroll.

PART TWO
Murder trial: 1985

'Court procedure has little to do with truth or justice. Once we are in court, we play this game called Courtroom. The idea is to win this game using this set of strange – at times, impenetrable – rules.'

John Dobies, Sydney lawyer

17

Themis, the Greek goddess of Justice, guards the leafy entrance to Brisbane's Supreme Court. It is a statue that many a defendant facing trial has afforded a nervous passing glance as they leave behind the sunshine and traffic on busy George Street and enter the sombre cloisters of the court's interior.

It is a statue that former Supreme Court Judge Angelo Vasta passes daily. Before the Fitzgerald Inquiry, before the night of the long knives in 1989 when he ignonimously became the first Australian judge ever removed from the bench by Parliament, he wore the judge's robes.

Justice. Angelo Vasta wonders if he will ever get it in Queensland. Hounded by Fitzgerald's anti-corruption crusaders and excluded from the hallowed inner circle of the legal fraternity, he wonders whether he will ever clear his name. He wonders, too, if there will ever be justice for Deidre Kennedy.

His was an ambitious climb to the bench. The son of poor Sicilian immigrant parents, who had left a Europe fractured by pre-war tensions and come to the lucky country in search of a happier life.

His father Salvatore's hard work eventually paid off: he could proudly boast that on a meagre wage and with no government handouts, he had paid for his three sons' education in Engineering, Medicine and Law, and his daughter's training as a dressmaker.

Married with three children, Angelo was admitted to the Bar in early 1968, and he quickly rose to the position of Crown Prosecutor, a move that created huge ripples in the small pond that was the Queensland legal fraternity. Once dismissed as a 'wog' and a 'dago' by Anglo-Saxon schoolmates, he was now outcast by those who regarded him as an interloper from down south.

At 38, he took silk and the resentment amongst his peers deepened. Just 16 years after he was admitted to the Queensland

Bar, he became its first Superior Court judge of Italian ancestry and the first judge not appointed by the Bar. Now, the animosity spilled out in unparalleled venom. Once whispered behind closed doors, the battle cry from the Queensland Bar was now loud and overt. Vasta, they sniffed into their brandy balloons, was an undesirable appointment. He should go.

But he didn't.

The Deidre Kennedy trial is finally starting today. February 1985, and Angelo Vasta is the judge who is to sit on it. *Before Mr Justice Vasta, Court No. 4, 1st floor, 10am: Queen v Carroll. Trial.*

Today's headlines have drawn crowds to the court. Many still remember the murder, how scared they were for the safety of their own children, and where they were at the time. *I was visiting my sister in Brisbane and heard about the baby on the radio. I thought, how hideous . . . I cried when it came on television. Those poor parents . . . I still remember thinking, if it was my daughter, I'd string the bastard up with my own hands . . .*

Public defender Kerry Copley tries to sway the court to grant bail to his client. Since his arrest and being committed for trial, Carroll has neither taken flight nor refused to cooperate, he argues. 'In my submission, there is no need for him to remain in custody . . .' Justice Vasta doesn't agree. Bail is refused. For the duration of the trial, Carroll will be held in the remand section at Brisbane's notorious Boggo Road Prison.

Faye is relieved. She has not seen Carroll since the committal hearing, but finds it extremely traumatic to be in the same room as him. This was the man who police had charged with murdering her baby and, to Faye, he looked so arrogant, sitting there with his arms folded and his legs crossed. She wanted the earth to open up and swallow him.

Carroll's defence also seeks to exclude two pieces of evidence from being aired before the jury: the slashing of undergarments belonging to female members of the RAAF; and his former wife Joy's allegations regarding his biting their own baby. This, they say, is highly prejudicial and outweighs any probative value. Vasta allows the former to be excluded, but rules that Joy's evidence should stay.

Justice Vasta surveys the jury, pared down to six men and six women after intense questioning to weed out people with prejudicial extremes. They appear a moderate group, ranging in age from their early twenties to fifties. They have a hard task ahead of them: any murder trial is tough, but one involving an infant can be emotionally overwhelming. Vasta warns them early about what they may face. 'I might mention that this charge of murder relates to a matter that occurred in 1973 and is a matter which received a good deal of publicity . . . reported in the paper as the murder of a Deidre Kennedy, a child of very tender years. Now, there may be some reason altogether separate and distinct from your knowledge of any one or more of the witnesses that may cause you to feel that you cannot deliver an impartial verdict in this trial. If so, now is the time to speak up.'

Vasta pauses to give them time to answer.

Silence.

Unable to cope with the emotional trauma, Faye and Barry choose not to stay for the duration of the trial. John Reynolds advises them to give their evidence and then go back to Richmond, where they follow its progress through the press. Barry knows the horrific details of Deidre's death, but he has sheltered Faye from them. What he cannot shelter his wife from is the graphic, heartbreaking press reports of the details revealed in the trial, and it is in this way that Faye learns that Deidre was dressed in women's underwear the morning she was found. Horrified at the implications, she sobs for days.

It is a packed court – police sneaking a few moments on their shift to have a listen and young lawyers sent to watch the 38-year-old Crown prosecutor on his feet. Imposing at 185cm, with a barrister's wig perched atop dark brown hair and a large, open face compliments of his Germanic heritage, Adrian Gundelach naturally commands attention. Known for his cheerful disposition and passion for criminal work, he started as a judge's associate at 18 and was a clerk to the Crown Prosecutor by 1968. Graduating with a law degree in 1972, he has prosecuted some nasty cases since graduating with his law degree in 1972, but nothing as abhorrent as the Deidre Kennedy case.

His case is three-pronged. To prove opportunity – that Carroll was not, as he claimed, on the base at Edinburgh when Deirdre was murdered. To demonstrate his predilection for biting young children on the legs. And to focus on the opinion of the three forensic odontologists that the prosecution would call, that Carroll's teeth had caused the contusions on the baby's thigh.

Emotion is high, even before the opening address. It is a hybrid mix that fills the public gallery. Mothers have come to ogle this person accused of murdering a child, shaking their heads as they see Carroll for the first time in the dock and providing home-spun commentary in the breaks. The media has outlined the gruesome details of the crime and those in the gallery have already made up their minds. Forget the trial, the Westminster system that an accused is innocent until proven guilty. Carroll did it, they think, and they are here to witness his metaphorical public execution. The men stand beside their women, faces grim. John Reynolds hears them talking in the corridors outside the court. 'Bring back the gallows,' they huff. 'Hang the evil bastard.' The case seems to have touched a raw nerve, Reynolds thinks; everyone seems to have an opinion. He realises Carroll's family must feel this sentiment and that the trial must be a shocking ordeal for them.

Gundelach delivers his opening address to the jury in strong voice and with raw force. No histrionics, no courtroom theatre, just a powerful, stark rendition of the facts. 'On Saturday April 14 1973, about 6.20am, little Deidre Maree Kennedy's bruised and sexually abused body was found dumped on the roof of a toilet block in Limestone Park, Ipswich. Her death at 17 months was due to asphyxia from strangulation.' It was, he continues, a warped and sadistic attack on a defenceless child – 'a child that would never have been in a position to identify or speak out against her assailant. This type of murder is the most abhorrent of murders . . . The facts indicate quite clearly there's a deep disturbance in the man who committed that crime.' He tells the court the motive was some sexual fetish known only to that man and that, if Carroll was guilty, the jury should give him no sympathy.

Already, women in the public gallery have started weeping.

Carroll, unable to afford a lawyer with the knowledge and experience to challenge the Crown prosecutor's, has had no recourse but to come through the Legal Aid system. QC Kerry Copley, though in private practice, opted to take the high-profile brief. A strong believer in the 'cab rank rule' – first come, first served – Copley is known to his colleagues as a compassionate, charming master of spin and equally known for his legendary cross-examination skills, meticulous research and encyclopaedic knowledge of the law. He has never refused a brief because the cause – or the client – was unpopular. Raymond Carroll – a man already branded a paedophile and baby murderer by the public – was proving a stand-out as one of the most unpopular clients of his career. But he was prepared to fight as hard for him as he did any other person he defended. Who killed Deidre Kennedy? It was his job to convince the jury that it was not Raymond John Carroll.

Copley tells the court that the case against his client rests on circumstantial evidence and that there is no evidence to prove he was in Ipswich at the time of the murder. The central issue, he says, is identity: the murderer is the same person who stole underwear from the veranda of the house next door. Carroll does not fit the descriptions given at the time, and nor were his fingerprints found at the scene or the Kennedys' unit. Evidence has been destroyed and the opinions of the forensic odontologists are unreliable. His client is caught up in a nightmare that is not of his own making.

Arresting officer John Reynolds is first on the stand and is attacked by Copley. He shows Reynolds no mercy.

'Included in the documents that have been lost, I would suggest to you, would be details of statements obtained from the defendant's family back in 1973 at the time of the murder . . . ?'

'If it refers to the doorknocks, yes, they are lost.'

'No complete records presently available of statements obtained from the occupants of 13 Quarry Lane?'

'No. Just some on the running sheet.'

'That does not show the defendant was at Quarry Lane on the night of the murder . . . Police records that have at all times been in police custody, gone . . . So it is not only air-force records that are lost, police records that are lost, it was in fact part of a systematic process of the investigation with a doorknock?'

Reynolds nods after each question. *Correct.*

'The defendant maintained to you at all times that he was not in Queensland on the date of the murder . . . there is nothing to show he was at home, seen at home, or present on the weekend of the murder . . . Nothing in air-force records to suggest he was not at Edinburgh, travelling by service air to Amberley, or being given compassionate leave . . . not one document showing he was in Queensland at the time Deidre Kennedy was murdered?'

'That's correct.'

By applying reason, Reynolds tries to salvage the damage Copley has wreaked. He fights to keep the irritation from his voice. Coppers have worked hard on this case; bloody hard. Many have taken it home with them, for years, sometimes unwittingly; going to work the next day tired but desperately wanting a resolution. Reynolds is one of these. Sometimes, in the twilight juncture between sleep and waking, he sees a rag doll, lying on the ground. Drawn to it against his will, he walks up, almost on tiptoe, to where it lies on a carpet of leaves. And the pale, forlorn figure that is not a rag doll but a battered child, looks surreal and terrible, dappled sunshine blinking on her bruises as if she is under a strobe light. He struggles to back away but can't, riveted to the spot, wanting to gag and when, fully awake he does finally leave her to go about his business, she stays with him, clinging. Deidre has stayed with him for years and is a nocturnal visitor to a lot of the coppers. But Reynolds doesn't tell Copley any of this. Courts are factories for airing facts, not nightmares.

Many documents, he says, were destroyed and thrown out when the Ipswich police station basement was waterlogged in the floods that swept through – not the 1974 flood, but one that came later, a seepage of water and fuel that swept all before it.

Prosecutor Adrian Gundelach has forensic scientist Kenneth Cox in the witness stand when Carroll's chest, head and pubic hair are handed up. While some similarities with his hair were found, they are not, Cox testifies, what he would call 'a very good match'.

On the other hand, he says, there are two portions of hair that do not have sufficient dissimilarities to rule out Carroll as a suspect. 'All I can say is they could come from Carroll and he cannot be eliminated.'

'Would you,' Gundelach persists, 'ever be in a position to say a hair came from a particular person's head or some other body?'

'No.'

The defence seizes on this. 'There is really no positive presumption of identification as to the defendant Carroll being the person here in this matter as a result of the hair sample; do you agree with that?'

'I agree with that.'

Cox recalls mounting hair samples on microscopic slides in 1980. At that time, he says, there was a Tasmanian suspect for the murder. But there was no match.

Neil Raward, officer in charge of the scientific section at Police Headquarters, says he examined hair samples from both the Kennedy family and people who lived in the Borchert household next door. After testing, he eliminated them all as suspects.

On day two, 27 February, Dr William Josephson, who attended to Deidre at Limestone Park, agrees with Gundelach that he was present at the Institute of Forensic Pathology in Brisbane on 14 April 1973. Vasta, known for cutting to the chase and keeping language simple for the layperson, peers down from the bench. 'Forensic pathology? Is that a fancy name for the morgue?'

Shown nine photographs, including close-ups of the bruise marks, Dr Josephson – by now, deputy superintendent at Brisbane's Prince Charles Hospital – is clearly unimpressed. After studying them, he makes his announcement. 'They are not,' he intones, 'an excellent representation.' Josephson later adds what he had adduced at the park. 'I would say the bite marks were inflicted probably at or around the time of death, though they may have been inflicted earlier.'

Press journalists scribble furiously. This is exactly the sensational type of evidence that headlines are made of, and they use it to full advantage. 'Baby Bitten Near Time of her Death – Doctor'. The story has now taken on proportions of its own, gathering a huge audience outside Queensland. But even hardened reporters struggle with some of the detail. Sometimes stories cut too close to the bone, and this is one of them. Other news items need attention but they seem shallow, empty against the tragedy that is the murder of an innocent child. Even 12 years on, the story has lost none of its resonance. There is a whiff of death in the courtroom, an unnerving spirit that hangs over proceedings. The main players, now paraded one after the other in the witness box, have aged, and there is sometimes a weariness in their answers, as if they wonder whether this horror will ever end.

It is only early in the trial, and there is no promise it will get any easier.

Josephson is still on the stand. He found, he reiterates, bruising on the air passages consistent with violence, but the small bones in Deidre's neck were not broken. 'I formed the opinion that death was caused by asphyxiation due to strangulation.' Cross-examined by Copley, he said he could see no indentations in the bite marks.

RAAF policeman John Rowley, called from Malaysia to give evidence for the prosecution, is extremely unimpressed with the entire exercise. The Crown puts a few blokes up at one of the best hotels in Brisbane for six weeks, and four of them, including Rowley, aren't called to give evidence. Rowley turns up each day not knowing if he's going to the witness stand or not. He is bored to death.

Time and memory can play tricks, especially through an inquest, committal and a murder trial. A lot has happened between 1973 and 1985. Cecil 'Nugget' Carroll died early in 1974 and Arthur Borchert has long ago left Short Street, his de facto Kathleen and the brood of kids. And Borchert can't remember now if Nugget had described the prowler on the veranda as having blondish-to-fair hair. Maybe he did, maybe he didn't. He doesn't know for sure. Borchert had definitely thought it could have been his son Paul, who also had that colour hair, but then . . . It was a long time ago; he can't remember that far back. He had been drinking that night, though he wasn't drunk and he didn't see the prowler. 'I never seen him,' he tells the court. But Copley reads his own words back to him from the committal, so he understands what he said at the time. 'And you were asked, "Blond-headed . . . ?"'

'Yeah,' Borchert concedes. 'It must be right. If that's what I said at the time, then, yeah.'

Reynolds is amazed at how little Borchert has changed. Same beatnik hairstyle, trailing down to his shoulders in greasy tendrils identical to the cut worn by Albert Einstein. Dressed in a suit that has obviously been hired, like something a man would wear to a wedding. Or a funeral.

Copley is testing Borchert's memory about the fellow he saw walking toward the flats that night, an exchange that degenerates into farce. 'A little earlier today you said you saw the person next door . . . who was walking between the flats for about five minutes.'

'Mmm.'

'You mean about five seconds, do you?'

'Five minutes, five seconds. I didn't time him. I wasn't timing him.'

'I suggest to you, as a matter of fairness to yourself, it wouldn't take five minutes to walk a distance of 25 feet?'

'No, I don't suppose so. Depends how fast you walk.' Borchert grins when he says it and looks around the courtroom as if he may take a bow.

Copley doesn't appreciate the humour. 'He wasn't doing hand-stands or anything?' he asks sarcastically.

'No.' Borchert shoots Copley a filthy look.

Copley is also impatient with Detective Morris's recollection of how police tested whether Nugget Carroll could so clearly have seen a prowler on the veranda. 'Do you know if the light was on in the bedroom when you went in to conduct this experi-ment? Surely there wouldn't be you and Carroll and other police-men trooping around the bedroom with the light off all the time, groping around in the dark, would you? You would have had the light on at some stage, surely?'

Morris cannot remember. 'I am not 100 per cent sure.'

Arthur Bocherts former 'missus' Kathleen is on the stand. Time has not been kind to her. Her skin is leathery and hair lifeless;

petrified to be in court, she looks as stunned as a deer in head-lights as she recalls events before Deidre was abducted. Weeks before, she says, 'Old Nuggie' had tripped over after a drinking binge. He was on tablets for the pain in his head 'and to stop him being wobbly on his legs'. He had got up to get his tablets and gone back to bed. She and the kids were watching television and Arthur was in the kitchen playing records with his mate.

She had done her washing the day before, she says; hung most of the clothes on the Hills Hoist downstairs and strung the rest on the veranda with a long rope. A pair of step-ins, a little pair of blue panties that belonged to her five-year-old daughter, and a few other items. She is unsure, now, what time she washed but, she stutters, 'she usually started in the morning part.'

Gundelach has missed something Kathleen said. 'That's not surprising, the way she mumbles,' Vasta growls, just audible enough for the court reporters to pick up.

Reporters move forward in their seats when RAAF dental surgeon Brett Halliwell takes the oath on the witness stand.

He had worked on Carroll's teeth in 1976 and specifically remembers him. 'His oral hygiene left a lot to be desired,' he tells the court, 'and he had a number of treatments with my hygienist at the time, which I deemed more than essential.' Adrian Gundelach remembered that outside court, the dental witnesses were not so circumspect in their descriptions. Carroll, they said, had a mouth like a sewer.

18

Former instructor Ray Martin looks comfortable in the witness box, telling the court that Carroll had left Edinburgh after he had told him someone was sick in his family. 'You had no other contact whatsoever with Raymond Carroll after you told him to report to the orderly room in headquarters?' Copley asks. 'No,' Martin replies. 'None whatsoever.'

The recruits agree that they recall Carroll's absence from the passing-out parade, and that they never saw him at Edinburgh again. Darryl Stephenson is the exception. Informed by telegram that his brother had died on Friday 30 March, the funeral was to be held the following Tuesday. He had left the RAAF base on Monday and was away for three days. But, he tells the court, he is fairly sure that he spoke to Carroll in the canteen on the day of the graduation.

Each recruit has his own recollection of Carroll. Some admit they remember very little. Others describe him as having 'buck-teeth' and unpleasant breath. Neil Hurst, who had the nickname 'Tooth', remembers Carroll's teeth were bigger than his own. He also recalls that Carroll had told him that, since the death of his father, he was the head of the family and responsible for them.

Former recruit Trevor Kitson does not take kindly to being cross-examined about his memory of Carroll being absent from the base. Leaning over the witness stand, the veins are prominent in his forehead. 'I couldn't give a damn what you bloody think!' he snarls at Copley. 'I am telling you what my memory tells me and that's it.'

Sergeant Robert Matthews had been attached to the clothing store at Edinburgh in 1973. The clothing register books filled out for uniform supplies when RAAF personnel moved bases would now be either destroyed or archived at the base, he says. But, he admits, he had failed to locate them when he had looked a month before the trial started. They were, simply, nowhere to be found.

Former Base Administration Officer Wing Commander Peter Moxey has no knowledge of Carroll being granted compassionate leave. No knowledge, in fact, of him being granted *any* leave at all in April 1973. Gundelach rises. Would any checks have been made if a chaplain from RAAF Amberley rang with a message regarding a recruit's family? Moxey shakes his head. Provided the officer receiving the call was confident that the information was true, then no. Training leave would not appear on a recruit's leave card that stayed on records whilst they were in the RAAF, and any request for interstate leave would be passed internally to the recruit's superior officer, who would make the decision that they could go. There was no requirement to keep these forms.

Warrant Officer Ronald Oldmeadow says he had pulled out Carroll's file in April 1973 but he cannot recall the reason why he did so. Unless there was a death in the family, he says, Carroll would not have been granted compassionate leave at public expense because a recruit could resign within three months of enlisting. There was no particular routine about granting leave because every case was different and it was ultimately the Commanding Officer's decision. Leave cards were only signed after a recruit had started at his first posting.

From where the reporters are sitting, the prosecution and defence are neck and neck. And then William Jordan, Carroll's neighbour from Quarry Lane, drops a bombshell. He just can't remember, he says, whether or not he saw Carroll prior to the murder. He was away that weekend and had volunteered to give his fingerprints to police when he returned home. 'Would you,' Copley asks, 'agree with me there was no suggestion of any family crisis in the Carroll family on or about 12 April 1973?'

'No, I would not agree with that,' Jordan replies. 'In the back of my mind, I remember Mrs Carroll was sick and Raymond had to come home from the air force on compassionate leave.' He has a vague recollection that he discussed this with his wife in 1984 after police had approached him and told him that Raymond was being questioned.

There is an uproar in court following this evidence. Although

Jordan had not suggested this to police back in 1973, he is now saying, unprompted, he remembers that Carroll's mother was sick.

Dr Graham Cruickshank was the Carroll family's GP in 1973, practising at an Ipswich clinic. He has located stamped attendance records for Raymond's brother, Peter Carroll, then 12, and sister Leanne, five, for a visit to him on 12 April 1973. They had been stamped to show the children had attended, but there were no notes from him regarding the visit. There are, he ventures, a couple of possibilities for this: either the children had not been sick enough to warrant him writing notes, or their files had been stamped on arrival but they hadn't waited to see the doctor. He had not received a call from the RAAF and it would be wrong to assume that because there was a date stamp on the card the children had received treatment. No, he says emphatically, he cannot show his appointment book. They were systematically destroyed after 12 months.

Gundelach thinks long and hard about how to best present the dental evidence to the jury. It is, he knows, a huge challenge. Beyond the circumstantial evidence and the key witnesses, the prosecution's argument about the identity of the person who produced the bite marks would be the crux of its case. It is this evidence that must convince the jury beyond reasonable doubt that, having conducted tests on the casts of Raymond Carroll's teeth, it was he, and no one else, who had bitten Deidre and left the pattern of bruising on her thigh. The prosecution must walk a fine line: to ensure that its message is clear and easily understood, while not confusing or boring the jury with scientific jargon. The last thing the prosecution needs is six men and six women baffled beyond comprehension. The evidence is further complicated by the passage of time: the odontologists had had to remove the restoration work done after Carroll joined the RAAF and reproduce his teeth to the condition they were in at the time of the murder. This needs to be explained, in layperson's terms. And if they can't sell this to the jury, the prosecution's case will be most certainly sunk.

The prosecutors also know that this is a landmark case, based largely on odontological evidence, that is being closely watched around the world. The challenge was to pull it off, convince the jury that none other than Raymond John Carroll's teeth had made those bite marks, that it was his dentition and his dentition alone.

Editors have warned their journalists to correctly report the three witnesses' professions. Under no circumstances are they to call them orthodontists: they are people who correct dental deformities. The correct title of the witnesses is 'forensic odontologist': people who specialise in the application of dental knowledge to questions of law. And, if they don't know that 'forensic' means matters relating to courts of law or legal proceedings, then they shouldn't be covering courts.

Out of earshot of the journalists, Kerry Copley has his own term for people who work in dentistry. Fillers and pullers.

The three expert witnesses – Dr Brown, Dr Sims and Dr Romaniuk – all agree that the bite mark consisted of two areas of bruising on the upper surface of the left thigh. The top mark was an irregular pattern of small bruises; the bottom had two separate diffuse bruises adjacent to each other. The top row of bruises was left by the biter's upper teeth, the larger area by the lower. It is crucial to the prosecution's case that the jury understands this. The row of bruises on the top part of Deidre's thigh was left by upper human teeth and it is their contention that it was Carroll's dentition, and *only* Carroll's dentition, that caused the marks. The three odontologists all reach the same conclusions. But they use different methods of identification to find that different teeth caused the marks on Deidre's body.

Unlike Sims and Brown, who used overlays, Romaniuk applied the casts directly onto a photograph of the bite marks. While his colleagues argue the upper bruising was caused by the four upper teeth, Sims's opinion is that it was caused by only three. Brown and Romaniuk agree that one particular tooth made a particular mark; Sims believes it was a different tooth. They differ, too, in their opinions regarding the lower teeth. Romaniuk relates bruising to all four. Sims sees only three and Brown cannot indicate which teeth formed the marks, pointing to a 'scraping mechanism', which he says caused diffuse bruising.

On the eighth day of the trial, plaster casts of Carroll's teeth, mounted on a wire jaw frame, and photographs of the bite marks on Deidre's thigh are handed up as exhibits. Kon Romaniuk's answers are considered, carefully weighed. 'In your opinion,' Gundelach asks him, 'is there a possibility that someone else's dentition could have made that bite mark that we see depicted on the thigh of Deidre Maree Kennedy?'

Romaniuk is unequivocal in his reply. 'No. I have done so much work on this and I have convinced myself quite clearly and it is my opinion that the only person who could have made the bite mark was Raymond John Carroll.' When everything is taken into account, he explains, including the relationship between Carroll's teeth and the deficiencies in them, he had a unique dentition. And no two people – not even identical twins – share the same dentition. He tells the court that, as a result of his tests, he has come to the conclusion that there is a definite pattern between Carroll's teeth and the bite marks. The headlines are forming as he speaks. 'Accused Man Bit Baby on Thigh, Murder Trial Told.'

The next day, Romaniuk reads to the court the statement he gave in October 1973 – that a panel of 10 dentists had admitted it was impossible to establish with any degree of certainty exactly who was responsible for biting Deidre Kennedy. That he had changed his mind between 1973 and now does not go unnoticed by the defence. For the reporters, it is easy pickings. Dentists have disagreed on the bite marks, and that is what they will relay to their audience.

'Have your views on the bite marks changed since 1973 because of any developments in odontology?' Justice Vasta asks.

Romaniuk nods. There have, he agrees, been some quite considerable advances made in the interpretations since then.

Romaniuk is on the witness stand all day long and loses copious amounts of weight due to the stress. The defence goes in hard to trip him up and query his academic qualifications. Copley quotes from a standard medical textbook. 'In cases where only bruising is present, a definite opinion should not be given concerning the identity of a suspect.'

Romaniuk waits until Copley has finished reading. 'I don't recognise that as an authoritative textbook on the subject.'

Copley will not give up. Weren't bite marks still a developing scientific technique?

Romaniuk holds his ground. Yes, he says. It is both an art *and* a science.

'That is not the answer to my question.'

'It is. It is the complete answer.'

'Is it?'

'Please don't interrupt me,' Romaniuk retorts, 'until I complete my answer.' He will not be bullied. 'I find your questions aggressive, confusing, devious and very often intellectually dishonest,' he complains to Copley.

Voicing strenuous objection to the witness's comment, Copley asks that Justice Vasta rule it out.

'Exchanges between witnesses and counsel are part of trial atmosphere,' Vasta responds. He will not rule as asked.

Romaniuk, Reynolds recalls, would not back down. They could, he says, have belted him with a cricket bat and he still wouldn't have changed his story. It was his unequivocal opinion that the only person who could have made the bite mark was Raymond John Carroll.

In his chambers during recesses, Justice Vasta discards his judge's robes and quietly reflects on the progress of the trial. The law, he knows, can be cumbersome and slow, jurors an eclectic mix, cases rarely watertight. Defence lawyers cannot always preserve any vestige of dignity for their clients, and prosecutors cannot always win a conviction. The scales of justice can dip erratically, sometimes on the slightest piece of evidence. Vasta can see all from his lofty position: the faces of the jurors, the angst of Carroll's family, the dour expression on police faces, the press and the parasites in the public gallery, often there just to gawk. It is their right, unless a court is closed, to see the law in all its transparency. But this is such a sensitive case that even he finds himself, on occasions, still shocked at the evidence.

Right now, Vasta's main concern is to ensure the jury does not drown under the weight of the forensic dental evidence. He has noticed, at times, that the media seems unsure of how to translate what they are hearing, occasionally shooting sideways glances at each other and rolling their eyes in exasperation as they try to unscramble what is being said in the witness box and how best to translate it to their audience. But it is not the media that is Vasta's immediate concern, it is the jury. As cumbersome and slow as the law can be, the pathway for them must remain clear and unobstructed.

But it appears, after all, that the press has a very clear view of proceedings. Readers in Queensland wake the next morning to read: 'Court Told Dentists Disagreed on Bite Marks'.

19

Bernard Sims, a genial bear of a man, takes the stand on 1 March 1985 and begs the court's indulgence to read out his curriculum vitae. It is a sure sign to seasoned observers that it will be lengthy, and it is. Senior Lecturer in Forensic Odontology at London Hospital Medical Centre. Member of numerous academies and societies of forensic science. Author of journals and editorials, including a forensic paper on 'Bite Marks in Battered Baby Syndrome'. Qualified in 1960 and working in forensic odontology within two years, he now boasts nearly a quarter of a century's experience and has seen about 200 bite mark cases in both adults and children. Of the battered babies he has seen, 400 were dead and 200 living.

Sims's stomach bulges over his belt and his ruby lips stand out against pallid skin, compliments of equally pallid English summers. He is clearly at ease in the witness stand. At the present moment, he says, he is the only full time forensic dental surgeon and forensic odontologist in the United Kingdom, and his full time occupation is examining bite marks, age assessments and identifications. He tells the court, with a broad smile, that he is so highly regarded in his field that he has had cause, on a number of occasions, to remind his mentor – one of the world's leading odontologists – that he has seen fewer bite mark cases than Sims.

Copley makes a flamboyant display of looking at his watch and the jury gets the message. Sims is well qualified. They have enough proof.

It was long before television shows such as *CSI* brought forensics into people's lounge rooms. In 1985 forensic dentistry was an exclusive profession. This was true of all forensic disciplines.

When Sims spoke, the masses listened.

Sims had not long been in Australia before the trial started and the court was adjourned while his opinion was typed up. He had made comparisons with Carroll's original dental study models and with black-and-white photographs of Deidre's bruises. Caused by rupture of the subcutaneous capillaries, blood escapes into tissue, which in time comes to the skin surface and fades, creating the blue-black discolouration that is a bruise. Within an hour, Sims had satisfied himself that it was Carroll's teeth that had made those bruise marks.

The exhibits are up again in the courtroom, a black-and-white horror show: tragic remnants of a life cut short. Tiny, plump legs and exposed bottom. Deidre's thigh embroidered in ugly bruises. A sickening reminder of a baby murdered.

The court is silent, apart from a cry somewhere within it: a thin, shrill cry that lingers like a soprano's voice in the dying moments of an opera. Reynolds feels the hairs go up on the back of his neck. It is now that Gundelach pounces, exploits his witness's expertise, to compare the photographs – these obscene exhibits – with the cast of Carroll's teeth. Could it, he asks Sims, be possible that someone else's dentition caused those bite marks? Sims has an air of authority, accentuated by his pukka British accent. He plays to the jury, moving his large hands to mold his words as though he is working a piece of pottery. 'In my opinion, no, because this is a very significant set of teeth. They appear to have been fractured and refilled and there are significant features of the bite mark . . . which fit the pattern as it would be for fractured teeth. Also . . . it would appear that the accused cannot close his front teeth together at all . . .' It is, Sims adds, all a matter of patterns. 'It is these patterns which convinced me that I was looking at the teeth responsible for this bite.'

Bastard. The word emerges as a hiss, loud against the sombre silence in the courtroom. Reynolds looks around to see who has said it, but the faces portray nothing but shock and revulsion at the exhibits. Justice Vasta looks up, quietly surveying all before him. It is enough, without him needing to speak. Heads are now bowed as though in prayer and the only movement in the room is the convulsive rise and fall of Carroll's sister's shoulders as her body is racked with sobs.

Bite mark study, Sims continued with some obvious pride,

was a field for an expert, requiring a person with expertise in their interpretation and assessment. It was certainly not a job for dental practitioners, who lack both the necessary experience and knowledge.

He is not able to say that a particular part of a tooth made a particular bruise; they simply made a pattern that may be *consistent* with the teeth. Each bite mark case is unique and must be dealt with on the evidence available.

Copley hits hard at Sims's expert evidence. Would he agree that many experts hold the opinion that dental evidence is more reliable as a means of *eliminating* suspects rather than identifying offenders? Sims nods agreement. And yes, he adds, there are leading world authorities who do not agree with his work.

Does he, Copley asks, believe his role is to confirm that the dentition fit the marks? No, Sims replies, adding there were other problems inherent in the identification by bruise marks alone, problems that would be magnified later. The bruise marks, he says, were on a curved surface, and this might cause distortion when photographed. The shape of the marks can also alter if the body is placed in a different position from that in which it was when the marks were made.

Sims disagrees with Copley that tongue pressure was a factor in the bite mark. 'Definitely not, because you are referring to love bites. This is not an erotic bite. You don't put your tongue out when you bite things, otherwise you bite your tongue.'

The defence does not call any forensic odontologist to challenge, but Gundelach has the parting shot.

'In answer to one of my learned friend's other questions, you said that the accused's lower jaw could move forward but I would ask you this: can his dentition as you see it represented in the models meet in an edge-to-edge relationship?'

Sims shakes his head. No matter how far Carroll moved his lower jaw forward, there was no way his upper and lower teeth could meet.

Those listening in the public gallery can now understand why there were no indentations on Deidre Kennedy's little body.

20

Dr Brown is on the stand. Like Sims, he is highly qualified: Senior Lecturer in Dental Surgery at the University of Adelaide, consultant odontologist to various departments, including coroners' and police departments, and experienced in lecturing in Australia and overseas. The press is particularly keen to hear his evidence: the last time he was an expert witness in a case concerning teeth marks was in the controversial Azaria Chamberlain trial. Talkative, but less affable on the stand than his colleague Dr Sims, Brown occasionally seems to forget he is explaining odontology to laypeople, not experts. But the jury, nonetheless, listens intently to Brown's opinon. He agrees with his colleagues that Carroll's teeth could not make edge-to-edge contact and he is visibly more relaxed as he moves into his area of expertise. Now he can demonstrate with his hands the intricacies of dentistry, guiding the jury through his analysis in the same way he lectures his students. 'The upper jaw is fixed to the skull . . . and chewing movements are carried out by the movement of the lower jaw and . . . you get sort of a gliding or a grazing movement of the teeth . . .'

The lower teeth do not move, acting as anchors like spikes on a meat tray that hold the joint still. It is the upper teeth that close and bite, and the inside of those teeth which closes on the tissue surface first.

'Do we,' Gundelach asks him, 'see evidence of that gliding movement in the photographs?'

Brown shakes his head, '. . . there are no well-defined marks . . . due to the inability of the teeth to make edge-to-edge contact . . .'

Gundelach wants him to be specific on his opinions about whether the bruise marks in the photos were caused by the casts of the defendant's teeth. 'After making your comparisons, did you arrive at an opinion?'

'I came to the conclusion that the marks were produced by the teeth represented by those casts.'

'And, in your opinion, is there a possibility that someone else's dentition could have made that bite mark which you saw depicted on the thigh of Deidre Kennedy in that manner?'

Brown nods. 'I had considered that possibility . . . It might be possible, if someone was to sculpture down someone else's dentition to be identical with the ones on the cast, that may be a possibility, but I think it's most unlikely.'

Carroll does not flinch.

After opting to postpone his cross-examination, Copley attacks Brown's experience in identifying a person by bruise marks left by teeth. Had he written papers on the subject? If so, had they been published, and where? Copley is theatrically exasperated. 'Dr Brown, don't you understand my question? I am suggesting to you that you have not written an article on the topic of identification of some person by bruises produced by the teeth . . . ? What was the topic of your article?'

'The investigation of bite marks.'

Copley slips it in, quietly, deliberately. 'But the investigation of bite marks may range from bite marks produced from dingoes in clothing, mightn't it?'

'It can range and include areas where teeth produced marks.'

'Of, for example, bite marks by dingoes in clothing?'

'Or human beings, as well.'

At the committal hearing, Brown had based his opinions on three photographs of Deidre's bruises and the model on an articulator. When he originally received the cast of Carroll's dentition, the fillings had not been removed. They were, he tells the court, removed in his presence by Dr Romaniuk, prior to the committal hearing.

In what degenerates into a combative exercise, Copley insists that Brown was influenced by Dr Bernard Sims, just a week before the trial started. 'I suggest to you that if one were to get in any way . . . an accurate picture of the shape of the teeth before restoration work, the first thing you would have to do is to remove as best you can from the cast all the restored material . . . do you agree or disagree?'

'Well, yes and no.'

'You agree and you disagree, and you are going to qualify both of those? Off you go.'

What marks, Copley demands, were made by teeth, by skin and by the tongue?

'I can't understand what you are wanting me to do,' Brown tells him. 'I have marked the bruises that correspond to the teeth.' He agrees there are no indentations on the photograph that appear to be made by teeth but strenuously disagrees that without indentations it is very unsatisfactory to try and relate bruising to teeth. He agrees with Sims that some scientists hold the view that bruising alone is not sufficient for identification, but by no means do all scientists hold this view.

Would you agree, then, Copley later asks, that, in the absence of indentation, there can be no degree of certainty as to which set of teeth caused a particular set of bruising?

Brown remains patient. 'I think I have answered that question before, that it is possible to reach a conclusion without indentations . . . You would have to recognise the pattern.'

It follows suddenly, without warning. Producing a photograph of the bite marks, Copley asks Brown to mark the top teeth that produced the bruises. He does so.

But Copley is clever. He knows that when a dentist faces a patient, the left side of the patients mouth is on the practitioner's right. Brown is never asked a question to explain this simple fact.

At home in Richmond, his stomach tossing like a clothes dryer, Barry Kennedy follows the trial's progress from updates by John Reynolds. He doesn't give a damn about how the forensic dentists have reached their conclusions; this is his daughter they're talking about. The science of the evidence makes him nervous. He regards himself as an average punter, just like the jurors. He hopes they understand the technicalities.

The dental evidence complete, Copley decides to go straight for the jugular. Carroll's first wife, Joy Meyers.

She had given evidence at the committal hearing that she

had seen bite marks on their daughter, Kerry-Ann, four, maybe five times during her marriage to Carroll, and that when she had asked him why baby was crying, he wouldn't say anything. She is extremely nervous, her voice so faint Copley can barely hear her. Meyers has already agreed with him that she raised no allegation of ill-treatment by her former husband against their child, even when she applied for custody. Agreed with him, too, that she never took the child to a doctor or the hospital and that the first time she made any allegations about her ex-husband was when the police knocked on her door. Meyers shakes her head at each question. No, there was never any suggestion that Carroll had dressed their daughter in adult female clothing. No suggestion of sexual assault. No question he had ever tried to strangle their baby. She had never asked Carroll if he had bitten Kerry-Ann.

Copley leans toward her. 'The fact of the matter is, there were no bite marks on her legs; is that not so?'

'No, that is not true.'

Meyers's reply is strident, louder than her previous responses. This witness is going to be tougher than he had anticipated. 'You see, the question of your husband's spanking or smacking the child – you would agree with me that he did smack her on the bottom, on the backside, on more than one occasion?'

'Probably, yes.'

'But he never bit her, did he?'

'Yes, he did.'

Copley moves to another topic: names they had suggested if their baby was a girl. Meyers had said her former husband had wanted to call the baby Deidre but, Copley muses, that wasn't right, was it? Hadn't he wanted to call the baby Desley, the name of his ex-girlfriend?

Meyers is adamant. Desley was not a name they discussed at length.

Well, Copley says, raising his eyebrows for the benefit of the jury; if they hadn't *discussed* it, had her husband written her a note?

'No.'

'Well, he didn't just walk around the house saying "Desley,

Desley?'" He sweeps his eyes around the courtroom, a mocking smile on his face.

'He didn't, no.' She is no match for Copley's intellect, but she is standing her ground.

Copley changes tactics, now playing the gentle patriarch, a patient father dealing with a recalcitrant child. 'Look, I don't want there to be any semblance of triviality about this matter, but Desley was not going to be the name for a pet or the name of a house or anything, was it? It was in the context of the name for the child to be born?'

'It was in the context, yes, but it wasn't a main name for it because I didn't like it in the first place.'

Now Copley is showing her a copy of the statement she gave police. 'You are,' he questions sarcastically, 'able to read?'

He is hammering her now, trying to break her down. *I put it to you . . . I suggest to you . . .* But Meyers is stubborn, digs in. 'You may suggest it, but I don't agree with it. I know what I'm saying.'

Immensely relieved to be leaving the witness stand when the questions are finished, away from everyone staring at her, she does not pause to speak to her former husband's family. She has no doubt about what they would think of her evidence.

The headlines in the next day's *Courier Mail* spells it out. 'Carroll Bit Daughter on Thigh, Wife Says'.

21

'**D**id you kill Deidre Kennedy?'

There is a collective intake of breath in the court. Carroll has opted to speak in his own defence, taking the witness stand with a seemingly calm demeanour. It is his right to refuse to give evidence; that he has chosen to do so, Copley will now deftly turn to his advantage. Fluffing his gown, he stares at his client, his voice steady and firm. 'Did you kill Deidre Kennedy?'

Raymond John Carroll returns the stare without blinking and answers immediately. 'I did not.'

'Did you have anything to do with that child's death?'

'I did not.'

Staccato questions. Name, age, address. He is 29 years old. Stationed at Amberley Air Base since 1979 with his second wife, Jennifer Anne Carroll, their five-year-old twin girls, Raylene and Samantha, and son, Saun, 18 months.

Bland, ordinary in beige trousers and shirt. A 29-year-old father of four in the witness stand, watched by lawyers, strangers and the press, answering questions about events from a long time ago.

Carroll reiterates what he told John Reynolds. He was 17 years old when he joined the air force. At the time of joining, he had lived with his mother and family at 13 Quarry Lane, East Ipswich. He did not go to Queensland in April 1973 and did not go to Ipswich. He never took any compassionate leave during training. He does not have a good memory for things he deems unnecessary. He did not march on the parade but he can't recall the reason why he didn't.

'Do you now recall?' Copley asks.

'I think I either asked the member if I could be excused from the parade or I was told to excuse myself from the parade.' He watched the parade from the sidelines, he says, just beyond the march-on area, and he wasn't present when the photograph was taken.

'When asked by the police about not marching, you made mention about a blank file?'

'That is correct.'

'What can you say about this blank file?'

Copley has been looking down at his papers, and slowly raises his head. This is theatre: let the jury think that what they are about to hear is casual, unimportant. A mere slip of the tongue from a young man with a bad memory.

'That reason that I gave the police is just absolute stupidity, as any member of the air force will know,' Carroll responds. 'As regards a blank file or not, you will still march. The reason I told the police that – they asked me questions and they wanted answers, I thought, and it was about the first thing that came to my head and, without actually thinking about it like I have done now, it seemed a possible excuse.'

It seemed a possible excuse. Gundelach takes note of the answer. *A possible excuse?*

Carroll continues with his evidence. He travelled from Edinburgh by service air to Richmond. Caught a train to Sydney and then on to his new station at Wagga. He never bit his daughter, Kerry-Ann on the thigh, the leg or any other part of the body. Never hit her across the face or head. Carroll's mouth moves, but his face remains impassive when asked what he thinks of these allegations by his former wife. 'They're just a bunch of lies,' he says. He produces six photographs of Kerry-Ann, taken when she was 12 months old. She is smiling, happy in a swimming costume. No marks on the child. Anywhere.

It is Gundelach's turn for the questions. Didn't Carroll tell his section commander in Darwin that his second wife, Jennifer, had accused him of murdering Deidre Kennedy, and cried as he told him the story? Carroll does not change expression. 'That is incorrect, because I did not murder her. My wife has never accused me of that, Sir.'

They have moved through all the evidence, and now Gundelach is asking why Carroll had looked at a photograph during his records of interview with the police and pointed to someone who may have been him. 'Are you seriously suggesting to this court that you mistakenly identified someone else as being you in that photograph?'

Polite, his voice even as though addressing a Commanding Officer. 'That's possible, Sir. They showed me a photograph, I studied it, and I said it was possibly me who I pointed out; I didn't say 100 per cent certain it was me. I only stated possibly me.'

Gundelach struggles to keep the sneer from his voice. 'Do you agree with me now he looks nothing like you?'

Carroll nods. 'Having studied the photograph, no, there isn't much comparison at all between us.'

Gundelach is staying in the past, on the topic of Carroll's first marriage. Why did he and Joy argue when he returned to Darwin from a trip home?

'One of my NCOs at the section I was at at the time had been propositioned by my wife and he confronted me with the facts to that effect, and then I confronted my wife over it.'

Gundelach does not take his eyes from Carroll. 'What is this NCO's name?'

Carroll can't recall.

'You are making it up,' the prosecutor snorts.

Carroll's denial is insistent. 'No. No, I am not, Sir.'

Desley Hill's love letters to Carroll are spread out for the court to see, the sad, lovelorn writings of a woman at first hopeful of romance, and then rejected. Aren't these letters, Gundelach accuses, the real reason the marriage ended? 'Your wife inter-cepted some letters from your girlfriend, Desley, didn't she?'

'She didn't intercept them, Sir; they were written *to* her.'

'Did you ever promise Desley that you would buy her an engagment ring?'

'Not that I can recall, Sir, no.'

Gundelach produces one of the letters, in which Desley asked him if he was serious about buying her a ring. 'I will ask you again; did you promise to buy her an engagement ring?'

'Not that I can recall, Sir, no.'

'Did you ever talk to her about going to Darwin with you?'

'I don't recall it, no, Sir.'

'Did she ever ask you?'

'I don't recall, Sir.'

Gundelach scratches his head at the base of his wig and raises his eyebrows. Perhaps Carroll will recall more of why he asked John Reynolds, during the records of interview, about fingerprints found on the body? 'You said,' Gundelach reminds him, '"In my mind, I am innocent," and, in relation to fingerprints, you said that "the prints on the body are not necessarily those of the offender . . ." Where did you get the idea that fingerprints had been found on the body of the child?'

'I have always assumed –'

'I beg your pardon?'

'I have always assumed, and when Mr Reynolds was talking about the scene of the crime, I thought the body was also included and I thought that they could lift prints from the body.'

Gundelach doesn't believe a word of it. 'I am suggesting you made that answer because, in your own mind, you knew that you had been very careful with respect to prints being left at the Kennedy household and also at the park, but, when you touched that young girl's body, you were worried that you had left finger-prints there. What do you say to that suggestion?'

Carroll stares at the prosecutor, his eyes betraying nothing. He says that that suggestion is incorrect.

Gundelach addresses the bench. 'No more questions, your Honour.'

Faye and Barry watch snippets of court evidence on the nightly news, and read about it in the newspaper. It is hard to stomach, and mostly they can't. Eleven-year-old Derek had only been told of the trial just before it started, sitting down with his father who explained what had happened to Deidre 12 years before. Barry left out the terrible details, spared his son the horror. There would be time for him to learn them, but he didn't need to know yet. Stephanie is 17, old enough to perfectly comprehend what is happening in court, old enough for the full implications of her sister's murder to sink in. Whoever had taken Deidre had loitered in the same room where Stephanie had also been sleeping. Why had he chosen Deidre, and not her? Was it because she was younger, unable to form sentences, less likely to create a stir in the sleeping household? If Deidre were alive, she would be 15, experimenting with Stephanie's make-up, borrowing her clothes. Stephanie struggles to understand any of it. She watches her mother stumbling around, eyes blank, reliving every moment; sees her father staunch and silent, holding back an emotional dam. It is like a wound in the family's heart, which no one can heal.

22

Jennifer Carroll is so nervous in the witness box she admits she can't remember anything properly. She wipes her hands on her sleeve, stares fixedly at the prosecutor. No, she does not know that her husband had been spoken to by police about this matter in October 1983. He did not mention it to her for a couple of weeks afterward. Gundelach lets the ramifications of her statement sink in. *He did not mention it for a couple of weeks afterward.* The wily prosecutor resists asking why. Why would a man who had been questioned by police about the murder of a baby not mention it to his wife?

Jennifer says that Raymond is an excellent father. He rarely disciplines the children; instead, he leaves that for her to do.

Gundelach is on his feet, summing up. He will go in hard, discount what Jennifer has told the court. *Raymond is an excellent father. He rarely disciplines the children.* The prosecutor will paint an entirely different picture of this man sitting in the dock, this man accused of murdering an innocent 17-month-old girl. Raymond Carroll, he tells the jury, has a perverted interest in little children. He allows his words to wash over them, allows the magnitude of what he is saying to sink in. *A perverted interest in little children.* He knows the jury will be appalled. Sickened. It is society's greatest taboo. And what, he asks, was the *motive* for the killing? Gundelach shrugs, nonplussed. It was a sexual fetish known only to her killer. A fetish involving stolen underwear.

This case, he tells the court, is based on identification of bite marks and circumstantial evidence that is overwhelmingly weighted against Raymond Carroll. The defence case has been nothing more than an academic exercise. 'The Crown has no evidence to show he was in Ipswich, but [we] say his teeth identify him.' Carroll, he continues, is no more than a shoddy liar who has created a web of lies and vagueness to protect himself over the years since the murder, a man who could provide no detail whatsoever that hangs together in a credible fashion.

'The defence would have you believe that Carroll was dead unlucky and that a series of unfortunate mishaps came into his life in 1983 which led to this charge against him.' The truth, Gundelach says, is that it was intensive police investigation that brought the charge. Warning the jury it would be wrong of them to guess why police interviewed Carroll almost 11 years after Deidre's murder, he adds that they had started to find 'astonishing coincidences' in their early investigation. 'Carroll's interview with police,' he continues, 'must strike you as a bit of a damp squid. It's not like the shows we see on television. The police are not permitted to trick people into confessing. They're not allowed to belt them or force a confession out of them. They're not even allowed to cross-examine them. The rules of propriety have obviously been observed. He was able to put his story over to the police with the greatest of ease – a story he has dreamt of for years.' His responses to police questions were not those of an innocent man, he tells the court, but the evasions and circumlocutions of a very guilty one.

Gundelach moves through all the evidence. Why didn't Carroll's first wife report that their daughter had been bitten on the thigh? Because, he says, it is a sad truth that child abuse and incest is often kept silent within the family and that shame and fear prevent people from going to the police. There is no reason why Joy Meyers, a poorly educated woman completely out of her depth in legal proceedings, would wait nine years to invent a pack of lies about her former husband. She has re-married, started a new life. And what of Carroll, when he was accused of molesting his own child? Instead of denouncing it as a scurrilous lie, he had to be prodded into a denial during the record of interview with police. He knew perfectly well that this was the clearest evidence of his evil and perverted preoccupation with children.

What of Carroll's family – his mother, present wife, and sister, Debbie? 'Of course they'd stand by him. It is a very natural, although . . .' There is a bloated pause, deliberate, 'one could think morally a wrong way for a family to behave. And,' he adds, 'it is certainly not essential to the Crown case that Carroll was staying in Quarry Lane with his family.'

'What does the Crown know?' Gundelach asks. He uses his fingers to tap out each point – that Deidre Kennedy was murdered and that whoever murdered her bit her on the thigh and dressed her up in underwear stolen from the clothesline next door. 'The only question to be resolved is who committed it? The Crown says it was Raymond John Carroll.'

His closing address over, Gundelach re-arranges his gown and sits down. It would be interesting to hear what his opposite number, Kerry Copley, makes of this address.

Copley rises with a sombre air. His client, he says, has been 'led like a lamb to slaughter' in putting his trust in air-force records proving he was not in Ipswich in April 1973. He has poor recollection, but he had not been given compassionate or any other leave and had not asked people to support his story because he believed the RAAF records would do that. He has been cooperative with police at all times and volunteered hair, dental and fingerprint samples. These, he says, are not the actions of a guilty man. The teeth marks are not Carroll's. Experts have agreed that movement of the baby's body could have changed the position of the bite and there are too many variables to warrant positive identification. To compare the teeth marks in the photograph and Carroll's plaster casts is comparing a two-dimensional picture with a three-dimensional object. There are just too many variables.

The defence rests.

Vasta's summing-up is lengthy. Warning the jury that a great body of the evidence is circumstantial, he says if the jurors return a verdict of guilty based on this alone, then guilt must be the only rational inference they can draw. If not, it is their duty to acquit.

Vasta later continues that there are two features that must be considered to bring in a verdict of guilty. If the jurors are not satisfied that Carroll was at Ipswich at the relevant time, then they must acquit. 'The second feature,' he notes, 'concerns the evidence which was given by the three forensic odontologists.' Referring to portions of their evidence, he says: 'The issue for you is as to whether the Crown has proved to your satisfaction beyond reasonable doubt that the accused was the person responsible for the bite on the child's thigh which caused the diffuse bruising . . . if you are in a state of reasonable doubt about that fact, it is your sworn duty to acquit . . .'

Is it reasonable, Vasta asks, that the accused would have forgotten as much as he says he has? Is a poor memory a convenient refuge? Counsel, he says, has mentioned that the matter of identification looms large in this case. How much weight could be placed on Cecil 'Nugget' Carroll's evidence? 'Mr Copley has submitted that the description of that person indicated that it would not have been the accused, Carroll. Now, that is perfectly correct . . . The question is: was it reliable, tested in the light of what you know of him from the evidence that is before you . . . ?

Vasta sees fit to direct the jury with regard to the evidence of Carroll's first wife.

'Now, the sole issue in this trial is one concerning the identity of the person responsible for the murder. As I have said to you, the person who was responsible for the bite mark is undoubtedly the person responsible for Deidre Maree Kennedy's murder. For this reason, it seemed to me that the evidence as to what the accused's former wife could speak about concerning the accused's treatment of their child, who was of an age similar to Deidre Maree Kennedy at the date of her death, would assist you with regard to the identity of the offender.'

Vasta has another warning for the jury. 'All three forensic odontologists, although they reach the same conclusion, do so in a route which is different, and the counsel for the defence would say is quite inconsistent and also a basis for your rejecting this evidence completely . . .'

And so it is on the nineteenth day of the trial – 14 March 1985 – that the jury retires for its verdict. It is 10.47am. Carroll's family paces outside the court, smoking and anxiously checking their watches as they tick into the afternoon. A jury can stay out as long as it needs, but legal wisdom dictates that the longer they deliberate, the more hope it gives a family of the accused that they are wrestling with some or all of the evidence.

Not, it appeared, this time. At 3.30, the court clerk gives notice that the jury is back in. The atmosphere in the court immediately shifts a gear. The tension is acute.

23

The jurors file into their seats, some glancing at the prosecution team and then to the defence. They do not look at Carroll, who is gazing intently ahead, mouth firmly closed, large hands resting quietly on his lap. One of the jurors, a portly man in his early forties, pulls out a hanky and wipes his forehead, sighing as he sinks into his chair. The weight of this duty has been onerous. Two female jurors quickly sweep their eyes around the court before they creep into one of the seats they have inhabited for the six weeks of the trial. *This is judgment day*, Reynolds, sitting in the public gallery, thinks to himself. His knuckles are white as he waits for the verdict.

The associate stands. 'How do you find the accused: guilty or not guilty?' One by one the jurors rise from their seats, staring straight at Carroll as they answer. 'Guilty.' 'Guilty.' 'Guilty.' 'Guilty.' 'Guilty.' 'Guilty.' Their voices resound in the silent courtroom. Twelve unanimous verdicts.

'Guilty.'

'Guilty.'

'Guilty.'

'Guilty.'

'Guilty.'

'Guilty.'

Sandra's hands, that had trembled violently as she waited for the jury's decision, now fly to her mouth in shock, and Ilma buries her face in her daughter's shoulder, weeping. Sandra looks at Raymond, who has not moved. He is like a rock, she thinks. Protected by a pane of glass from the public gallery, the shock of the conviction – hearing those jurors, one by one, saying he is guilty – is so overwhelming, he stands stock still. The press would condemn it as a vacant, emotionless reaction, but his family see it differently, as a natural reaction for a man who always bottles everything up, who has never shown emotion.

Carroll stares fixedly at Vasta when asked if he has anything to say. This, too, is interpreted by reporters and onlookers as a cold, insolent reaction.

'I didn't do it. I am not guilty.'

Justice Vasta pauses for a brief moment before pronouncing the sentence in his trademark gravelly voice. 'You have been found guilty by a very careful jury on what I consider to be the cogent and compelling evidence of the brutal murder of an innocent child. It was a killing in respect of which an outraged community had long since given up any hope of having the offender brought to justice. The fact that an arrest was made, some nearly 12 years after the slaying, is a tribute to the excellent efforts of the law enforcement authorities in this state, particularly the Queensland Police Force.

'The law provides but only one penalty for this crime. I sentence you to imprisonment with hard labour for life.'

Ilma, stunned by the ferocity of the jury's decision, cries quietly. She has punished herself throughout the trial for not having had the money to straighten her son's teeth. Now he has been convicted, partly on bite mark evidence, and she blames herself.

Carroll's wife, Jennifer, is so stunned she can barely move in her seat.

Carroll, held in custody since the start of the trial, doesn't turn back to look at his family as he is led out by security guards. The only sound in the courtroom is the muttering from the packed public gallery and Sandra's loud voice, catching with sobs. 'I love you, Raymond,' she calls after him as he disappears from sight.

John Reynolds regards the verdict as a personal and professional victory. In all his years in the police force, he had never seen such an emotional reaction from a jury. Every man and woman.

Reynolds had made a promise to Barry and Faye, who are still living at Richmond air base in NSW, that as soon as the verdict was in, he would ring them. They have purposely not been there for the verdict; Reynolds has to race right around to the other side of the building to use the phone and is near tears when he tells them the jury has found Carroll guilty.

By trial's end, Faye, who has always enjoyed good health apart from high blood pressure during pregnancy, needs anti-depressants to try to clear the black cloud that hovers over her like a vulture. She breaks down when she hears the verdict, clinging tightly to Barry. Thank God it is over.

Legal experts immediately hail the trial as a landmark case because the circumstantial evidence has been solely forensic, based on the interpretations of dental experts of the bite mark on Deidre's thigh. Like technology had reached out its hands from the grave. Bernard Sims speaks to the media outside the court. 'We like to rule out people, to say to police, "This is not your man." There are some cases where there are a number of suspects and some experts say that you can only determine who it is *not*, rather than who it is.' This, he smiles, was not one of those cases.

Carroll's wife, Jennifer, is not smiling. 'Bastard cops,' she spits. The media has been lying in wait outside the court, unsure who is who in Carroll's family. It is an uncertainty that results in family members being badly misrepresented in the press: Sandra mistaken for her mother, Jennifer for his sister, his sisters for his wife. They cover their faces as they brave the onslaught, deliberately exiting through different doors to dodge the photographers. 'Pack of vultures,' they mutter as they hurry past, their heads down.

Military police and civilian coppers all head to the pub, saluting the victory with beer and backslapping. From 1973 until today's verdict, the cost of the investigation and trial has run to over a million dollars. Now they can finally say it has been worth it.

Two hours into the celebration, John Reynolds calls for quiet. 'Let's raise our glasses,' he says, 'to the most important person in all of this. Deidre.'

PART THREE
Murder Acquittal: November 1985

'I beseech you, in the bowels of Christ think it possible you may be mistaken'

Oliver Cromwell

24

Carroll has never been so scared in his life. The prison guard is snarling, leaning close to his face. So close, Carroll can smell his fetid breath. 'I've waited 12 years to get hold of you, arsehole.'

Well, you're gunna have to wait another 12 years, mate, 'cause you've got the wrong bloke. It is what Carroll recalls saying to the prison guard, recounted with a swagger in his tone. But it rings hollow, smacks of false bravado. Scared men generally cower in silence.

Newly arrived, Carroll looks around the yard to see if anyone is watching. A seething audience of bored men, hungry for action, are leaning against the wire and leering at him, their tattooed arms folded and muscles taut. Ready to circle, watching, waiting.

Welcome to Boggo Road.

Two days after his unceremonious entry into the prison system, Carroll is given his marching orders from the Air Force. Bluntly told to 'sign here', kicked out because of civil incarceration. Automatic dismissal, no ifs or buts. It irked Carrol to no end. His career and retirement benefits gone, straight down the drain.

It starts as soon as he enters the yard. 'You're dead, maggot.' Calling out to him everywhere he walks, sidling up to him as he eats his lunch and hissing in his ear. 'You're dead, maggot.' The prison code is strong; despised by guards and prisoners alike, rock spiders – slang for those who sexually abuse children – are kept apart from the general prison population. The reasoning of the prisoners is basic: while they're doing time, it could be their kid that is copping it from a paedophile. Difficult as it is, inmates invariably find ways to get protected prisoners. Their food is pissed on in the kitchen before they eat it, a sly fist crunched under their ribs when no one is looking, shit stuffed into their shoes. Carroll learns fast. He is scared for his life, told by other prisoners he should look out for himself and sooner or later those who picked on him would tire of it, told that if he cowered down, he'd cop it even more.

He cops it anyway. Relentlessly taunted, just as he had been at school. *Hey Carroll, Sabre-tooth.* This time the abuse is different. Calling out to him when he is in the toilet, hissing in his ear as they pass him in the yard. *Scum bag. Child killer. Rock spider.*

You're dead, maggot.

Placed in the general area, Division One, which houses 550 other prisoners, Carroll is held in protective custody in a single-bedroom cell three metres by 1.8 metres. The cell walls are engraved with the desperate etchings of desperate men and the floor is uneven in parts where thousands have tried to out-step their claustrophobic demons by pacing up and down. Nothing but a desk and a toilet. But at least the toilet flushes. On the old side of the jail, prisoners only have a pan pail to use.

Escorted from his cell in the morning and returned in the after-noon, Carroll is locked down at 4pm until just after dawn the next day, when the same routine starts again. Lying on his bed through the long nights, his hands entwined under the nape of his neck, staring at the ceiling. Going over and over what had happened during the trial. The way they had spoken about his personality in court – *he was disliked, a loner* – and his teeth – *stained, protruding*. Like he was something out of a freak show. Paraded in court as if he needed a good hose-down. Seeing his mother's face, gaunt and scrunched with pain, and hearing Sandra's voice echoing after him – 'I love you, Raymond' – when he was escorted from the court-room, down the stairway to hell. The voyeurs in the public gallery – curious, contemptuous – and Reynolds, hard as concrete, staring him down when the jurors came back with their verdict. *Guilty, guilty, guilty* . . . Standing there gawky, panicked, like the arse had fallen out of his world but registering nothing on his face. His entrails knotted, not moving, as the jurors' voices enveloped him. *Guilty, guilty, guilty* . . . Vasta, sitting up there pompously pronouncing judgment, and feeling the relief in the court from everyone but his family. At least the Kennedys weren't there. He couldn't have dealt with them eyeballing him as well.

He has got to get out of this prison, this steaming hell-hole filled with mad, bad bastards and plastic gangsters who roam the periphery of the yard looking for trouble and usually find it, somehow. Brawls break out at the slightest excuse: a terse glance, an ill-chosen word, an accidental bump as someone walks past. The advice to the new blokes coming in is always the same: watch your back, watch your front and keep your peripheral vision clear. Standing high on the hill, Boggo Road is an illusion of grandeur, save for the wire that marks it as a fortress; inside, the men are trapped like spiders in sticky glycerine, subjugated to the bells and the orders and the sudden lock-downs: rhythmically, systematically institutionalised.

Carroll has told his solicitor to hit the ground running with any grounds for appeals he can find. It will take them a week to lodge it from the Public Defenders Office, and Christ only knows how long after that while it churns through the system.

The wheels of justice turn slowly.

The same old abuse, every day and now Carroll says he heard a new, strange voice join the throng. 'How would you guys feel if you were convicted of this crime and didn't do it?' It is something of a salvation for a man shit-scared, a man despised and condemned by prisoners, guards and the outside world. From then, according to Carroll, the inmates actually started listening to him. After that he was out in the yard, in mainstream, not protective custody but in a solitary cell at night. He was given the option and chose mainstream. Carroll didn't want to be in protective, he says, with those sick bastards. Didn't want protection with those pricks.

The prisoners, he reckons, started to make their own decisions, started taking notice of him. They came to their own conclusion – that he was fitted up.

Nine months in Boggo Road. Physically unharmed but the taunting rarely stopped.

Scum bag. Child killer. Rock spider.

You're dead, maggot.

His family feels as though they are in prison, too. Stalked by the press who seem to materialise at every turn demanding comment, they are also verbally attacked in the street. 'Your brother's where he belongs. They should throw away the key.'

Judgments come in less obvious messages, too: people turning to look over their shoulder as they walk past them in the street, muttering to their companion; cold gazes from shop assistants who recognise their photographs; the wordless, malevolent thinking, expressed in their eyes, that the family must have known *something*. It is as though they, too, are publicly condemned and branded, as if it is somehow their fault that Raymond has gone down for killing a baby. Within a short time of Raymond's conviction, his younger brother Peter is picked up twice on the same night for drink-driving. His mother, Ilma, tormented with grief and outrage that her son has been convicted, has aged overnight, her once brown hair fading to shades of grey. Raymond's sister Sandra would shoulder the burden that gnawed at her nervous system until it collapsed and she had a complete breakdown.

Raymond has been at Boggo Road for seven months. The prison grapevine has been beating like a bongo drum that a jail verbal is coming down against him. Word is that a prisoner is going to grass him up, repeat something that Carroll has allegedly said, drop the information in the ear of a screw. *Raymond Carroll told me . . .* It is the currency of prison, to give and receive. Give information, receive reward. Whether the information is true or not is irrelevant; coming shortly before the appeal, it has made his lawyers extremely testy. He is shoved back into protection to try to head it off, but his counsel decide the date set for his appeal is too close to take the risk of any detrimental evidence that may adversely affect the outcome. They want their client moved to Wacol Prison on the other side of Brisbane. It suits Carroll just fine. Wacol is a dream home in comparison to Boggo Road – a five-star hotel with modern facilities.

His reception into Wacol is not much better than it had been at Boggo. He has a cell to himself, is woken early in the morning to work in the kitchen and returns late at night to his quarters. The kitchen is one of the most dangerous places in the prison to work: stainless-steel knives, boiling water and heavy pans make perfect weapons for edgy, caged men. He keeps mainly to himself, tense and cautious. It would only be later that he would find out that the inmates in the kitchen had been cautioned sternly that if anything happened to him, they would lose all their privileges. Sleeping in protection and working mainstream, he copped a bit of abuse, but nothing major. Same old shit that he got at Boggo Road, he felt.

Scum bag. Child killer. Rock spider.

You're dead, maggot.

Lying on his bunk at night, staring at the ceiling, his hands entwined behind his neck, he wonders how much longer it will be until he knows whether the appeal will be allowed. He has to get out of here, away from this wild rabble.

25

Raymond Carroll is pacing the yard, waiting for word to come through from his lawyers. He has been told the Appeals Court would make a decision today: 15 November 1985. It is stifling hot, five weeks before Christmas, heat prickling already prickly tempers. The other inmates are circling, restless; just the sniff of another man's freedom makes them edgy. Carroll had earlier boasted to them that he would be out of here by tonight, but they know better than to take bets. Many a man has mistakenly reckoned on his freedom on pre-judging what a jury or an Appeals Court will decide.

A screw is walking toward Carroll. The inmates lean against the yard wall, smoking, watching. Waiting.

Carroll's counsel had clear instructions: to pursue each and every legal ground against the jury's verdict. They have done so, raising numerous grounds for appeal: an attack on the admissibility of evidence, suggested defects in the summing-up, Carroll's lack of knowledge about the Kennedy family, the description of the man seen on the veranda that did not fit his description, and the adequacy of the Crown case as a whole.

Lawyers devour the issues, taking each apart thread by thread. Trevor Hartigan, QC, and Kerry Copley appeared for Carroll; Philip Nase, for the Crown.

The hearing lasts for two days. Faye and Barry are on tenterhooks, waiting for the result. Faye buries herself in work, in her management role at the local supermarket. Barry doesn't say much, keeping his thoughts to himself, but Faye finds it almost impossible to concentrate.

Carroll doesn't have to say a word. The other prisoners know, by the way he holds his thumb up in a victory salute, that he is out. Cool, detached, he doesn't turn to say goodbye after he collects his belongings, exiting through the electronic doors. An inmate watches his disappearing back, crushes a cigarette under his boot and spits on the concrete.

Angelo Vasta is in chambers when one of the appeals judges advises him of the acquittal. It is a blunt summation of their decision, delivered by verbal guillotine. 'We've rolled you, Angelo.' Common courtesy dictates he be told before it is made public. But the decision is irreversible.

Vasta stares out of his chamber's window, and ponders the appeal outcome. As Chief Crown Prosecutor, he has worked on hundreds of cases of rape and serious sexual assault, but never of a child of such tender age. It is, for him, truly a horrifying case. He doesn't grieve for himself when he hears that Carroll has been acquitted; he grieves for justice, for the overturning of a jury's decision. It was a decision which they took very seriously, believing that the evidence against Carroll was strong, and which Vasta believes has been overturned on technicalities and points of law. To his knowledge, this has not been done before. Usually a re-trial is ordered, which does not happen on this occasion. For Vasta, that raises serious concerns. Usually the Appeals Court says 'the evidence as we read it is unsatisfactory' and orders a re-trial; they didn't do that in the Kennedy case. Instead, they allowed the appeal, quashed the conviction and directed a verdict of acquittal. The consequences of the appeal are the same as if the jury had returned a verdict of not guilty. Essentially, the appeal court's verdict has locked the door on the case and thrown away the key.

He ponders a possible scenario. 'Imagine if an Appeals Court overturns a jury decision and the next week the accused says, "I did it." With our double jeopardy laws as they are, it would not be possible for that person to be re-tried.'

Double jeopardy. The principle of law that says no person shall be twice tried for the same offence for which they have previously been either acquitted or convicted. The courts may also consider it an abuse of process for additional charges to be brought, following an acquittal or conviction, for different offences that arose from the same behaviour or facts.

Seated at a vast desk in a study lined with legal texts, Angelo Vasta does not have the slightest air of pomposity. Warm and personable, his face, creased with laughter lines and years of worry, appears as though it has been rinsed in eons of Sicilian sunshine. Look closer and it could be his father, cutting cane in the muggy heat of an oppressive North Queensland summer.

'Look,' he says, settling into his leather chair, 'Appeals Courts *do* overturn decisions – that is a fact of law. It is the function of that court to look at evidence if an appeal is raised, and it is their right to decide accordingly. So I didn't take it personally. But I knew the jurors would wonder at the decision. And they did wonder.'

Faye is at work when John Reynolds, who has been keeping track of the appeals process for the Kennedys, advises her of the appeal decision. A sound escapes her, like the noise of a wounded animal, a cry he will never forget.

It is Carroll's first weekend of freedom in nine months. As he is walking out of Wacol Prison, his lawyer is representing him in the Ipswich Magistrate's Court where he was granted bail on the 17 charges from the break-in at the women's quarters in 1982. Ten break-and-enter charges, six of wilful destruction and one stealing offence. He finds out by telephone that he has been granted bail on the undertaking he reports weekly to police. Carroll has not taken any chances with anyone knowing his whereabouts. On his lawyer's advice, he meets Jennifer and the children and scarpers straight into hiding.

Twelve days after the order for Carroll's release, reasons for the judgment are delivered. Three judges – Chief Justice Dormer Andrews, Justice George Kneipp and Justice Tom Shepherdson – had presided and each agreed with the rulings given by their brothers. Their findings were:

(1) That a reasonable jury could have been satisfied beyond reasonable doubt from the evidence presented by the Crown witnesses that Carroll was not on the RAAF base at

Edinburgh when Deidre was murdered, but that there was no direct evidence that he was in, or near Ipswich at that time.

(2) That the similar fact evidence of his first wife, Joy Meyers, was not sufficient to outweigh its prejudicial effects and ought to have been excluded.

(3) A jury must have entertained a reasonable doubt as to Carroll's guilt based on the odontological evidence of Romaniuk, Sims and Brown.

The similar fact evidence given by Carroll's ex-wife, Joy Meyers, had afforded the three appeals judges much grief. Andrews had pondered whether to order a new trial or simply to quash the conviction, but was satisfied that the alleged biting of Joy and Raymond's own child, Kerry-Ann, and the fetishism shown by Deidre's killer was not sufficient to prove identity. For these reasons alone, he said, he had been able to come early to the decision that the verdict could not stand. Kneipp and Shepherdon were equally adamant. There were, Kneipp argued, not sufficient similarities between the alleged physical abuse of Joy and Raymond's own child and that occasioned to Deidre.

> It was suggested for the Crown that it could be supposed that the alleged acts of the accused in relation to his own child did not go further because of the circumstances in which they took place. That may be so; but one cannot build a sufficient series of similar acts on mere speculation. In my view . . . it should not have been admitted.

Shepherdon noted that Meyers's evidence did not in any way suggest that Carroll was a man who had a fetish for putting adult female clothing on a baby or of sexually interfering with the baby – both elements that were present in the Kennedy murder.

It was also ruled that Joy Meyers's evidence of Carroll biting his daughter could not justify its admission into evidence. The most it went to prove – if, they wrote, it were true – was a propensity to bite a 12-month-old child's leg. It did not show a striking similarity to the Kennedy killing. And, as for Joy Meyers's evidence that Carroll had allegedly wanted to call their unborn baby Deidre, this was nothing more than a highly prejudicial invitation to the jury to speculate that, because Carroll had mentioned the name Deidre in 1974, then that showed he must, beyond reasonable doubt, have been the killer of Deidre Kennedy.

What of Carroll's alibi? Kneipp was satisfied that a jury, notwithstanding conflicts in the evidence, could find beyond reasonable doubt that Carroll was *not* at Edinburgh Air Base at the time of Deidre's murder. But that was not enough. This, in itself did not necessarily place him in Ipswich and there was not any direct evidence that he had been there. The other judges backed this opinion. Carroll had not been seen in Ipswich and his family had said he was not there. There was conflicting evidence as to his presence in South Australia and RAAF records did not reveal whether he was absent or otherwise. Denials regarding his guilt were persistent and consistent. He had cooperated with police. And 'Nugget' Carroll's eyewitness account? Carroll did not fit the description Nugget gave police the day following Deidre's murder.

But it was the evidence of the forensic dentists – the linchpin of the Crown case – that came under the most savage attack. Kneipp noted that, apart from the evidence of Mrs Meyers, the only evidence available to the Crown as to identity was that put forward by the dentists.

> It cannot be said that there was not any evidence on which to find in favour of the Crown. Each of them qualified as an expert, and as has been said, each expressed the view that the marks on the child's body were made by the teeth of the appellant . . .

But this was not the end. 'In the present case, there were not any lacerations or indentations and . . . one can only have serious reservations as to its reliability where there are bruise marks only,' Kneipp had noted.

Romaniuk's earlier assessment, that the individual bruises caused by the bite were not sufficiently defined to enable one to arrive at any definite conclusion, was also highlighted. His change of opinion, between 1973 and 1985, was not adequately explained, the judges ruled.

Shepherdon noted that whilst the jury had only to accept the evidence of *one* of the experts, he was still left with an uneasy feeling. The altered plaster cast did not accurately reproduce the state of Carroll's dentition as it was in April 1973, and it was this cast that was one of the basic pieces of evidence on which each of the three experts founded his opinion. 'Admittedly,' Shepherdon conceded, 'Dr Romaniuk has become more experienced with bite marks since 1973. This, however was his first bite mark case and . . . he stated [in 1973] that "it would be impossible to establish with any degree of certainty as to who would be responsible for this bite mark to the dead child . . ."'

Recognising Dr Sims's eminence in his particular field, Shepherdon noted that his sense of unease was caused by discrepancies between the dentists on identification of certain bruise marks with certain teeth. 'I accept that each man was concerned with only the pattern of bruising.' Then, he added: 'I am conscious also that I must be careful not to let myself become an expert by viewing the exhibits and substituting my opinion for those of these three men.'

The odontology evidence, the judges reasoned, could not safely support the jury's verdict. Though they reached the same conclusion, the different way they achieved that result was cause for concern. On their evidence, the judges decided, a properly directed jury must have a reasonable doubt as to Carroll's guilt. In conclusion, Shepherdon noted that even if there were no errors made in the summing-up, and assuming the jury was properly directed on circumstantial evidence, on that which was properly admissible, any verdict of guilty would be such that it would be unsafe and unsatisfactory.

Dormer noted:

The matter has given me a great deal of difficulty. But in the end result I have concluded that a properly instructed jury, properly considering the matter, could not be satisfied beyond a reasonable doubt on this evidence that the accused was guilty. I would allow the appeal, set aside the verdict and quash the conviction.

The Appeals Court conclusion was final: the prosecution had not led any reliable evidence to identify Raymond John Carroll as Deidre Kennedy's killer. He was a free man.

Dr Brown is initially deeply shocked at the outcome of the appeal. When he reads the reasons for it, his shock turns to disgust. He perceives that it simply came down to legal issues, doesn't think the judges had any understanding of what the odontology evidence was all about. The fact that the odontologists disagreed on which teeth made the bruise marks was not relevant. What Sims meant was that he had enough evidence with the three teeth and he wasn't interested in the others. That, according to Brown, didn't contradict what Romaniuk said at all. He seethed that although the odontologists used different dental terms, they all meant the same thing. *The same thing.* They just used terminologies recognised and understood by dentists everywhere, but the appeal judges didn't clarify that point.

In Brown's view, those judges are wrong, very wrong, in their decision.

John Rowley, living in Malaysia where he was posted with the RAAF, is incredulous when he hears the news. He thought the murder case had finally been put to rest and can't imagine how the Kennedy family must now be feeling. He thinks this is a sad, sad decision for them.

For weeks after the appeals decision, Faye Kennedy wanders aimlessly around her house, withdrawing into a torpid stupor and sitting quietly on the bed where Deidre's doll has pride of place.

When she ventures out again in Ipswich, where they are now re-posted, she can feel the anger, the simmering resentment about Carroll's acquittal. For months afterwards, total strangers, stunned at the decision, would approach her on the street, offering to take the law into their own hands. One bloke from a bikie group tells her that if she 'wants the job done, to just say the word'. Another woman says she owns a transport company, and that Carroll will need to be careful on the road. Faye shakes her head at every suggestion. Thanks for the offer, but no thanks.

She is concerned about Barry. From the moment the acquittal decision came down, he has become increasingly withdrawn, going to the pub and staying there for hours. She frets for him, and for their marriage.

Ilma Carroll's phone is ringing, and a stranger is on the line. Cold, detached. 'You can't protect your son forever,' the voice says. 'We'll get the bastard.' The phone line goes dead. She has come to dread the voiceless callers who ring, say nothing and then hang up. And, day after day, the death threats continue – so many, she is forced to change to a silent number. It is an extremely traumatic time for the whole family. They hear that people want to distribute Raymond's photo with the caption 'Baby killer lives here' accompanied by his address. People just cannot accept that Raymond Carroll has been acquitted.

John Reynolds has not been able to accept the acquittal, either. He had been confident that Carroll would lose the appeal. Nearly all of the people in the jury that found Carroll guilty have called him, wanting to know how the hell their decision has been overturned.

He was out of Brisbane when the Appeals Court announced its decision. His then wife rang and said she had just had a phone call from the Commissioner's office. 'Carroll has been released and your instructions are not to talk to the media under any circumstances,' she told him. Confident that Carroll would lose the appeal, Reynolds went right off.

Shortly after news of the acquittal, Reynolds receives a phone call from a nurse who had worked at Wagga Base Hospital. She tells him that Kerry-Ann had been brought into hospital with a broken arm when she was six months old.

Carroll would later remember the incident. He was, he says, giving Kerry-Ann her bottle and her arm was behind him on his back. He says he went to sit her up and she suffered a green stick break. Joy wasn't at home when it happened. He was on his own with Kerry-Ann.

Carroll, Jennifer and kids move to Jennifer's home town, Leeton, in New South Wales. His lawyers had been blunt with their advice. Get out of Ipswich for your own safety, they warned him. The public is baying for your blood.

26

If Carroll was hoping the law would leave him in peace once he left Queensland, he was mistaken. The Attorney-General, Mr Harper, ordered a High Court appeal as soon as Carroll was freed. Tony Fitzgerald, QC, would head the Crown legal task force, his juniors Adrian Gundelach and Philip Nase. The Director of Public Prosecutions, Des Sturgess, lodged the motion for special leave to appeal.

The Crown does not just want the jury conviction restored. It is seeking a re-trial.

The High Court appeal is heard in June 1986. John Reynolds and Carroll's family are present. Fitzgerald has based his appeal on the grounds that the Criminal Court of Appeal had made an error in principle. Discrepancies in dental experts' evidence had not been considered, he argues, and nor had Carroll's false alibi that he was on a course at Edinburgh at the time. The court had misunderstood the expert evidence and, even if Joy Meyers did not give evidence again, there was enough for a re-trial.

Chief Justice Sir Harry Gibbs peers at Fitzgerald. Could he please tell the court what principle was broken? Yes, Fitzgerald replies. The court was required to consider the whole evidence and not certain aspects of it.

Ruling there is no question of an error in principle, Chief Justice Gibbs says Carroll did not know there was a baby in the Kennedy household and evidence showed he was not in Ipswich when she was abducted and murdered. Nugget Carroll's statement had identified the man who stole the clothing from the line as having long hair; Carroll had short back and sides.

Fitzgerald has taken an hour to outline the Crown case: it takes the five judges of the Full Court just 10 minutes to reach their decision. They refuse to grant the Crown special leave to appeal. It is all over.

Ilma Carroll and her daughters, Sandra and Debbie, loiter outside the courtroom just long enough for Reynolds to see their smiles.

Since the murder trial, Adrian Gundelach has kept much of the evidence pertaining to the Kennedy case packed and boxed in the basement underneath his house. It has seemed as good a place as any to store it, but, with the Full Court decision in, he thinks it best it be returned to Homicide Branch. He speaks to an officer at the desk, asking that it be picked up from his place. With Carroll's full acquittal, it is now, essentially, an open inquiry again.

'We know who did that murder,' the cop says yawningly.

Eventually returned to Homicide and discarded into an exhibit room with little organisational care, the boxes of evidence are not in prime condition. A flood that had gone through Brisbane after 1985 had caused water damage to Gundelach's basement and damaged some photographic exhibits. It would fall to the police photographer in the next trial to try and mop up some of that damage.

Adrian Gundelach delivers lectures in America on a paper he wrote two years after the appeal decision came down, which focused on the problem forensic scientists repeatedly face in having their evidence accepted in court. It is a carefully prepared, caustic attack on the appeal decision.

A fact-finding tribunal, he says, is often required to understand the scientific detail of expert evidence even though it is uninitiated in that area of expertise. And if the tribunal cannot understand the conclusions it must, like St Thomas, remain a doubting tribunal and reject the evidence as inconclusive. Each juror becomes his own Sherlock Holmes.

Gundelach tells his audiences of scientists and police that the Court of Criminal Appeal had quashed a jury's verdict of guilty because they were unconvinced of the reliability of three expert dental opinions that the marks on the murdered baby's thighs had been caused by Carroll's teeth.

Most of the police are drawn from outlying Midwest areas

around Kansas, baked hard under severe blue skies. Appeals Courts and high-falutin' legal decisions do not sit well with these officers; the way they see it, it takes enough time and money to round crims up in the first place, without watching them walk in one jail door and out the other.

Although Gundelach says the experts' reasons for their conclusions did not coincide in all respects, these so-called 'discrepancies' did not affect the basis of their conclusions that Carroll was responsible for biting the deceased child's thigh, and no other person gave evidence to the contrary.

The lesson, Gundelach concludes, is clear: that when expert evidence of three eminent scientists is rejected by an appeal court, it demonstrates the real danger of judges (or jurors) playing Sherlock Holmes in an area beyond their competence and expertise . . .

The lesson to expert witnesses? That unless their evidence is unshakeable and totally unanimous, judges and jurors may not feel inclined to accept it.

27

The Fitzgerald Inquiry. Regarded by many as long overdue, a cleansing of Queensland's police corruption, money laundering and prostitution, its name would inexorably be linked with disgraced Police Commissioner Terry Lewis. By its conclusion, Terry Lewis, four politicians and several police officers would be charged and jailed. And Angelo Vasta would become the only judge in Australian history to be de-benched.

Many regarded the 1989 inquiry as little more than a blood letting, a witch-hunt carried out in an atmosphere of sensationalism and hysteria. Asked to provide a statement against Terry Lewis, Angelo Vasta refused. He went further, attacking the basic tenets of the Inquiry.

To speak out against the Inquiry, Vasta says, was tantamount to speaking out against motherhood and the Queen. He wanted a separate inquiry to prove whether any actions they were talking about had compromised his office.

Eventually given his inquiry, headed up by three fellow judges, it was more far-reaching than he had imagined. Accused of tax scams and unbecoming conduct, Vasta told the Queensland Parliament in June 1989 that he would go to his grave and to his God with a clear conscience, knowing that he had done no such wrong.

In his opinion, he says of the Kennedy appeal, two of the appeal judges were misguided, but genuine; and the other judge had a reputation for being over-technical. It was most unfortunate that there was this combination of judges; if it had been a different combination, he is certain there would not have been the same result.

John Reynolds had watched the unfolding Inquiry with interest. In the past, police officers were regarded as God, and that's how corruption survived and flourished in Queensland. It worked on the MERIT system: Mates Elevated Regardless of Intelligence or Training. Reynolds was dismayed at the outcome for Angelo Vasta. He was known as a fair judge, but very tough when it came to paedophiles and other crimes against children. If the accused was found to be guilty he gave them a long custodial sentence – no ifs or buts – and it was a fact that the criminal element would do everything they could to avoid coming up before him. He was tough on lawyers, too, who might try to take the easy way out of cases.

Reynolds chuckles as he recalls a memorable exchange between Vasta who, during a trial, complained that he was tired of his opposing defence, Kevin Townsley baiting him. Townsley rose to respond. 'Your Honour. I have been called a lot of things, but I have never been called a Vastabaitor.'

Raymond and Jennifer's third daughter together, Tabatha, is born in early November 1989, but the marriage is in trouble. Jail does strange things to a person, breeds paranoia. After they move to Leeton, he goes out playing cards on a Friday night but Jennifer doesn't like it. When he tells her he is going to go to Mildura to watch the bike races for three days, she tells him to go, but warns if he does, not to bother coming back.

He goes.

Jennifer has a neighbour Marilyn, with whom she often associates on a friendly basis. When Raymond goes to the bike meeting, Jennifer tells her she is going to put his stuff out the front, cut up his photographs and his personal items. Marilyn responds that that's not a nice thing to do. On Tabatha's second birthday in 1991, Jennifer and Raymond's marriage ends. Within a short time, Marilyn and Raymond are together.

Faye and Barry had returned to an Ipswich posting in 1988, but their marriage has been quietly eroding, sliding away beneath them. In 1992, the year they celebrate their twenty-fifth wedding anniversary, the union that had started with passion and love collapses under the weight of unresolved sorrow and guilt.

Barry has fallen apart. Since the acquittal, he has simply shut down, as if a light has been turned off in his eyes. Not living, just surviving, with a blank, pensive look that never goes away. He carries all his hurt inside, and it has consumed him. Haunted by guilt that a stranger entered his home and abducted his daughter, he has constantly berated himself that he should have done more. He feels it is his fault. He feels he is a failure.

The RAAF had offered some counselling sessions, but they were of little help to Barry. He found unburdening his soul to a virtual stranger awkward and embarrassing. He is a private man, who deals with his problems in his own way.

Alcohol blurs the pain. He is drinking heavily now, rarely home. Month after month, Faye goes looking for him. He had always been spotlessly turned out, his shirts starched and ironed; always an exemplary serviceman. But now he has gone AWOL, and the service police pick him up. They barely recognise the bleary-eyed, dishevelled man as Barry Kennedy.

Faye's old fears resurface when she sees Barry drunk. Just the smell of the alcohol is enough to bring back the dread she had felt with her father, and how the drinking had destroyed her parents' marriage. But Barry has never been violent, never even raised his voice. Just quiet, maudlin, drowning his demons.

Money is haemmoraging from the household, swallowed by his gambling habit. They don't bicker, but icy silences last for days and there is simmering resentment. Faye tries to understand, asks him why he does it. His answer stuns her. When he is drinking and gambling, he says, he can block out the real world. He doesn't have to think about Deidre. Doesn't have to think about what happened.

But he will stop. He will straighten out. Everything will be all right.

'You need to get help, Barry.' Faye seems to be saying it all the time, now. 'Please, Barry, get some help.'

I will, mate, I will.

He props a goodbye note on the sideboard and quietly closes the door behind him.

The house is so empty without him. Faye is still in love with Barry, and desperately lonely years follow as she withdraws with her grief.

Barry was all she knew; they had done everything together since they were teenagers, and it is such a waste of a good man. She thought they could get through anything together, and after Derek was born, they tried to make their lives full. The years they had before the first trial were good, wholesome years as a family. But it wasn't enough.

In her darkest moments, feeling as though she is disintegrating, she flirts with the idea of suicide. There is a cliff in front of her, beckoning. She won't turn the car, will keep accelerating and free-fall into oblivion. She plants her foot on the accelerator, grips the wheel tighter.

But she can't do it. She sits at the steering wheel trembling, crying. After all the grief Stephanie and Derek have been through with her, she doesn't want to make them suffer any more. She sits sobbing for hours in the quiet womb of the car, before she drives home.

There is solace in the familiar comforts of home, and in hard work. But peace does not always come easily. She is stunned, inconsolable, when a stranger approaches her in the street and berates her for being a bad mother because she hadn't locked the doors and window on the night Deidre was abducted. Right up close to her face, spitting out her venom. 'It's your own fault. You can't blame nobody else. You're a bad mother, Faye Kennedy.'

Faye weeps for days.

Dr Kon Romaniuk is walking across a busy road in Sydney, dodging the frantic traffic of weekend drivers rushing to enjoy the hot January 1994 day. He doesn't see it coming, can't remember feeling anything as a motorbike slams into his side and he lies sprawled in the gutter.

Months in hospital follow, and the best the doctors can say is he is lucky to be alive. So visually impaired as to be legally blind, he has damage to the frontal and back lobes of his brain and has lost all cognitive ability.

Romaniuk never works again. He becomes a shadowy figure who goes into the university office, like a homing pigeon, but cannot always remember why he is there.

*

The years turn slowly, season after season through the 1990s. The snap of winter, when dew forms diamond drops on windowsills; spring, when flowers peek shyly from their buds; summer, when butterflies float in the warmth of blazing sunshine; and autumn, when leaves turn russet. Year after turning year, Faye's four grandchildren – two each from Stephanie and Derek – grow older and the pages of her photo album start to wither at the edges.

Faye lives quietly. Late on summer afternoons, she sits out alone on the back patio of her suburban Ipswich house on the fringes of bushland, watching time pass with the heralding of a changing sky. At dusk, the harsh blue infused with streaks of watermelon, and then darkness encroaches, gently. It is at these times she feels the loneliness most, an exquisite loneliness when she aches for all she had lost. Losing Barry has been hard enough. But whoever had abducted her daughter had also kidnapped the sunshine.

She keeps to herself, wary of strangers. When one of the uniformed police from the original investigation approaches her in the street, she shies away, skittish and scared. He only wants to wish her well, says he kept up with proceedings from a distance. She thanks him, abashed at how many people have looked out for her, without her even knowing.

28

Queensland journalist Peter Hansen has been in the game so long there is little he doesn't know about the Kennedy case. But Hansen is of the old school. Don't boast about who you know, and never burn a contact. Off the record means off the record. With a voice as smooth as warmed whiskey, an old-fashioned turn of phrase and a brain that zeroes like a radar on to a good story, he lacks the brash abrasiveness often seen in younger reporters. Seduced back to part-time journalism from retirement, Hansen is mindful of sensitivities, particularly those of Faye Kennedy. He frets for her that, already debilitated by grief, each time something new breaks in the inquiry into Deidre's murder, her hopes soar only to be dashed again in despair. Journalists, he ruminates, should walk gently on this patch.

Could computer technology be used to solve the Kennedy case? Senior-Sergeant John Garner, specialist in forensic imaging and freehand drawing with Queensland Police, was determined to find out. Devising a digital analysis system in 1997, he and forensic odontologist Dr Alex Forrest, a lecturer in Oral Biology at the University of Queensland, believe they discovered that it elicited information about the bite marks on Deidre's thigh not seen at the 1985 murder trial. The Deidre Kennedy case, in theory unsolved and re-opened since Carroll's acquittal, has, in reality, been sitting gathering dust for 12 years through lack of leads or suspects. It is a reality that is about to change.

John Garner trusts Hansen. He is, he reasons, the perfect person for him and Alex Forrest to speak to about the new technique they had devised to reconstruct a human face from a skull. And, while they were there with him, they would mention the breakthrough they had made in the identification of bite marks using digital technology. Perhaps it could help solve the Deidre Kennedy murder?

Garner is more scientist than cop, a lateral thinker who grates evidence to shreds and re-builds it, piece by piece, as if it were a Lego set. Each piece on top of the other, layering, gluing them in place. And when the pieces don't fit, he mentally sets them aside. There are pieces that don't fit in the Kennedy case, and he is dying to have a crack at it.

The technology had discovered two more bite marks on Deidre's thigh.

Forrest and Garner go over what they know. Bite mark number one was the obvious bruising referred to in the dental evidence at the first trial. But closer to the back surface of the thigh, to the right on the photograph they can now see a faint bite mark bruise. They will call this bite mark number two.

On bite mark number one they can see a curvy mark, near the top of the thigh that almost touches the bruise made by one of the lower teeth. This, they have ascertained, is a bruise made by the clip attached to the step-in in which Deidre was dressed. It is close to the bite mark, but independent of it.

The new technology took years to perfect, but the techniques were simple.

Garner is looking at the post-mortem photo of Deidre. Her skin has very faint, directional scratches caused, he thinks by the scraping action of the teeth over the surface of her skin just prior to the actual bite. If no pressure had been applied in the bite, that would explain the lack of indentation marks. There was nothing to cause them.

Deidre, Garner believes, was not lying down when she was bitten. Years spent photographing horrific scenes – murder, suicide, accidents – has hardened his shell, but he is still ashen when he explains what happened to her. He speaks in rapid-fire voice, layering his scientific knowledge of the case with insightful comment and opinion. As a circuit breaker to tension, using his skills as a free-hand artist, he often draws caricatures of people involved in different cases. Some have a sour edge, others are bleak. The Kennedy case affected him so deeply, he drew scores on the subject.

Garner illustrates with his hands how he believes Deidre was held. It is like watching a macabre puppet show, hynoptically following the strings as they move up and down. 'She was picked up by her left leg, like this' – he turns his hand over – 'and held upside down. Picked up by this animal like she was a leg of turkey, her right leg flailing. She was in this positon when he bit her, raking the skin with his teeth. We can only imagine how distressed she would have been. The poor, pitiful little soul.' His description is so vivid I am stunned speechless and tears dampen my shirt. It comes as a boot in my gut, and bile burns my throat, rising swiftly on a tide of horror and disgust. She was only a defenceless, vulnerable baby. The poor, pitiful little soul.

Forrest and Garner needed to solve some basic theoretical problems before they could move on. How best to analyse a three-dimensional dental model against a two-dimensional photograph? On a curved surface, such as an arm or a leg, the angle changes when teeth close, and a wave of tissue moves ahead of the upper teeth, which leaves an impression of the *insides* of those teeth. The lower teeth drag less and tend to leave more sharply defined wounds.

With the help of Dr. Peter Adams from the University's Department of Mathematics, they devised a formula to calculate distortions made by curvature. Using the formula and taking a photograph of the thigh, they worked in reverse to 'unfold' the leg and show how the bite mark would look had it happened on a flat surface.

To demonstrate which tooth touched in which order as it came into contact with the surface of the skin, they placed the dental model into a Chinese takeaway food container and slowly poured in ink and detergent. It was rudimentary science, but it did the trick. Garner took photographs vertically from above, clicking away as each tooth in turn submerged until eventually they were all covered. The result was a series of pictures which showed the contours of the teeth at each given ink level, allowing them to analyse the parts of the dentition in contact with a surface as the bite became deeper. They then ran the digital image in reserve, watching as the teeth gradually grew and emerged from the ink.

They knew that Carroll's front teeth could not come together without a lot of effort, if at all. He had developed a habit of biting on the side, off-centre. Because of that, Garner said, they knew his teeth were going to be at an angle when they hit the skin. They could not hit flat on, as someone with a normal bite does.

Another challenge was to compare similar things, to ensure they were precisely the same scale. Instead of comparing teeth with the wound, they produced a wound from the teeth and compared the simulated wound with the original. Both the teeth and the wound had to be scaled correctly, and they had to be able to demonstrate that they had been scaled the same.

To compare the drag marks on Deidre's skin, they dipped the cast of teeth into powdered dental wax, dragged the teeth across a surface like fingers down a blackboard and took photographs which they then put on the computer. Irregular teeth would leave a barcode effect as they dragged. Garner superimposed the drag marks on the original photograph to see if there was a corresponding bite mark pattern. It was a visual test, and he was satisfied it worked.

29

eter Hansen is very interested in what Garner has to say.
Where, he wants to know, would they use their new techniques?

It is Garner's chance, a calculated opportunity to try to bring on another shot at the Carroll case. 'Had this technology been around at the time of the Deidre Kennedy trial,' he says, in a tone that he hopes does not give too much away, 'I am confident that we would have had a different result.'

The interview pays dividends. Headlined 'Give me Peace – Mum Wants Justice for Murdered Baby Deidre', an article, printed in February 1997, trumpets that a breakthrough in the case that horrified Australia is now possible because forensic experts could identify the murderer from bite marks on the toddler's body. Faye speaks with Hansen about her hope that Deidre's killer will be convicted. Hailing the advances in forensic dentistry as a 'modern miracle', Hansen recounts how Garner and Forrest have identified a deceased North Queensland man by building a face from a skull with astonishing accuracy. 'But,' he writes, 'the case that cries out for answers is the one which caused Australia-wide outrage 24 years ago . . .'

There is an incredible response to the newspaper report. Unlike the hundreds of reports that had been written about Deidre before, this one prompts a stream of people to telephone this newspaper and the police.

One of these people is Graham Bradshaw, a fair-haired, gentle-mannered man who had served in the RAAF. The story he tells the newspaper is astonishing. He had, he claims, been drinking with friends in the convivial atmosphere of an airmen's club in 1974 when another RAAF member, whom he believed to be Raymond Carroll, approached him. 'Do you know anything about the murder of a little girl at Ipswich?' Carroll allegedly asked him. The question startled Bradshaw. 'I said I had read about a baby's body being thrown on to the roof of a toilet block in an Ipswich park, and he replied that was the one he was talking about. He then said, "I did it."'

Bradshaw was stunned into disbelief. What sort of person would want to boast about something as evil and deranged as the sexual assault and murder of a defenceless baby? He looked at his mates, perplexed, and then stared hard at Carroll. 'Are you really trying to tell us that you killed this little girl?'

'Yes, I did it.' Carroll, according to Bradshaw, was impassive, offering no explanation for the murder. 'I didn't know what to make of it,' Bradshaw told Hansen. 'It seemed so unreal and the man was as cool as a cucumber.' Bradshaw's drinking companions had apparently warned him not to believe Carroll, as he was unreliable. 'The man's a bull artist. A storyteller. Full of shit.' He had not gone to police earlier, Bradshaw said, as he knew that Carroll had been arrested and everything was under control. He figured police had enough evidence already to get the murder charge through, and afterward he became busy at work and never thought of the incident again until he read that Carroll had been released.

In 2000, conducting a review of cold cases stretching back 40 years, Detective-Superintendent Peter Barron, the officer in charge of Homicide, Brisbane, asks Detective Senior-Constable Cameron Herpich to look at the Kennedy file. 'Let me know what you think,' he instructs him.

Days after the *Sunday Mail* report appears, Barron receives another phone call from a man, who chooses to remain anonymous, telling him that a 'certain person' had admitted to him that he had killed Deidre. The level of detail he offers is chillingly accurate and Barron makes a public appeal to the man to call back. 'I believe there are other people out there in the community who could provide us with valuable information,' he said. 'It has become quite obvious that at the time of the investigation people had information, but for one reason or another – through fear or not wanting to be involved – they did not come forward.'

Another man with a thorough knowledge of the park crawls

out of the woodwork and contacts John Reynolds by phone, telling him that he had seen Deidre dumped on top of the toilet block. The killer, he says, was driving a white Holden panel van and had climbed on the roof-racks to reach the top of the block. He cries as he explains to Reynolds why he hadn't come forward earlier, describing himself as 'young, stupid and naïve'. Refusing to give his name, he promises to contact Reynolds again. He never does.

Two weeks after the *Sunday Mail* article is published, another titled 'Exclusive – I Didn't Kill Baby: Carroll Speaks Out' appears in the same newspaper.

> The man convicted and then cleared of one of Queensland's most notorious child murders is living and working only kilometres from the death scene . . . Carroll, 41, was confronted by workmates at a meat-processing factory near Ipswich last week. They asked if he was the subject of renewed police interest in the murder and whether it was his photo in the *Sunday Mail*.

'That's me,' Carroll told them. 'But I didn't do it.' Carroll's only comment to the journalist was 'no comment' and the basis of the breathless 'Exclusive' tag was simply a letter from his solicitor denying allegations that his client had confessed to two people.

The hysterical hype continues, with a mother of three with whom Carroll works reportedly asking to go on stress leave when she realises who he is.

The one-man detective outfit is upgraded to a full team after the second phone call. Herpich, assigned to head the investigation, is convinced that the fresh leads are worthwhile. He believes that while it wasn't a confession, per se, it certainly indicated some guilty knowledge by this person, alleged to be Carroll, to Graham Bradshaw. But from the start police look at the legal implications of what they can do even if they did find something that can support Bradshaw. They look at the grounds on which the Court of Appeal had overturned the verdict and how they can identify why the appeal ran. Herpich zeroes in. Determined. Meticulous. Dots the i's and crosses the t's. He was 11 years old when Deidre was murdered; now in his early forties, a sturdy, serious man with a thick-set oval face, brown hair streaked with grey cut severely short, and dark eyes that glower suspiciously when he is annoyed, Herpich appears as hard as granite. It is not a side he will show to Faye.

'May I speak to Faye Kennedy, please?'
   'Speaking.'
   'Faye, this is Cameron Herpich from the Homicide Branch of the Queensland Police Service. I'm about to turn your life upside down.'

Married with three young children, from the start Herpich becomes Faye's protector, building an emotional moat around her. She has been hurt enough, and he will not allow anyone to trespass on her emotions. He is the buffer between Faye and the outside world. And she trusts him. From the moment he made that phone call, warning he was about to turn her life upside down, Faye has trusted him.

There have been promises made. He will keep her informed of every step of the investigation. She shall never ask him a question if she doesn't want to hear the answer. And he will try, within the boundaries of what he has to work with, to bring her daughter's killer to justice.

Herpich has no sympathy for Deidre's Kennedy's killer. In his career he has seen some stone cold people and others who have caused a death, and he feels sorry for them. He doesn't feel sorry for this person. It is a case that has stuck in people's minds and that they remember more than anything else. Not just because it was bizarre, but because Deidre was completely defenceless.

Trevor Swifte's hands tremble as he picks up the phone to call Detective-Superintendent Barron. He introduces himself, a preliminary that is unnecessary. In and out of jail all his adult life, Barron knows him by reputation only too well. Known as a character, one of the old-time crims, police simply refer to him as 'Swifty'. It seems fitting: whenever he lags on someone, they muse he may be, to quote a colloquial Australian expression, 'pulling a swifty'.

'I've got some information that may be of some benefit to you . . . ' Swifte tells the Superintendent. He seems to be half-whispering, as if he imagines his walls have ears. And he is talking flat out. '. . . About an ex-crim who was inside with me at Boggo Road Jail. Name of Raymond John Carroll.'

Swifty is a grass. A snitch. Perfect fodder for police information, if his evidence could be deemed reliable. Cameron Herpich does not waste time, tape-recording an interview with him on 12 March. On 19 July, five weeks before he is due in the District Court for yet another appearance, this time for receiving, Swifte gives a written statement to Herpich. 'I am a married man, 38 years of age and reside with my family at an address known to Police . . .' It is an innocuous start to what will colloquially become known as the 'jailhouse confession'.

On 17 February 1984, Swifte had been remanded in custody in the special protection yard at Boggo Road Prison. Designed for the special protection of prisoners such as paedophiles, informers or those deemed a suicide risk, he was placed in there for his own protection because he was a grass. He had been warned that Aboriginal inmates were wanting to 'knock' him – jail slang for kill. Carroll, he writes, was marched into the protection area by five screws sometime after Swifte had gone in, and his entrance was accompanied by a lot of racket. 'I spoke to one of the screws through the cell window and asked what all the commotion was about,' Swifte alleges. 'He said something like "Just another scum".' The next day, Swifte approached Carroll's cell. 'I looked in and saw him looking toward me. I recall that he looked at me as if to say "What are you fucking looking at, cunt?" . . . There were a number of crims in the next yard – H yard – who were always at the fence wanting to know about Carroll or to give messages to other crims . . .' Either 'the next day or a couple of days after', Swifte claims he approached Carroll again and asked him what he had been pinched on. 'The murder at Ipswich . . . a dozen years ago,' Carroll allegedly told him. Some 'over-zealous military copper' had got him, he added. Swifte remembers Deidre's murder. Then 15 years old, he was incarcerated at a boys' home for delinquents and police had made inquiries there as to whether any of the juveniles had absconded that night.

'I think it was the next day,' Swifte continues in his statement. 'I was in the jail surgery with Carroll . . . He said, "What do you know about teeth marks?" I said to him, "They are as good as fingerprints . . . and you're a shot duck . . ."' Carroll, he says, went quiet but appeared to be mumbling to himself. Later, Swifte pressed Carroll to tell him more. 'What went wrong?' he asked him. Carroll, he claims, was pacing up and down his cell. 'He held his arms out to the side of his body with the palms up and said "Those fucking bite marks . . . I used to go snowdropping and I was pinching women's underwear and it all just got out of hand."'

Swifte claims he collared a prison officer, Denzil Creed, through the steel gate of the SOBS yard and told him what Carroll had said. He asked Creed to get hold of the investigating police officer who was working on the case. The message never got through.

'Creed said words to the effect, "Don't worry, they've got him cold," and I said, "Fuck, he looks the part."'

Swifte allegedly spoke to Carroll again afterward, asked him why he did it. 'It got out of hand,' he claims Carroll said. 'It wasn't meant to happen.' Swifte kept pressing. How did he get the kid out of the house? 'Through the window.' Carroll, he says, then 'mumbled something about a van, said he dressed her up in woman's underwear and sexually abused her.' Swifte, who did not want to go into details about the sexual abuse, offered Carroll help on the proviso that he tell him what happened. 'I've always had a fetish about women's clothing,' Carroll allegedly ventured, adding he strangled Deidre with pantyhose and left her on the toilet block.

There was a ruckus behind them from 'H' block fence, a prisoner screaming to get Carroll's attention. 'You fucking mongrel dog,' he shouted at him. Any minute, the whole prison could erupt. A powder-keg at the best of times, prisoners held in the protective yard are prime targets for violence and abuse. Swifte, an 'old head' who knew his way around the system, ignored it and kept digging. 'Are you into raping women?' Carroll shook his head. 'No, it's easier to get a pro.' He became agitated when the bite marks were mentioned again, hurled off, according to Swifte, with a stream of expletives. Swifte was distracted by another prisoner speaking to him. 'You had better give that prick a miss otherwise you'll get yourself into trouble. They'll think that you are buddying on with him.'

'Not fucking likely,' Swifte replied, and walked away. 'About a week after this,' Swifte continues in his statement, 'I was moved to "H" wing . . . but after the warning from the crim, I kept away from Carroll.' Moved to another prison, Swifte again encountered Carroll when he was transferred back to Boggo Road after Carroll was sentenced for the murder. Carroll, then in 'H' wing, was hosing the yard. 'I walked up to him and said, "You got your right whack, cunt."' Carroll, Swifte writes, did not recognise him and turned his back.

> I can't remember seeing Carroll around the jail after this occasion. In June 1985 I was discharged from Boggo Road jail and travelled around Australia. The next thing I can recall about Carroll was when I read in the paper that he had been acquitted of the murder. This was earlier this year [1997]. I contacted Police at the Homicide Squad . . . Everything that I have said in this statement is true and correct.

He signs it 'Trevor Jonathon Swifte' in a tremulous hand.

Swifte's sentencing remarks on the receiving offence, heard in August in a closed court are placed in a sealed envelope, and the judge makes an order that they can only be opened by an order of the court. Carroll's defence will successfully be granted disclosure to have the remarks opened.

John Garner and Dr Forrest are approached by Cameron Herpich who asks whether they would be willing to apply their new techniques to the Kennedy case. They agree and on 30 April 1997 they are given post-mortem photographs of Deidre and dental models of Raymond Carroll. Dr Forrest, Garner and later odontologist Dr Ian Davies examine the dental models. They believe that the new technology will enable a precise match to be obtained between these and the injury photographs and will dramatically reduce the reliance on expert opinion. Dr Kon Romaniuk, Cameron Herpich, Detective-Superintendent Peter Barron and Angelo Vasta's son Sal Vasta — now a lawyer representing the DPP — are in the room when they do the preliminary match with the case photos. There is a sense of expectation, of growing excitement. The match comes in. The *top* bruise nearest Deidre's knee is a match with Carroll's *lower* teeth. The bottom bruise is a match with his uppers.

There is one person in the room who should know that the match — the top bruise caused by lower teeth — is vitally different from that which had been presented at the first trial. Kon Romaniuk. The three years since his accident has not reduced the trauma to his brain. Kon can't even look down a microscope, let alone know what he is looking at anymore. From the time of his accident he scored very high on the dementia scale but he is bright enough to still occasionally fudge his way through situations if he needs to. He can appear lucid, but only for very short time.

This is not one of those times. John Garner is devastated to notice that Kon appears to be in a fugue state, staring vacantly out the window, lost in his own world. If the once brilliant odontologist noticed that there is a difference compared to the way he and his colleagues had oriented the teeth marks at the murder trial, he does not comment.

Herpich also contacts John Rowley and John Reynolds to ask if they are available to help with the investigation. They immediately agree. But Herpich — nicknamed 'Bulldog' by John Garner for his tenacity — faces major hurdles. All the exhibits relating to Deidre Kennedy, including the way she was dressed the day she was murdered and the hair samples found on her were missing. They had disappeared. John Reynolds doesn't think anyone deliberately lost them; when police headquarters shifted, around 1990, things became messed up. He went in one day and found a box marked Deidre Kennedy. But as soon as he lifted the lid off the box, which was full of tapes, he knew it had absolutely nothing to do with that case. It was so frustrating. They had been put in the wrong box. The police were getting nowhere.

On the back of a rumour that evidence had been stored under Adrian Gundelach's house after the first appeal, Reynolds calls him and asks whether Gundelach has any of the exhibits. His answer is indirect enough for Reynolds to assume that he had had them, but no longer did. Reynolds has tapped into an important question: what to do with evidence when a case hangs in limbo? Gundelach knew this case inside out, and Reynolds has no doubt that he thought taking it home with him would be the best course of action. The safest place, so it couldn't get mixed up.

Herpich would find that missing evidence was not the only hurdle he would face.

Within a short time, Garner and Forrest have identified what they perceived as critical problems with the original bite mark examination by the police and odontologists. According to John Garner, the G-scale, which had been placed adjacent to the bite mark, had partially obscured some details of the mark. The acetate tracings made by Dr Romaniuk were also inaccurate and the scaling method used in the photograhy of the dental models flawed, which resulted in a scaling error. But it is what they find that has not been previously identified in the photograph that will prove explosive. The original photographs were *under printed* which resulted in a significant loss of detail in Deidre's injuries. Careful photographic printing reveals what Sims, Brown and Romaniuk had missed: a second bite mark. It is this mark that is to become the cornerstone of the Crown's new case and form the basis of the controversy that will irreconcilably divide expert dental opinion. The point is impossible to ignore: the possibility, Garner says, that these three eminent specialists could well have orientated the teeth the way he and and his colleagues did, if they had had the benefit of correctly printed photographs. And if that is the case, he believes, the failure of the first conviction can be attributed to the printing of the original negatives.

As Deputy Director of Public Prosecutions since 1995, the task of re-examining the Carroll case has fallen to Michael Byrne. But he has misgivings. In his opinion, on the evidence before him, there are no prospects of conviction. To get this case before a jury – let alone achieve a guilty verdict – would be tantamount to convincing non-believers of a miracle Resurrection. He came into it on the basis of the first trial – that Carroll had been convicted on evidence that was all over the place. The challenge was how to resurrect that.

Byrne knows that double jeopardy laws prevent the Crown from pursuing Carroll for the offence for which he had previously been convicted and then acquitted: murder. He also knows that, within that law, it is the court's discretion to not allow additional charges following an acquittal or conviction for different offences arising from the same behaviour or facts: this is known as an 'abuse of process'. Byrne is a criminal lawyer, involved in the drama of human lives that plays out before him on a daily basis, and the starchy, dry arguments of double jeopardy, written on ancient pages and enshrined in British common law 800 years ago, leave him cold. To its detractors, it is a vestige of history that needs dusting off and has no place in the twenty-first century. To its supporters, it offers a safety net of balance between the power of the state and the individual accused of a crime.

Those who argue against the double jeopardy rule point to numerous problems with the law. It does not allow for a re-trial in response to the discovery of compelling new evidence, such as DNA not available when the case went to trial.

Another argument against the double jeopardy principle is that it does not allow for a re-trial in the event of a 'tainted acquittal', where jurors have been bribed or documents forged. Therefore, it is argued that the principle is biased in favour of the defendant.

There are further arguments against it. Once a defendant has been found not guilty, the rule prevents additional police inquiry, even if further incriminating evidence comes to light.

Those who argue in favour of the double jeopardy rule do so on the grounds that it prevents the persecution of defendants who have been afforded a 'not guilty' verdict. High Court Justices Gleeson and Hayne, who heard the Carroll case, argued that without safeguard, the power to prosecute could readily be used as an instrument of oppression. Finality, they say is an important aspect of any system of justice.

Innocent until proven guilty – the cornerstone of legal systems based on English law – would, critics claim, be threatened by changes to double jeopardy rules. The onus of proof beyond reasonable doubt lies with the Crown; changes to double jeopardy would burden the accused with having to re-establish innocence.

The centuries-old law, supporters note, also protects defendants who are uneducated and disadvantaged by the cost of legal representation. They voice other concerns. Protracted legal battles are expensive, and, without resources available to police and lawyers, it is often extremely difficult for a defendant to financially challenge DNA or other new evidence. Critics of change also argue that an overturning of double jeopardy would invite shoddy police work. If police didn't get it right the first time, they say, they could be rewarded by knowing they could have a second crack at a case. They point to the Stephen Lawrence case in Britain as proof that failure to secure a conviction was largely due to sloppy police work. It would open the floodgates for arbitrary, malicious or careless prosecutions.

Former High Court Chief Justice Anthony Mason – an advocate of a review of the laws – has warned against opening the door to change too wide. That, he has said, would invite a way for the prosecution to retry an individual because the prosecution overlooked something at the first trial.

Opponents also warn of media hysteria backing calls for change. Civil libertarian Terry O'Gorman argues that the Carroll case is a classic example of the press pushing for a popular result in a case with an unpopular defendant.

Academics wade into the debate. Robyn Lincoln, Assistant Doctor of Criminology at Queensland's Bond University, writes in February 2003 that justice agencies should not have the opportunity to keep coming back to try suspects afresh whenever they wish. The concept of finality in the criminal justice system, she believes, is under threat from proposals to scrap the double jeopardy rule and to introduce sex-offender notification laws, which operate in 45 United States jurisdictions.

Byrne works late into the night, considering how to get around the double jeopardy laws. The only charge the Crown could bring, he believes, is perjury: to somehow prove that Raymond Carroll had lied when he said he did not kill Deidre Kennedy. And to bring perjury, the Crown has to have fresh evidence.

Byrne was in Grade 12 when the first trial ran, but he still vividly remembers the story. How it impacted on the public because of the bizarre nature of the murder. Such a sad, stark image: a dead baby with bite marks, dressed in women's underwear. And it is because he remembers the story that he will prosecute it with zeal.

It is the pictures that finally convince him. Alex Forrest and John Garner move through their area of expertise, showing Byrne the computerised images they are sure will persuade him to run with the case. 'Look at the bite marks through the digital imaging,' they say. 'Then tell us you're not sure.'

It is a pivotal moment for Byrne. He knows it is a high-profile case that will be closely followed by lawyers, a challenge with inherent difficulties – not the least of which is the time since the murder and the death of some key witnesses, such as 'Nugget' Carroll.

Fuelled by a passionate belief in justice, Byrne knows he needs to bypass the double jeopardy laws and avoid any vestige of this being a re-trial for murder. The evidence had to prove that Carroll had lied when he gave evidence at the murder trial that he did not kill Deidre Kennedy.

30

Dr Ken Brown has carefully stored the two sets of Carroll's dental casts – one given to him from John Reynolds in November 1983 and the other by Kon Romaniuk after he had made his modifications – at the Forensic Odontology Unit at Adelaide University. He shakes his head, mystified that the original casts needed for corroboration of Romaniuk's modification had simply disappeared.

Housed in the old medical school at the end of a labyrinth of corridors, the Odontology Unit – the first in Australia established in 1980 – has the quiet, faintly musky air of scholarly research, its walls adorned with charts of cases where forensic odontology has triumphed over crime. Even here, two stories above the medical laboratory where bodies offered to the University for scientific research lie on the slab in bloated degrees of embalmment, the dead seem to speak louder than the living.

Brown has retained all the material he had used at the first trial. On 24 April 1997, he hands to Herpich two sets of upper and lower casts of the teeth of Raymond John Carroll. He wants to use his casts, as the originals have been lost. He also asks for photocopies of any relevant material Brown has.

Garner assumes that the jury will know nothing about computers and that he will need to explain the equipment they will use. When he gets this to court, it must be clear that no wizardry or sleight of hand has been used.

They use the standard, commercially available software program Adobe Photoshop to compare scanned images taken on a flat-bed scanner. When a photograph or any other object is scanned, it distorts and stretches and every scanner introduces some degree of error. He will explain how to correct those errors in simple language. But the second bite is trickier; he will need to use a more elaborate comparison method to twist the image to match the photograph, at the same time keeping it in scale with the original.

In the months leading up to trial, there is a constant development of technology, though Garner has some practical problems to sort out first. Photographs taken at the time of the initial investigation – aerial shots of Ipswich, street orientations, houses – have been glued together, damaged by floodwaters that had seeped into Gundelach's basement. Garner has to separate them as best he can, in order to present originals. Many photographs need reprinting, and some are beyond repair.

To maintain impartiality, Garner and Forrest start from scratch, untainted by evidence given in the first trial. They know their evidence will have to stand up to scrutiny, not just by experts in Australia but also overseas. They decide to check the digital evidence they have with the three experts from the original trial.

Kon Romaniuk, disabled by his head injuries, is unable to be of assistance. The next person on their list, Dr Bernard Sims, lives in the UK and it takes six months to get clearance from the Queensland Police Service to go to London. By early September 1997, Herpich and Garner are on their way to speak with Sims and show him their new technology.

Genial as ever, Sims is happy to share his expert opinion on the Deidre Kennedy case. Then he makes an unheralded announcement. He rather likes the technology, he says, but in his opinion they have the teeth *upside down*. Because Garner and Forrest have deliberately not looked at the earlier evidence, this is the first time they realise that the way the odontologists had aligned it in the first trial was opposite to their orientation. Garner questions him further about what was said at the first trial.

Sims's response shocks Garner. He wasn't asked, he tells Garner, about which way was up. It can go either way – right side up or upside down, he says. It doesn't make any difference. It will make the same mark.

Garner looks at Cameron Herpich, who has turned deathly pale. They thank Sims for his time, and hastily depart. Back at their hotel room, Herpich is ready to write off the case. He is less than impressed that, having taken months to get clearance to come to London and interview the world's leading authority on bite marks, Sims, was now telling them they had the teeth upside down. Herpich is more than just nervous; he can see his entire career sliding down the tubes.

But if Herpich is concerned at what Sims has just told them, Garner is amazed. 'Think about it,' he tells Herpich. 'How can a set of teeth make the same mark from both directions? It is anatomically impossible.'

In the hotel room, Garner demonstrates the method they had devised in Australia. 'The basic failure in the original Crown case,' he tells Herpich, 'was that Sims *thought* the teeth would make certain characteristic marks, without testing to see if this concept was valid. I'm going to prove to you by *demonstrating* that his notion could not be right.'

Garner sits back after the demonstration and grins at Herpich. 'See? It's anatomically impossible.'

Sims had also advised them to show the computer imaging to the Director of the Met in London, which they do shortly after. He says little when the demonstration ends.

Herpich and Garner next want to speak to British forensic scientist Colin Bamford who works at New Scotland Yard, helping police identify victims and criminals from dental evidence. The Yard is near Westminster Abbey and Britain is in preparation for the funeral service of Princess Diana. The streets near the palace are awash with flowers, and Garner and Herpich's initial conversation with the brilliant scientist and barrister concerns only the princess's sudden death. But now they need to get to work. They do not mention the real reason for their visit, that they are re-examining the Deidre Kennedy case. As Garner would later admit, they had to con him to get in his door. They ask to take some of his time to show him an interesting program they put together and for his opinion as to its value. They start with facial reconstruction and superimposition.

Bamford is underwhelmed. 'If we can get a family photograph of a deceased, we can superimpose the soft tissue onto the skeletal remains,' he tells them. 'This is certainly a good program, but nothing new in the UK. Do you have anything else?'

'We've also got a program we've been working on in relation to bite marks,' Garner volunteers. 'We'd like to show you that.'

The presentation takes the entire afternoon, and this time Bamford is impressed. 'It's certainly more advanced than anything I've seen to date. The computer technology is very good.' The odontologist still uses the tracing method.

Garner senses the time is right, hands him a photograph. 'Can you tell us what this is?' he asks.

'Yes, of course. It's a bite mark.'

'Animal, mineral or vegetable?'

'It's human all right.'

'OK.' Garner draws an unsteady breath. 'This is actually a case which is up and running now. Could you please tell us which are the upper teeth and which are the lower?'

Bamford immediately orientates the mark. 'The top bruise has been left by the lower teeth, the bottom bruise by the upper.'

Garner can't believe what he is hearing. 'Are you sure? You can clearly see that?'

'Um . . . yes.' Bamford raises a quizzical brow. One of few scientists in the world experienced in bite mark identification, he was clearly perplexed at the questioning. 'Why do you ask?'

'Well, that's how we read it, too.'

'Well, there *is* no other way to read it. Why are you so concerned about the orientation of the teeth?'

Garner looks at Herpich. It is time to come clean.

Bamford listens and shakes his head. 'Sorry, but it is absolutely impossible for teeth to go either way. And the way I've just told you the mark is oriented is the *right* way. Look, what's this all about?'

'We should perhaps have mentioned this at the start,' Garner admits. 'We didn't, because we wanted a completely independent judgment. It's about a little girl who was murdered in Queensland —'

Bamford cuts him off. 'Deidre Kennedy? You're working on the Deidre Kennedy case?'

Garner nods vigorously, a habit he has when he is excited at a turn in an investigation. Bamford keeps talking. 'Every time I go into court that story is raised. It put bite mark cases back into the dark ages. There's not a forensic odontologist in the world who doesn't know about that baby.'

Impressed with their digital technology, Bamford provides Garner and Herpich with a statement for court purposes about how he orientated the bite marks and a copy of a British Court of Appeal judgment given against Sims, relating to an earlier misdiagnosis he had made. He will, Bamford assures them, make himself available to fly out to Australia to give evidence any time he is required.

31

A month after returning to Australia from London, Cameron Herpich, Detective Fredericks (now working on the case), John Garner, Dr Alex Forrest and Dr Davies attend a meeting of the International Association of Cranio-Facial Identification at Melbourne University. Dr Ken Brown was a founder of that association and intended going to the meeting, but a last-minute phone call about his gravely ill mother has forced him to cancel. She dies the next morning.

The team has organised to show people at the meeting a presentation of their new computer imaging and Dr Brown is outraged when he hears about it later. They called each person in separately, he says, showed them the new evidence and then got each to sign a document to say they agreed with it. People with no expertise whatsoever in bite marks were presenting what he describes as this so-called 'new evidence'.

The atmosphere at the meeting is decidedly tense and Garner soon finds out why. This case is extremely controversial and their efforts are seen by many as a direct attack on Dr Brown. Every expert in that room knows that Brown's alignment at the first trial was similar to Sims, and so the new technology is perceived as a direct challenge to Brown, known in dental circles as the 'father of forensic odontology' in Australia. To their discredit, Garner says, many at the meeting simply refused to even look at the evidence, because they were seen as a major threat to the Forensic Odontologist 'order' and created factions within it. But, Garner argues strenuously, that is not what they were about. They were just trying to get to the truth about Deidre's murder.

Dr Brown's daughter-in-law, Jane Taylor – also a forensic odontologist – has attended on Brown's behalf and is horrified by what she sees. She refuses to sign anything.

Statements are provided by five dental experts from around Australia and overseas, including a Dr Pamela Craig who works at the Melbourne University dental school. These doctors, Garner says, gave *precisely* the same information relating to the teeth and the bite mark match as he and his colleagues had aligned it. The importance of this was that there would be no grounds on which the Court of Criminal Appeal decision could be repeated.

Shortly after the meeting, the head of the Melbourne University dental school, Dr John Clement, asks Garner and the team to leave the university. Garner believes it shows that the lines are now well and truly drawn between 'the old and the new order' of forensic odontology.

With Jane Taylor present, Garner and Herpich run through their presentation with Brown in Adelaide and offer him the chance to review it in his own time, using their computer if required. Dr Brown is far from impressed. He does not, he says, appreciate the way his opinion has been corralled. He tells them he doesn't need to keep their computer, as they have been using the same system for 12 months, and that he will review what they show him and write a report about it. Knowing that a new charge against Raymond Carroll is imminent, Brown makes his feelings plain to Herpich and Garner. The odontology evidence as presented to him by them should never go to a second trial.

For a start, he says, they have the diastema – the space some people have between their two front teeth – wrong. About a week after their presentation, they phone and tell him that they have fixed up the problem and send him down a photo. In Brown's view, they just do not know what they are talking about.

Brown asks them who else had seen the new evidence. They choose not to tell him, but they let enough slip for Brown to work out that they've been to London and spoken to Bernard Sims. He phones Bernard that night and, sure enough, his hunch is confirmed.

Brown asks his old colleague what he had thought of the evidence. There is a slight pause at the other end of the line.

'I advised them to take it around to the Director of the Met laboratory in London, to see what he thought.'

'And what did he think?'

Sims gives a grim chuckle. 'Not much.'

In June 1998, Brown writes his blunt assessment of what he calls the 'New Evidence in the Carroll Case', which is intended for both the prosecution and defence to read at any subsequent hearing or trial. He sends a copy to the officer in charge of Queensland Police Forensic Services, Terry Stewart, John Garner's inspector. According to Brown, Stewart agreed with his ideas completely and made it clear he had urged the police department not to support it. Brown also confers with a Doctor of Physics at the University of Adelaide, the former superintendent in charge of Forensic Sciences at the South Australian Police Department and with the DPP, Paul Rofe, who would later resign, under pressure from that office. He tells them the methods cause him no small concern, that it can impact not only on the Carroll case but on others where this technology can be used to review cases. Brown knows that his opinions will not go down well with Garner and Herpich. They are diametrically opposed.

Dr Brown's paper leaves the reader in no doubt as to his opinion. 'I had,' he has written, 'previously been informed by telephone that further investigation of the Carroll case had been initiated in the light of new evidence which, it was expected, would vindicate the original conviction which had been set aside on appeal . . .' He barely contained his sarcasm, and reserved special criticism for the second bite mark.

In view of all these issues, he concluded that '. . . it would require a courageous decision by a prosecutor to proceed with a prosecution.'

Brown wonders how long it will take Cameron Herpich to ring and respond to his report. He doesn't have long to wait. He rings and takes umbrage at what Brown has written. Brown is unperturbed. 'You asked for my comments, I have made my comments and I stand by them,' he tells Herpich.

John Garner has been using the QPS computer at the Photographic Section at police headquarters in Brisbane to work on digital imaging of the Kennedy evidence, but decides that the best way to continue to keep the material safe is in his own time on his home computer.

A benefactor gives Garner a powerful computer and high-resolution scanner, which allows him to re-scan all the images. The detail in the higher-resolution images allows superb detail.

From the time Garner starts using his home computer on the case, he and his associates each clock up more than 1000 hours of their own time.

The crown dental witnesses have made a breakthrough. Cameron Herpich has shown them a photograph of Deidre dressed in underwear, which clearly details the placement of the suspender clip. It will become central to their evidence: now, they will be able to demonstrate that the mark caused by the clip was independent of the toothmark, and part of bite mark number one.

32

12February 1999. Marilyn, now living with Carroll as his de facto wife in Ipswich, is completely dumbfounded. Cameron Herpich, Peter Barron and other detectives she does not recognise are standing on her doorstep, summer's unrelenting heat blasting through the open door. What do they want *this* time?

Herpich flashes his ID card. 'Is Raymond John Carroll home?'

'Yeah, he's sick in bed. Why do you want him?'

'Could we talk to him, please?'

She sighs, opens the door and gestures for them to come inside. Marilyn's children are getting ready for school, fretting about why the police are here, and she hurries them across to a neighbour.

Marilyn − flame-red hair cropped into short spikes, mouth crinkled from heavy smoking and face the colour of chalk − speaks in a suburban patois, laced with frequent additions of 'and that'. Herpich, she recalls with high dudgeon, sort of 'storms in', and when Raymond comes out, all they say is it's about Deidre Kennedy and they ask him did he do it? Raymond says 'no' and they just say, right, you've gotta come with us.

The detective follows Carroll into the room while he dresses, and Herpich stays in the lounge room with Marilyn. She is highly agitated. 'I've got a right to know what's going on! Tell me!'

He won't. Stock-still and stony-faced, he handcuffs Carroll and walks him out to the car. Carroll doesn't know why they need to handcuff him. All part of the show, he supposes.

Marilyn follows them, desperately trying to talk to Raymond through the car window. 'What do you want me to do?' she cries. They have started the engine and she is screeching over the top of the noise, standing in the street outside their housing commission home, knowing she looks a spectacle but not caring.

'What do you want me to do?' It is coming out in heaving sobs now, and the vehicle is moving away.

'Ring Sandra.'

Marilyn stands there, stunned and inconsolable, until the police vehicle disappears around the corner.

Sandra breaks down when she hears that her brother has been taken into custody again. The family is never going to get any peace, it seems. But she gathers herself to ring a lawyer, asking that Raymond have immediate representation. She is the responsible one, the person on whom the family relies. By the time she has finished her phone calls, she has paced the room countless times and smoked half a packet of cigarettes.

As the head of the re-opened Kennedy investigation, Detective-Sergeant Cameron Herpich is the point of reference for any media inquiries regarding the case. Herpich offers a firm handshake and an uncomfortable expression when we meet at QPS headquarters in Brisbane in May 2004. He carefully picks his way through his words, building sentences block by block in police parlance. Pleasantries are exchanged, tape recorder running, but, inexplicably, it already feels like high noon.

Part of the reason for Herpich's unease immediately becomes apparent. So many reporters, he says, have promised Faye things they have not delivered, dredging up emotions and leaving her depleted. There was a screenplay on the story, never completed. Contracts shoved under her nose, which made her nervous. And now this book. Would this be finished, or end up an unfulfilled promise, like the others?

I assure him that I have Faye's, and her family's, full cooperation.

Herpich often appears ill at ease, never more so than when he believes I may be attacking the QPS. 'It has been suggested to me,' I venture, 'that a dark angel has looked over and protected Raymond Carroll. What do you think about that?' What Herpich thinks is that I am subtly pointing the finger at the QPS. '*I hope you're not suggesting . . . ?*' It is a common refrain throughout the interview.

'Who,' he demands to know, 'said that about the dark angel?'

'Faye Kennedy,' I reply.

Herpich uses police speak from the outset. 'We *interview*

crooks. We *speak* with witnesses.' And so it was with Raymond Carroll.

Herpich tells Carroll he would like to interview him back at police HQ.

Carroll refuses to talk to Herpich at all times. Afforded his rights, he is conveyed from his home address to Brisbane; during the trip in the car, he doesn't say a thing. When the car arrives at headquarters, Herpich tells him that he has the right to contact a lawyer. He gives him a phone book and says, choose one.

Herpich studies Carroll's body language. He is quiet, nervously quiet and cold. The arrest had come out of the blue for him. It was, Herpich mentally notes, like he knows this is it. He also knows that he doesn't have to speak to police and that Herpich will have to prove anything he suggests.

Carroll's defence barrister, Jim Coburn, arrives at headquarters shortly after Carroll's arrival and has a brief meeting with him. His client, he flatly informs Herpich, will not be answering questions.

Police use Carroll's dental impressions from the early murder trial, and Carroll is informed that he is being arrested on perjury charges. Once he is arrested, police can, by law, take a new set. And they have to.

Alex Forrest takes further impressions of Carroll's teeth, and police photograph the procedure. They are graphic, disturbing images: Carroll's mouth stretched wide to reveal the outline of his teeth, his dark eyes haunted. He remains icily composed throughout, but Herpich knows that if looks could kill, he would be dead.

Deemed a no-flight risk, Carroll is bailed, but the biggest concern Herpich has is where police stand in relation to the law. But after the Director of Public Prosecutions, Royce Miller, QC, and his deputy, Michael Byrnes, say what he is doing is right, he has no doubts. Herpich is certain that it was Carroll's dentition that made the bite mark on Deidre's thigh. He has cause for confidence. Alex Forrest told Herpich, it's him. Colin Bamford said, 'it's him'. Pamela Craig said, 'it's him'. Another person in New Zealand said, 'it's him'. With so many experts saying the same thing, who is he to say the opposite?'

Barry Kennedy is at home in Longreach where he returned after he left Faye, sorting out his life, regaining sobriety, when he reads that investigators have re-opened the case on Raymond Carroll. John Reynolds had always kept him up to speed in the first investigation, though he had sheltered the Kennedys from unnecessary pain. Faye and he had separated but Deidre was still his daughter. Surely he could have been contacted, instead of having to read it through the press? Placid by nature, this was a slight he would neither forget, nor forgive.

Carroll utters only four words at his committal hearing for perjury. 'Not Guilty, your Worship.'

They are all here. Eight months after Carroll's arrest, the Kennedy and Carroll families, a sprinkling of lawyers and a gawking public have turned out to see him at the start of the committal. At stake, this October 1999, is not only Carroll's future, but the credibility of the digital technology used for the first time to prove that he had lied at his first trial when he gave evidence in his own defence that he did not kill Deidre Kennedy.

The DPP has flown Dr Colin Bamford out from England. Experienced in giving evidence on bite marks prevalent in rape and child-abuse cases, he tells the court that although Bernard Sims correctly identified Carroll as the person who had bitten Deidre Kennedy, he had made errors in some of his tests. Identification of a bite mark on the baby's body made by Carroll's upper teeth had been made by his lower teeth, and vice versa. There have, he says, been advances in technology since Sims gave his evidence, but it is a '100 per cent certainty' that it is Carroll who made the marks. Sims had once been Bamford's teacher, but, while he is highly regarded in his field, Bamford says his mentor is 'not infallible'. Lawyers scribble furiously: Dr Bamford is saying that Dr Bernard Sims – by his own admission one of the world's leading odontologists – got the bite mark upside down in the previous murder trial.

Garner and Bamford go for a sandwich in the lunch break, a welcome diversion from the bleak evidence being given in court.

Bamford, renowned for his large appetite, hoes into huge slabs of thickly sliced bread with roast beef. It is the height of the mad cow disease outbreak in the UK, and Garner watches him devour the sandwich, waiting until his mouth is full. 'Good, is it?' he asks.

Unable to speak, Bamford can only nod. 'Mm, mm.'

'Glad you're enjoying it,' Garner casually says. 'We're getting all this really cheap beef from the UK at the moment.'

Back in court, Carroll's counsel Liz Wilson suggests the new technology is simply more 'showy' than the technology of the past, but is still based on much of the old subjective methods of the eighties. Bamford disagrees, telling the court there was a 'lot of information' left by the marks and that the computer technology is a breakthrough. Bite mark analysis, Bamford continues, is a form of pattern recognition and comparison. He refers to the paper scale that appears in some photographs of the bite marks, which has the large letter 'G' written on it. Bamford, a barrister as well as a forensic scientist, knows what he is doing. 'What letter is this?' he asks.

'G,' Liz Wilson replies, with a look that indicates that this is obvious.

'Pattern recognition,' Bamford crows. What Wilson has identified is pattern recognition and any similar letter 'G' would be recognisable by comparison. This is the classic spider-and-fly exchange that earns Wilson the sobriquet 'G-Whiz Liz'.

Wilson could not have chosen a more challenging adversary. Legendary for calling a spade a spade, prior to the committal Bamford had used his skills to identify victims from London's Paddington underground rail disaster. All the bodies, bar two, were horribly dismembered. It was total chaos and carnage. Bodies were strewn up and down the railway line and in carriages. Working in the morgue for more than 30 hours without a break, Bamford had heard a commotion outside the building. An ugly crowd had formed, a wild, unruly mob of Afro-English, hurling abuse at him. 'You just identifying all the white bodies first!' they screamed. 'What about our people?'

Exhausted, Bamford appraised the crowd through roadmap eyes.

'Who's in charge here?' he barked. A couple of people, with a local politician, stepped out of the throng, their chins jutting out. 'Come inside,' Bamford ordered. 'Leave the rest of this lot out here.'

Row upon row of blackened bodies, burnt beyond recognition by the diesel, were laid out on slabs. One of the men started gagging and the politician turned away. 'Now,' Bamford said, 'tell me which of these people is white, and who is black.' He had made his point. 'Now fuck off and take that mob with you, so I can get on with my job.'

Back in the office, after the committal hearing had finished for the day, John Garner asks Reynolds and Herpich to consider a question. If Carroll had been in Ipswich on April 13 1973, what was he doing the night before Deidre was abducted?

They shrug their shoulders. 'Dunno. Gone out to buy fags or something?'

'There aren't any shops in the area.'

'All right, he's gone snowdropping.'

'He travelled from Edinburgh to Ipswich to steal undies? Doesn't make a whole lot of sense to me. What about this idea?' Garner outlines his theory. 'He's in the air force. The bloke who owns the block of flats Deidre was abducted from is also in the air force. Every person who lives in those flats is in the air force.'

'So?'

'So, there are too many air forces here. Suppose he had a married girlfriend who lived at the flats? He went to visit her, the old man was home, she slammed the door in his face. That would put him in the right place and in the right frame of mind. What do you think?' They don't think anything.

Garner plugs on. 'He was only 17 then, not married, but we need to find out what sort of bloke he was, whether he would play around. I reckon the best person to ask would be his ex-wife, see what she knows.'

The witnesses continue in the committal hearing. Former recruits repeat what they said at the first trial and Joy Meyers hammers her ex-husband about his treatment of Kerry-Ann. 'I could hear her crying, really crying, really badly. When I went to change her nappy again I found these bite and bruise marks on her leg.' No, she says indignantly when asked, the marriage did *not* end after she was accused of having an affair.

Garner waits until after Joy has given evidence before he speaks to her outside court. 'I know what you've said about Carroll as a father, but what was he like as a husband?'

She looks at him. 'As a husband? Well, he wasn't a very good one.'

'Did he play up on you?'

'He played up, all right, but he reckoned he didn't. His girl-friend's name was Desley. Desley Hill she is now. She sent some letters to Darwin when we were living there. Love letters and stuff. I don't know where she's living now.'

Garner corners Michael Byrne and Cameron Herpich after he speaks to Joy Meyers. Not an authorised investigator on the case, he has to be diplomatic. 'I've spoken to Carroll's ex. She is none too fond of the man, to put it mildly. And there *was* a girlfriend in the picture. Name of Desley Hill.'

Herpich nods.

33

Detective-Sergeant Herpich tells the court the case was re-opened after the discovery of two people who alleged they had heard confessions: a former RAAF officer, Graham Bradshaw, and a prisoner who claims to have spoken with Carroll about the murder while incarcerated with him at Boggo Road Jail.

Herpich says it is the first time that digital analysis of the bite marks has been used anywhere in the world. He concedes that RAAF records that would prove Carroll was in South Australia at the time of the murder have been destroyed. His brief to John Garner, he says, had been simple: to find out whether anything could be done to enhance the photo-imaging, to counteract part of the problem at the original trial in the quest to try to match teeth to a photo.

The sight of the prisoner who claims to have spoken with Raymond Carroll about the murder, Trevor Swifte, scares Faye who is sitting in the court when he is brought in. He is in his early 40s, a big rugged bugger. It is the first time she has seen him, and they brought him down for the Committal in handcuffs. Faye has never encountered someone shackled like that and gets a terrible fright. Swifte's evidence stuns the court. Carroll, he says, admitted to him that he had abducted the baby, sexually abused and then strangled her. 'He said that he was out "snowdropping" – pinching underwear . . . He took the baby and murdered the baby and whatever else, I don't like talking about what he done . . .' He says Carroll told him he had bitten the child on the 'buttocks or something' and that it was the bite marks that had 'fucked him' when Trevor asked him what went wrong. Under cross-examination, Swifte vehemently denies that he told police about Carroll's confession to help him in an upcoming court appearance. He adds that the only person he told about Carroll's confession, a prison officer, has since died.

The court is also told that, while they were living in Darwin in the late seventies, Carroll's second wife, Jennifer, had accused him of murdering Deidre. RAAF officer John Gnezdiloff – known to his colleagues as 'A–Z' because his name has so many letters in it – says that Carroll had cried during a private meeting with him when he made the revelation. 'He said something along the lines of "My wife has accused me of murdering that baby,"' he said.

Graham Bradshaw repeats the evidence he has told police, that Carroll had approached him whilst he was drinking with some mates at an airmen's club at Point Cook military base in Victoria. 'He said he did it,' he tells the court. 'I said, "Are you really trying to tell us that you killed this little girl?" and he said, "Yes, I did it."'

John Garner says using the digital imaging, he has discovered bite marks that had not been detected at the original trial and that he has matched the three bite marks found on Deidre's thigh to models of Carroll's teeth taken in 1984.

State forensic dentist Dr Alex Forrest does not mince words, saying that the dental evidence against Carroll at his first trial was wrong. The teeth had been analysed upside down and two further bite marks were discovered on Deidre when the case was re-opened. The accuracy of new digital dental analysis he and Garner had developed, he says, is 'right up there in the field of DNA' and similarities between models of Carroll's teeth and the marks left on Deidre's thigh are 'far, far better than would be expected to arise from chance'.

Forrest fares better than Victorian forensic dentist Pamela Craig, who is slaughtered for the evidence she gives and the way she delivers it. It is an ominous precursor to what is to come for her at trial.

The rest of the committal hearing is equally rigorous, and, after two weeks, Magistrate Brian Williams, SM, finds there is enough evidence to commit Carroll for trial on perjury charges. Remanded on bail to appear at the first sittings of Brisbane's Supreme Court in the New Year, he is assailed by reporters as he leaves the court. 'If convicted, you face up to 14 years' jail, Mr Carroll. Do you wish to say anything?'

Purse-lipped, he stares straight ahead and keeps walking.

Raymond Carroll receives six letters, sent to him via his solicitor from a stranger in West Ipswich, four of them mailed in November 1999 and two in March 2000. The envelopes have been re-used, the writing in a shaky hand. The man, who is 90 years old, includes his name, and says he got 'knocked up' when he travelled. It would be better, he has written, if Carroll's lawyer could go and see him.

Carroll has no clue about the elderly man's identity, nor his motive for writing letters. He passes them to his solicitors, who make a decision that his allegations do not strengthen their case in any way. Perhaps, they reason, the man is delusional or insane; perhaps he has a vendetta against his son; certainly his allegation is not proof that it is true. For Carroll, the bizarre letters, and the letter writer, remain a mystery.

'Mr RJ Carroll,' the first reads. 'If you tell me the name and address of your solicitor, I may be able to help you.' The letter is signed with the man's name. They continue to arrive, protesting that Carroll's lawyer has ignored his letters. 'I won't write to your lawyer asking him when the trial is due. He might send me a bill for $50.00 for seeking information! They don't call lawyers "sharks" without a reason.' The letters become even more bizarre:

> On 21st October [1999], I reported to Ipswich police that my son had admitted killing Deidre Kennedy. Later that day, 2 detectives called at my house and one of them asked me did he admit it before it was published in the paper. I said I couldn't remember . . .

By the end of November, the letters take a desperate tone. 'In reply to your letter,' he scribbled:

> your lawyer had better come and see me if he wants to talk to me. Last Thursday I fell backward twice in Ipswich Mall and a policeman did my shopping and the ambulance drove me home. I was all right next day.

The final letter arrives on 13 March 2000. 'I have received no word from the Brisbane Police or your solicitor about your coming court appearance,' it grumbles. Offering to go to Brisbane by train, the man concluded, 'I would of course tell the jury you are inosent of the crime and my son is guilty. Hoping to hear from you . . .'

Garner and Forrest are concerned. For some reason, there appears to be a reluctance by police to follow up on the information regarding Carroll's former girlfriend. They know that the more evidence they can bring to this case, the stronger it would be. Desley Hill may not be of any help, but surely she was at least worth talking to? In a meeting with Michael Byrne, they outline their apprehension. Byrne agrees, sending over a checklist to Criminal Investigation Branch. Tactfully, he slips in the query: *'Anyone had a chance to check on Desley Hill yet?'*

Herpich's offsider, Detective Bob Hitch, is quickly dispatched to locate her. It doesn't take long to find her.

Desley Hill opens the fly-wire door and squints as Hitch shows her his ID. It's a stinking hot March day and her chubby, round face is flushed and sweaty. How this policeman has found her out here, at Lee Creek in South Australia, she doesn't have a clue. Come all this way just to talk to her about Raymond Carroll.

Desley strikes Hitch as credible. 'Gawd,' she says, 'fancy after all this time, Raymond's name coming up again. Fancy.'

Hill talks in a flat voice. She knew Raymond had been charged with the baby's murder in 1985, she tells Hitch, but she reckoned if the police wanted to ask her anything then, they'd have found her, wouldn't they? She is happy to talk about Raymond, and Hitch helps jog her memory, taking her through the years. It was all such a long time ago.

She tells her story. Raymond had visited her at the unit where she lived with her parents, but they're dead now. Yeah, she can remember when it was. She was pregnant to a bloke who took off when she told him about the baby, and she was waiting for the cot to be delivered the next day. Well and she got a real shock because she hadn't seen Raymond in a long while and here he was. Then the news come on, about the dead baby they found in the park only that morning. She'd never seen Raymond shitty or moody before but he just took off, real quick, said he had to go home because his mother was sick.

Hitch has been around long enough to know a thing or two about appraising a witness. Desley probably didn't have the best education, but she seems honest. If her story is true, it's dynamite.

Garner knows it is, too, when he hears back from Hitch. 'But,' he says to Forrest, with whom he regularly bounces around ideas, 'Desley is only a silver medal. She puts Carroll at her unit in Brisbane the day *after* Deidre's murder. It's the gold medal we need. Where was he on the *night* of her murder?'

The defence team jumps as soon as they hear about Desley Hill. Preparation for a trial of this magnitude is lengthy and intense. Both prosecution and defence have a huge amount of groundwork to cover, checking witness statements, tying off loose ends, looking for holes in opposing pre-trial arguments.

Based partly on the unreliability of a jailhouse confession made 16 years before and the lack of opportunity for Carroll to test Desley's allegations, they argue in a voir dire – a hearing where the admissibility of evidence or the competency of a witness is tested – for a stay of proceedings. A stay, which halts any further action by order of the court, may be temporary or permanent, pending further legal argument or until certain regulations are met.

The trial judge, Justice Muir, rules that exclusion of Swifte's evidence would likely result in the prosecution not proceeding. It does not, he states, appear to him that a stay should be ordered on this ground. He rules Desley Hill's evidence admissible and the digital evidence 'plainly unobjectionable'. The application by the defence is rejected.

It is decided that Graham Bradshaw would not be called as a witness at the Supreme Court hearing. No records can be found of Carroll ever attending Point Cook, though this meant little, according to John Reynolds. RAAF personnel move around all the time and Carroll didn't have to be stationed there. He might have just gone in for a day or so. The RAAF records were never the strongest point of the murder trial, so it meant nothing to Reynolds that any possible visit there by Carroll wasn't recorded or kept. Bradshaw was a strong witness, because in that he never changed his story. He was adamant that Carroll spoke to him at Point Cook, and not at any other base.

Carroll is equally adamant that he never spoke to Graham Bradshaw anywhere. 'I do not know who this man is,' he writes to his solicitors as a rebuttal in May 2000.

> I have never seen him before except at the Committal and under no circumstances have I ever approached him and said words to the effect that 'I have just committed a murder'. I have never been stationed at Point Cook and I have never received any training – all electrical fitting training was always conducted at Wagga – there was no provision for it at Point Cook . . . there is no record of me ever being there and no reason why I should have been . . .

Peter Davis, Carroll's barrister, believes that no records of Carroll ever being at Point Cook indicates a credibility problem for Bradshaw and that he would be slaughtered by the defence if he appeared. The Crown was wise to jettison him as a witness.

Davis, in private practice but paid by Legal Aid to represent Carroll at the perjury trial, cannot recall seeing Brown's report. Brown did not forward it directly to him. The prosecution team did not offer it, which they were not obliged to do. 'And Herpich,' Davis wrote to me when questioned, 'never offered *anything* to me. *Ever.*'

Prosecution and defence jockey into position for the start of the trial. The case will be heard in a blaze of publicity, the lawyers' expertise under the spotlight. There is not long to go now, before it starts.

PART FOUR
Perjury Trial: October 2000

'Dental identification is as old as the Bible. The first mention was in Genesis. It had to do with a woman, a serpent and an apple.'

Dr Bernard Sims, Senior Lecturer, Forensic Odontology, University of London

34

'**A**rraign the accused.'
Indictment: that on the eighth day of March 1985 at
Brisbane in the state of Queensland in the judicial proceedings,
namely the trial of Raymond John Carroll, you murdered one
Deidre Maree Kennedy and knowingly gave false testimony to
the effect that you did not kill the said Deidre Kennedy and the
false testimony touched a matter which was material to a question
then pending in these proceedings.
Plea?
Not Guilty.

35

In the days leading to the start of the trial, Michael Byrne ticks off the strengths and weaknesses of the Crown case. To bring a new case against Carroll requires the Department of Public Prosecution to have substantial new evidence not available at the original trial. Byrne sees the inefficiencies in the first trial as being the expert dental evidence – corrected now, he thinks by the digital technology and the discovery of the new bite mark that had not previously been documented. Interpretation of that evidence in light of the mechanics of biting is also a feature, producing evidence that has not been recognised before.

The evidence of Joy Meyers, thrown out at the first appeal, has been re-admitted. The Crown now also has evidence of Carroll's presence at Edinburgh, bolstered by a new photograph that showed he wasn't there. They did not have this photo at the first trial. There is the jail confession, for what it is worth, by Swifte. Byrne takes that with a grain of salt, knowing jail confessions are easily manufactured, but he has the impression from Swifte that he is being truthful. And they have Carroll's former girlfriend, Desley Hill.

Mindful that a perjury charge can only be pursued on the condition they have fresh evidence and satisfied that they have fully tested whether that evidence breaches double jeopardy rules, the prosecution team is confident their case is strong enough to carry it through to a jury verdict in favour of the Crown.

Byrne strides across George Street to the Supreme Court of Queensland, pin-stripe suit under wig and gown. The DPP is ready to go.

Byrne is to face off against Peter Davis. Forty-year-old Davis had graduated in law with honours and was admitted to the Bar in August 1990. Known for his rapier wit and decimation of weak witnesses, he is a resolute and worthy opponent for Byrne, who is regarded as one of the state's sharpest prosecutors.

Like Byrne, he was only a young man when he first heard the Deidre Kennedy story – 13 years old, in Year Eight, numbed with horror at hearing a baby had been tossed on top of a toilet block. For the young teenager, it was a turning point in his understanding of human nature, but also the time, he now believes, that Queensland – sunny, perfect Queensland – lost its innocence.

Everything is in order, Court 14 packed on this twenty-seventh day of October 2000 for the opening of *The Queen v Raymond John Carroll*. The public, vying for the best seats in the house amongst the smattering of lawyers and students, settle into position. Monitors to display the digital evidence are provided to the judge, legal teams and jurors, and a projector with large white screen centred so expert evidence can be shown to the court.

It is a rectangular room, green carpet, seats set against cream walls and sombre dark wood-panelling. The dock, in front of the public seating at the back of the court, has a high glass back and a wooden rail in front. The jury is seated on the left, so close to the defence team they can smell their nerves and a small media table accommodates the press at the back left-hand section of the court.

Lawyers sip water and adjust their wigs, silently preparing their thoughts. Davis has his own theory, even before proceedings start: the Crown's evidence is ludicrous, the trial is an absolute circus, and the only living victims are the Kennedys.

Justice John Muir, dark-haired and of medium build, has presided over many controversial cases. Highly intelligent, he is skilled in the delicate handling of witnesses, lawyers and jurors and sympathetic to the needs of Faye Kennedy and her family. Muir is also extremely switched on with respect to technical equipment, capable of quickly picking up on inherent inaccuracies. Given the computer technology shown during the trial, it is a skill for which Forrest and Garner will be thankful.

Muir's instructions to the jury are succinct: they must reach a verdict according to the evidence and put out of their mind anything they may have seen, read or heard about the circumstances of the case. Their decision must be made on the evidence alone and the onus of proof must be beyond reasonable doubt. It is for the jury to decide whether the witnesses are credible and truthful.

He explains how the trial will unfold. The Crown will open its case and call its witnesses. The defence, if they wish, can cross-examine each of those witnesses in turn and the Crown may then re-examine to clarify any confusion. The accused — Raymond John Carroll — can give evidence but is not under any obligation to do so. The onus of proof rests with the Crown and never moves from the Crown. The accused is innocent, until proven guilty.

Still regarded as being a no-flight risk, Carroll is to be bailed every afternoon until the jury starts deliberations at the end of the trial.

Michael Byrne has the air of a conservative, shy boy on his first day at boarding school, an illusion that is quickly dispelled when he launches into his ruthless opening address. Some male jurors lean forward, resting their elbows on their knees. The women sit back, hands locked in their laps.

'Ladies and gentlemen. Deidre Kennedy was only 17 months old when she was abducted, sexually abused and brutally murdered. Her body, which had been grotesquely dressed in women's clothing, was dumped on the roof of a toilet block in Limestone Park at Ipswich, which is just a short distance from the home from which she was abducted. The Crown says to you, and makes no bones about the fact that it says to you, that the person who did that to Deidre Kennedy is amongst us in this court-room . . .' He pauses for dramatic effect, glancing at Carroll. 'The Crown alleges, and it's central to the Crown case, that the person sitting in that dock, Raymond John Carroll, is the person who the Crown will prove, beyond reasonable doubt, murdered Deidre Kennedy . . .'

The jury — six men and six women — turn toward the dock. Carroll looks as immaculate in the dock as he had in his RAAF uniform. Ironed shirt, tie straight, hair slicked down. A model of respectability, a middle-aged father of four. Sitting quietly composed, staring at something only he can see in his mind's eye.

It is a memory that will always stay with Michael Byrne. He recalls Carroll had the persona of a man who was thinking, 'what's going on here? It doesn't concern me.' He behaved like a man of straw. Flat, emotionless. No smile. No frown. No nothing.

Her brother's demeanour does not surprise Sandra. He has always been like this. In her opinion, the press again would misconstrue his body language. They always did.

Through the see-through plastic that separates Carroll in the dock from the rest of the courtroom, the jury can see Faye Kennedy seated behind him. The same hands that had ironed her husband's air-force uniform into perfect creases and that had lovingly held Deidre as she snuggled against her shoulder, now kneads a handkerchief like worry beads in one small fist, her other hand grasped in Derek's.

Byrne concludes his opening address and calls his first witness, Detective-Sergeant Cameron Scott Herpich. Peter Davis had wanted Faye and Barry up first, to save them the trauma of waiting, but Herpich had wanted to sit in court and hear evidence. He couldn't do that until he had completed his own evidence, and it had been a tense moment the day before between him and Davis, who was adamant he should wait. Herpich won.

He moves to the witness stand, walking in deliberate, precise steps. It has taken more than three years to prepare this case for court and, as its chief investigator, he feels the pressure. Not just for himself, but for his team, and for Faye. Especially Faye. He clears his throat, and waits for Byrne's first question.

Outlining how he was asked to re-investigate the case after Graham Bradshaw and, later, Trevor Swifte came forward following the *Sunday Mail* article, Herpich details his contact with Dr Bernard Sims and Dr Colin Bamford in London. Then, in response to Byrne's queries, he moves on to what he had done in relation to Swifte. 'I made inquiries in relation to the information that he told me . . . and I wanted to make sure that, in fact, Swifte and the accused were in jail at the same time.'

'Did you obtain a gate book from Boggo Road to that effect?' Herpich nods.

Yes, Herpich replies, he did. And a reception register for mail that showed Swifte entered the jail on 17 February 1984 and that Carroll followed 10 days later, on 27 February.

Shortly after this, Peter Davis starts his cross-examination. 'Your brief,' he asks Herpich, 'was to reinvestigate the matter and conduct a full review? And, when you commence an investigation, you commence it with an open mind, don't you?'

Herpich agrees.

'And normally you have no suspects in mind when you commence your investigation?'

'I couldn't agree with that.' Herpich has anticipated the defence questions and is as steady as a camera on a tripod. Solid, determined. He answers that his job is to either prove or disprove what he had been told, to see whether a further prosecution is warranted. He agrees Mr Carroll was a central point in the investigation but not the *whole* focus. He denies he set out to nail Carroll. If evidence had turned up to clear him, he says, then that's the way it would have gone.

Davis moves on to questions about fingerprints. Yes, Herpich says, he was aware that there were some identifiable, but not *identified*, prints taken from the Kennedy flat and that the fingerprints remained unidentified. He had asked the fingerprint bureau to run the prints against the national database again, but it was a huge task, with prints now piled up from 1973 to 1998. 'It is not my job as a detective,' he says with a hint of high dudgeon, 'to go and rerun fingerprints or to identify people from fingerprints.'

Davis has got under his guard, and now suddenly moves back to Swifte. Did he not do some investigations at Boggo Road Prison to ascertain whether it was possible for Carroll to have had the opportunity to confess to Swifte? And doesn't the reception book show when people are received into the jail, but not released from it? *Correct.* 'When was Carroll released?' Davis is waiting, poised.

'His prison file has been archived, destroyed. I can't tell you. All his release dates and so on would have been in that particular file.' RAAF records are gone, too. It happened 27 years ago; documents were archived and later destroyed. 'I can't tell you what documents were actually destroyed because of the way the RAAF record the destruction of records . . .' Herpich, his brown eyes set against a stern face that creases when he smiles, doesn't smile now. No, he admits, he could not locate any RAAF document that would put Carroll at Edinburgh or somewhere else.

Police had 24 boxes of evidence relating to the murder. Twenty-four boxes that he meticulously went through, reviewing the old files with, he insists, no pre-conceived ideas about who was guilty. But he couldn't check the doorknock evidence. All the 3500 males who were spoken to during the doorknocks were fingerprinted and their prints checked against those found at the flat and toilet block, but the doorknock evidence was missing. He is unsure in which floods it was destroyed. He knows there were floods in 1974, but doesn't know if they went in the floods that followed, in the late seventies or early eighties.

Faye Kennedy trembles as she stands on the witness stand, close to tears as she identifies police photographs of Deidre's bedroom. Gone is the open face and easy smile of the girl raised in the scrub, replaced with deep stress lines filled with sorrow. There is desperation in her answers, and Michael Byrne silently wills her to keep going, not to break. He wants this over, fast. Her heartache is unbearable to witness. The jury turns away when she falters, embarrassed at being voyeurs of her heartache.

It is Davis's turn to cross-examine. She had checked the aluminium sliding window when she went into the girls' room the second time that night, but did she, he asks, hear it click into a locked position? Does she know what happened? 'I couldn't say, yes, I did hear it click or no, I didn't hear it click at this point.' Davis pushes on. Wouldn't it be her automatic action to push it closed until she heard it click? *Slide and lock.* And she has no reason to think that wasn't what occurred on this particular night? Is that right? *Mmm.* Did she draw the curtains closed, for no other reason other than making sure the room would be as dark as possible in the morning so the girls wouldn't wake too early? A sudden frown crosses Faye's face, a look boardering on anger. 'That was never a concern . . . I remember leaning across the bed and swishing the curtains across. As to how far they closed, I had no reason to go into my girls' bedroom and lock it up as a fortress. It was just never in our upbringing.' Davis is on shaky ground. The jury's sympathy is firmly with Faye Kennedy and he senses it is an opportune time to back off. 'I'm not for a moment suggesting . . .' Right. Thank you.

Looking haunted and gaunt, Barry Kennedy takes the stand and admits the doors of the unit were closed, but not locked the night Deidre was abducted and that they would have pulled the window shut to self-lock. It was, he says, found slightly ajar the next day.

Byrne is gentle. 'Do you recall hearing anything that night?'

'No, I didn't hear anything.' Barry puts his head down as he says it, rubbing his forehead with a shaky hand. There is something in his demeanour that alerts the jury that this is more than an expression of his grief. Something deeper, more troubling.

Both Byrne and Davis are grateful the Kennedy's have finished giving evidence, at least for the time being unless they are recalled. The next witnesses' evidence won't be nearly as heartbreaking.

36

The police had found them, the Crown have lined them up and now they are here, in Brisbane's Supreme Court: RAAF witnesses reflecting on something that happened 27 years earlier.

Warrant Officer Roland Gay says he has given the matter a great deal of thought since he spoke to police. He tries to be as specific as possible but it sounds confused, convoluted. 'It started to fall into place, this particular thing involving an individual leaving the course early, and what hit me again was a period of time which was pre-Easter for the Easter break . . . It fell into place, an instant where a recruit was going to leave the course early.' It could be perfect evidence for the prosecution but, Gay admits, try as he might, he can't remember if that recruit was Raymond Carroll.

The Flight Sergeant in charge of administrative records, Ronald Oldmeadow, explains the different types of RAAF leave. For recruits, compassionate leave related to death or illness of a family member is known as 'special' leave and given at the discretion of the Commanding Officer. If a recruit has problems at home, that leave can be given. The story will be checked to see if it has substance, perhaps by the Commanding Officer, or the padre. There are no records kept.

Liz Wilson appears to struggle with the concept, and Justice Muir intervenes. 'It seems to me he has made his position perfectly plain. He's saying RAAF has compassionate leave and there are terms and conditions which are attached to it . . . but recruits . . . are treated on a different basis . . . which is called special leave . . . and dealt with at the Commanding Officer's discretion.'

Robert Matthews had worked in the clothing store, handling uniforms and clothing cards, signed by air-force personnel when they were moving to another base. If a recruit was absent, the notation was made in a leather-bound register book but, he tells the court, he could not find that book when police inquiries were made into this matter in the mid eighties.

Former recruit Darryl Stevensen cannot recall much of Carroll, except that he was once dragged outside by a group of fellow recruits and hosed down. The evidence he gave in 1985, he tells Byrne, was that he recalled introducing Carroll to his parents in the canteen after the passing-out parade. Now, he cannot remember if it had been Carroll he had introduced. It is just too long ago.

RAAF witnesses are milling outside the court, talking as they wait to be called to give evidence. It is obvious, Davis thinks, that there is discussion between them, an opportunity to jog their memories and present hearsay evidence.

Witness after witness has no recollection of Carroll being on the train with them leaving Edinburgh. It is possible he may have been in another compartment, they concede, but they don't remember seeing him. He definitely wasn't in their group. And now recruit Raymond Sager recalls there were two people missing from the parade. One was back-coursed and the other, Carroll, had gone home. He had omitted to tell police this in his original statement because he had forgotten, but just prior to the first committal, he signed an amended statement. 'I now remember that Raymond John Carroll travelled home on compassionate leave about one week prior to our graduation.'

There are also lighter moments to break the monotony of the stream of RAAF witnesses giving evidence. Trevor Kitson reiterates what he had said at the first trial – that he didn't relate to Carroll, didn't have much time for him at all. He also remembers, now that the course instructor, Raymond Martin, had gone and had a chat to Carroll, went to tell him something.

Wilson wants to be sure that false memories are not being carelessly aired.

'It's not something that came into your mind today?' Wilson asks.

'No.'

'Or you've been talking to others about this?'

'Negatory.'

'Sorry?'

'Negatory.'

'That would be "no"?'

'Well, when I went to school that's what it meant, yeah.'

Lunch breaks. Adjournments. Legal argument. Bowing to the judge. Taking the oath. The jury in and out of the courtroom. The legal banter: *I object. Overruled. May I seek instructions? You're excused. If your Honour pleases* . . .

Recruit Michael Sheean is confident, militarily trained to answer questions in a snappy voice. Yes *Sir*! No *Sir*! He is adamant that Carroll was called away, and that he and another recruit had had to pack up Carroll's weapons. He may have given conflicting evidence in the past, he admits, but it was not deliberate. He remembers everything now, and his memory is right.

Is this, Davis asks, some flash of inspiration, perhaps? Selective memory?

No, Sheean responds. It's just that he is nervous and frightened in the witness stand. But he knows what he knows. And he knows this: '. . . I don't want to get Raymond into trouble for something he hasn't done. I don't want to lie to you. I don't want to lie nor to the police. I don't want to lie to my bloody self, because this is what I can recall. I can only say exactly what I recall and how I recall it.'

Sheean also says that, even if someone didn't march, they would still be in the photo as it went into RAAF records. Each recruit got a copy, as did the instructor.

'Was Carroll present at the time of your parade?'

'No, definitely not.'

Raymond Martin particularly remembers course 1203 as it was the first time he had acted as an instructor to recruits. Raymond Carroll, he says, did not graduate with the rest of the course.

'And why was that?'

'Because he wasn't on the base to graduate.'

'Why was he not on the base?'

'Because he was in Ipswich or Brisbane; he left the base on leave.'

Former recruits have faded memories but similar recollections. Andrew Frankland, who had spoken to police in 1983 during early investigations, says he remembers that, some time prior to the graduation, Carroll left on compassionate leave. 'I recall he was late getting to Wagga. The train which travelled from Melbourne to Wagga arrived after the Anzac Day weekend and Carroll arrived days, if not a week, after that.' Other former recruits Flynn and Godwin, who did not give evidence at the murder trial, have been located and are now on video-link from London. They share similar recollections. *Carroll didn't finish the course. . . Left about a week before . . . Subsequent days he was missing from the course. . . He did not return, to my knowledge.*

Barry Kennedy sits behind Faye in court, watching as she dips her head in tears and Derek consoles her. The evidence is harrowing, and he wants to cry himself; does so when he escapes the public gaze. He has made eye contact with Carroll on numerous occasions, once passed him as he walked into the men's toilet. He held on tightly to his anger, knowing that hauling off wouldn't achieve anything.

He is riding down the court elevator to go outside and have a smoke, and the lift door has stopped. Ilma Carroll and her daughter Sandra are poised to step in, before they notice who is inside. Barry gestures for them to enter. 'You can take this lift, if you like,' he says. They ride in silence, go their separate ways when they reach the ground floor.

This whole nightmare isn't their fault, he reasons.

Day seven. The Crown calls Desley Robyn Hill.

By her own admission, she's not very bright. Left school at 14 with limited education. She can remember years, but not dates and times. Desley speaks softly, in little more than a whisper, like a breeze is blowing through her windpipe. Speaks with a dawdle in her voice. 'I thought he would stay the night, but he *never*. I *seen* him . . .'

She drives the defence to distraction.

She doesn't remember when her daughter, Natasha, was conceived but she remembers the place, on a weekend down at

Top left: Childhood sweethearts Barry and Faye Kennedy on their wedding day in Longreach, Qld, 1967. (Photos courtesy Faye Kennedy)

Top right: Sisterly love. Stephanie, 3, adored her little sister, Deidre. The girls were inseparable.

Doting dad. Barry with Deidre, 16 months, shortly before her murder, 1973.

Top left: Detective Senior Constable Morris examines Deidre's pyjamas found at Limestone Park toilet block, Ipswich, April 1973. (Courtesy Newspix)
Top right: Police fingerprinting at the toilet block in Limestone Park where Deidre's body was found. (Courtesy Newspix)

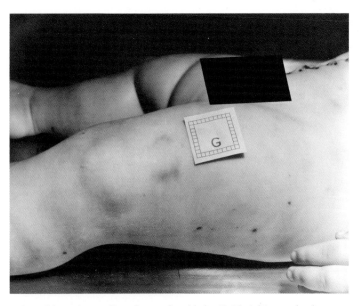

The tragic and haunting reality of a murdered baby. Deidre's bite marks shown at autopsy. (Courtesy Dr Ken Brown)

Raymond John Carroll as a recruit in his RAAF uniform at Edinburgh Airforce Base, February 1973. (Courtesy Peter Davis)

Comparison of Raymond Carroll's teeth with the dentition of a standard set of teeth. (Courtesy Dr Ken Brown)

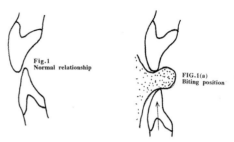

Fig.1
Normal relationship

FIG.1(a)
Biting position

NORMAL central incisal relationships

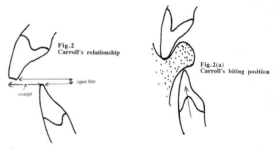

Fig.2
Carroll's relationship

open bite

overjet

Fig.2(a)
Carroll's biting position

CARROLL's central incisal relationships

Fig.2(b)   View of Carroll's upper incisor teeth (palatal aspect) as modified

A G-scale used to measure to scale the wound on Deidre's thigh. The scaling would come under attack at the trials.

Crown Prosecutor Adrian Gundelach. (Courtesy Adrian Gundelach)

As printed in the *Courier Mail*, murder trial judge Angelo Vasta, 1985.

Crown Prosecutor Adrian Gundelach (*second from left*) and forensic odontologist Bernard Sims (*second from right*) with police officers in Wisconsin, USA, in mid-80s. Gundelach was delivering a paper to a police conference on the Deidre Kennedy case. (Courtesy Adrian Gundelach)

Defence barrister Peter Davis who defended Carroll at the perjury trial. (Courtesy Peter Davis)

Raymond Carroll, 2 November 2000, being tried on a perjury charge following his 1985 murder trial for the sexual assault and strangulation of 17-month-old Deidre Kennedy. (Courtesy Newspix/Philip Norrish)

Faye and former husband, Barry Kennedy, outside court at Carroll's perjury trial, 2 November 2000. (Courtesy Newspix/Philip Norrish)

Special Awards Ceremony for Commendation of Services on the Deidre Kennedy case, Police Headquarters, 18 August 2003. Includes (*back, left to right*) Bob Atkins; Crown Prosecutor Michael Byrne; Detective Sergeant Cameron Herpich; Police officer, scientific section, John Garner; former police officer John Reynolds; Faye Kennedy (*front centre*) and forensic odontologist Alex Forrest (*centre right*).

Faye Kennedy with former police officer John Reynolds who worked tirelessly to gather evidence for Raymond Carroll's murder trial. (Courtesy Faye Kennedy)

(Left to right) Stephanie, Faye and Derek Kennedy in Ipswich, Qld, 2003. (Courtesy *Australian Women's Weekly*)

the Gold Coast. It wasn't like the bloke was a one-night stand or anything, she says: their fathers knew each other from work. But he wouldn't have a bar of it when she told him, instead snorted, dug his hands into his pocket and shook his head back and forth, his mouth gasping for air like a fish on dry sand. He doesn't believe her, he said; no, no bloody way. Well it's *true,* she insisted, her chin trembling, because her period is late and her mother guessed she was expecting even before she saw the doctor. A young woman in her late teens doesn't usually get sick just for no reason. No, no bloody way, he said again and he was out the door while she stood there, flustered and humiliated with fingers trawling across her belly and eyes swollen with tears. She is married now and that was years ago, but the memory has left a rancid taste, so bitter that even now when she mouths his name it comes out in a half spit, her lip curled around it. Desley was 19 years old, pregnant and alone, and now she is aghast when asked if she has any more children. No way, she says. One was enough. She was glad when the baby, whom she named Natasha, made her debut 10 weeks premature on 25 July 1973. A few months after she conceived, she says, she and Raymond started seeing each other again.

Desley reiterates what she told Detective Hitch. How Raymond just materialised, out of the blue, and then bolted when he saw a news report about Deidre Kennedy.

Davis can't believe what he is hearing. Could she help him calculate when Natasha would have been conceived if she had gone full term with the pregnancy? Surely she must have fallen pregnant in January 1973?

'I never thought about it. It's a time I wanted to forget . . .'

He tries to be logical, patient. If Natasha was conceived in January, and it took six weeks to realise she was pregnant, then she would not have known until some time in February? So was it then that she told the father, who didn't believe her? What did she do; strike up the relationship with Mr Carroll immediately after? Wasn't it a couple of months later?

Desley bites her lip. 'I know it was a while. I don't know how long.'

'Mr Carroll did not come and visit you around about the time Deidre Kennedy's body was discovered, did he?'

'Yes, he did.'

'You're just lying . . . it's a complete fabrication, isn't it?' It is not possible, Davis continues. She could not have known she was pregnant until February and by then, Carroll was in the air force. There was no time for her to have a relationship with him. She was living with her parents, but no one can check with them that he visited that night, because they are both deceased.

Watching the exchange between the defence barrister and Desley, Faye wants to cry for her. Davis is picking her apart like a crow.

And he keeps at it. She had not remembered anything of his visit for 27 years, until Detective Robert Hitch jogged her memory – is that what she is saying? *Yes, that's right.* Does she remember going to the toilet that particular day? *No.* 'See, you gave evidence about this . . . before the judge at the committal hearing . . . and you said, "When I got home, I went and used the toilet and just laid down." Do you agree you said that?'

'Yes.'

Davis is dripping now with unrelenting sarcasm. 'You just said a moment ago that you clearly remembered that you didn't walk Mr Carroll to the train station. You just said that, didn't you?'

'Yes.'

'But before the other judge on another day you say that you walked him to the station, didn't you? Didn't you?'

'Yes.'

'Well, which one is right? Did you or didn't you?'

'I walked him halfway.'

'Part way?'

'Yes.'

Davis tips forward on the balls of his feet, a dramatic gesture designed to grab the jury's attention. 'I see. So, before, you said you walked him to the station. That is what you said on another occasion. And now you are going to split the difference and say that you walked him part way. Is that seriously your evidence?'

'Yes.'

Unrelenting. She didn't see any news of Deidre's murder, did she? The truth was, that Detective-Sergeant Herpich had shown her the video of that news broadcast.

No, Hill says, she cannot recall seeing any other story about the murder, even though it had extensive coverage at the time.

So, Davis continues, how can she tie down Carroll's visit 27 years after the event? All of it is just lies, a nonsense. 'I suggest to you that my client did not visit you and did not have a relationship with you at all while you were pregnant with Natasha?'

'He did.'

'And that any relationship between you and he wasn't reignited until 1975 when he was visiting from Darwin . . .'

'He came down to see me that day. He only stayed a few hours. He said he had to go home because his mother was sick.'

Desley Hill is starting to tire but she will not change her story. The relationship petered out, she says. She heard he had gone to Darwin, that he had married and she wrote two letters. One was to his wife Joy, telling her about their affair. She looks hangdog when attacked on this. She thought the wife had a right to know her husband was playing up.

The defence doesn't think so. It was a vendetta, wasn't it, aimed simply to get back at Carroll? A case of hell hath no fury like a woman scorned?

Desley shakes her head. The other letter was directed to Raymond, apologising for the first. She never seen him again, she says, until her twenty-first birthday party in June 1975.

Peter Davis was exhausted at the conclusion of the Hill cross-examination. Desley, he recalls, is one of those people who just naturally looks bewildered all the time. Once, while asking her a very important question, she was staring over his shoulder, fixated on something at the back of the court. He thought, there must be something really spectacular back there, and turned around to look. There was nothing. He wanted to shout out 'Oi! Concentrate, please?' but Desley eventually re-focused. It was tough going.

But if Desley was hard work, it wasn't going to get any easier.

37

Joy Meyers avoids looking at Carroll when she takes the stand. She reiterates that, as it was so hot in Darwin, Kerry-Ann was usually dressed in singlet, nappy and plastic pilchers – clothing that easily allowed bruising to be seen. The courtroom falls silent as she again recounts the nightmare of how her daughter was abused.

Davis will have none of it. 'You've gone out of your way not to tell anyone about it.'

'I wouldn't say I've gone out of my way. It was just that I was very young and a lot of people would probably think, well, she's only a young mother; she's just, you know, being over-protective or whatever.'

'I see.'

'It was 20-odd years ago. Young mothers didn't have the system, you know, like they've got now.' Meyers concedes that she made the allegations in 1983 only after she was approached by a policeman in connection with the investigation into the murder of Deidre Kennedy. But she is adamant, defiant: she is not lying about anything. 'That's wrong,' she fires back at Davis, 'totally wrong, and stop trying to mislead me . . . and I know what I'm saying; that happened.'

'I put it to you that my client never bit the child.'

'You're wrong.'

'And that he never went in the room and locked you out while he was – '

'You're wrong.'

'. . . changing a nappy.'

'Wrong.'

'I put it to you that he proposed the name Desley for that child but never the name Deidre – '

'You're wrong in those cases, too.'

'Now, the break-up of your marriage – I suggest to you that

you received a letter from Desley Hill . . . suggesting there may have been some infidelity by Raymond. Did you get that letter?'

'I don't remember, I could have but I don't remember it now.'

This sounds preposterous to Davis: she can recall that Carroll accused *her* of having an affair when he returned to Darwin from a brief trip to Amberley Air Base at Ipswich, but not a woman alleging an affair? Davis reminds her that at the first trial she was asked the question and she had admitted she had received a letter. She hunches her shoulders, takes a glass of water with trembling hand. She hates being on display like this.

Davis moves to another subject. Yes, she agrees she knows Kerry-Ann was suffering, but she wanted to find out what was going on.

'You mean, you wanted to keep putting the child through the pain to see what occurred?'

'I didn't really want to put her through it but it was the only way I could find out to see what was happening again.'

'This is just an invention by you, isn't it?'

'No, it's not an invention at all.'

'It didn't occur.'

Although, intellectually, Meyers is no match for Davis, she is spiky when cornered. 'It did occur, and what right have you got to say that it didn't?'

Joy has finished her evidence, but RAAF canteen worker Diane Ferguson backs up her story, telling the court that Carroll had introduced his wife to her as Joy and his child as Deidre. On another occasion, she says she noticed Kerry-Ann had bruises all over her body, from her torso and thigh to her buttocks and soles of her feet. When she had asked Joy what had happened, she replied the child had fallen downstairs.

On another occasion, she claims she asked Carroll, in front of another woman, what had happened to the baby? He responded that the dog had bitten her. Ferguson's rejoinder was swift. 'I said it doesn't look like dog bites, and he said, "I think some kids have been biting her."'

Ferguson says she tackled him after Joy left Darwin. '"Raymond, how could you do such a thing to your own child?"'

He shrugged his shoulders and said "Oh well" and seemed really indifferent about it. And that was the last time I had spoken to him.'

Ferguson will not be swayed by the defence. There were definitely bite marks on that baby. She saw them.

Initially unaware that Carroll had been charged with murder, Ferguson read in 1985 that he had been acquitted. She then went to Ipswich Police Station and made a statement that she had seen the bite marks.

Why, Byrne asks her, didn't she raise the matter at the time?

She did, she says, but the service police did not go to interview her and, shortly after, she transferred with her husband to Malaysia. Her pudgy fingers caress the surface of the witness box as she waits for Davis's onslaught, which comes hard and fast. But she does not break under his cross-examination. There were bite marks on that baby, she insists. Adult bite marks.

Defence has been unable to locate the other woman who had allegedly been with Ferguson in the canteen and Davis turns it to his advantage. It was all such a long time ago. How very convenient.

After particularly gruelling evidence, Faye stumbles outside to get some air. Herpich has warned the trial could take up to six weeks. There's a long way to go.

Every day, Faye and Derek have come to listen and watch, Derek, now 26, missing only one sitting when he could no longer stomach the evidence. Fury and disgust rise within him when he sees the photographs, the terrible, terrible photographs of a sister he never knew, her plump little legs and exposed bottom frozen cold on a black-and-white picture. He has stared at Carroll hard, unflinching, willing him to stare back, do something – anything – that will help him understand. But Carroll has not obliged, stares straight ahead. On the rare occasions they make accidental eye contact, Carroll looks away, down to his feet.

Carroll would later admit he studiously avoided the Kennedys in the adjournments, but they could not always avoid passing in the corridor. No words were ever spoken between them. Ever.

Every day, Derek has waited for a sign, anything to help him understand. But there is nothing but the pomp and palaver of a Supreme Court proceeding, as though a dark play is being enacted, quiet and sinister while the world turned outside. Derek earns his living lopping trees, and is used to fresh air, bird calls and peace. This is way outside his comprehension.

It is as though the image is in front of him still. Dr Josephson, who had originally attended at Limestone Park, takes a wavery breath and recounts from memory. The teeth marks against the pale, fair skin of the baby were 'very clear', he says, 'and they did not look like perfectly symmetrical teeth'. Josephson recognises the photographs from the post-mortem, studies one in particular. 'The actual bite marks were much clearer than this photo would indicate. Much clearer.' The photos are handed around the jury and a female jury member looks as though she will break down, stifling her distress with a hand over her mouth and Byrne allows them time to view them. A good lawyer knows a picture speaks a thousand words. He finally rises. 'That's all I have, thank you, your Honour.'

Davis slides in. A few quiet questions, ingratiating, gentle, before he takes the first kick. 'You only saw one bite constituted by two bite marks; is that right?'

'Yeah . . . there were marks of upper and lower teeth.' Josephson adds that other marks appeared to be insect bites.

So, Davis continues, if the bite mark was inflicted when the leg was bent, and then the leg was straightened, the mark would be distorted?

Josephson nods his head. 'In general, you are absolutely correct, Sir. Yes.'

It is immediately obvious what Davis is leading to. If the actual mark was *distorted*, how the hell could the Crown purport to prove it was his client's dentition that had made that mark?

Defence and prosecution both make admissions to shorten the trial. Byrne tells the jury that no fingerprints recovered from any of the crime scenes were found to belong to Raymond John

Carroll. And he has another admission. 'The accused was arrested on 24 February 1984, a Friday, on a charge of murder and stealing Mrs Borchert's underwear. He was held initially at the Ipswich watch-house. He appeared in the Ipswich Magistrate's Court on 27 February 1984. He was received into . . . Boggo Road . . . the same day, a Monday at a time unknown. He was transported from prison to the Ipswich Magistrate's Court on 28 February 1984 at a time unknown prior to 4pm. He was released from the Ipswich watch-house on 28 February 1984 at a time unknown and he was not returned to custody prior to this trial in 1985.'

Carroll had been in Boggo Road the first time for no more than 24 hours.

Davis appraises the next witness as he takes the stand. No suit. Hard life, judging by the lines on his face and his bleary eyes. Trevor Jonathan Swifte is one of the prosecution's star turns, but, with Byrne's admission of Carroll's entry and exit times into and out of Boggo Road Prison, Davis hopes to annihilate him.

38

'**D**o you know the person Raymond Carroll?' Michael Byrne is leaning over the bar table toward his witness, a slight smile flickering around his mouth.

'Yes I do.' Swifte is skittish, alternately sitting on his hands and then wiping them on his knee. He talks fast, but his diction is clear.

'And, in February 1984, were you . . . remanded in the Brisbane prison, Boggo Road?'

'That's correct.' He adds that he was in there from January until September. In February, he was held in the Special Observation Unit – SOBS – for protected prisoners because he had been threatened by Aborigines that when he got to the jail he would be killed or seriously hurt for something that had happened years before. He was an old head – been in and out of the system all his life – and authorities had agreed to keep an eye on him in SOBS.

All Swifte's sentences are punctuated at the end with *yeah*. 'How many cells were there in the SOBS yard?' *Five or six, yeah.* How long had Carroll been there when he came in? *No longer than a day or two, yeah.*

Swifte asked what he was 'pinched on'.

Justice Muir interrupts, looking perplexed. 'Pinched on?'

'Meaning what are you arrested on, yeah.'

Shot duck. Old head. Pinched on. Screws. Michael Byrne suppresses a smile. He hopes the jury understands jail slang. 'Now,' he continues, 'did you have another conversation with him?'

'Yeah, I spoke to him over the couple of days.' He gets the days and times mixed up, he says, but he can distinctly remember talking to him over different periods. 'I asked him what he was arrested on and he said, "The murder at Ipswich of the baby." I said, "I remember that . . . I was in a boys' home at the time and the police had come in to find out whether anyone had absconded . . ."'

He is rambling, and Muir again interjects. 'What Mr Byrne is trying to get from you, Mr Swifte, is what you recall, if anything, of the conversation with the accused.'

'Yeah. I'm sorry. When we spoke, he spoke about the murder.'

'What did he say?'

'He murdered the baby.'

Sandra shifts angrily in her seat.

Swifte continues. '. . . Like he'd been out all night and . . . he found a window open . . . Told me that he been out pinching women's items, looked in and seen the baby . . . took her out, abused her and murdered the child. It was as simple as that.'

'Did you speak to him about taking women's clothing?'

'Yeah.'

'Did you speak to him about any connection between those clothing and the killing of the child or the abuse of the child?'

Yeah, Swifte replies, when he told him he had taken the baby, abused the baby and then dumped the body, he said he should have put the baby back.

'Did he tell you how he killed the child?'

'That he strangled the baby.'

'Did he tell you where he put the child after that?'

'He said he took it to a van, I don't know whether he said a van or a caravan; he took the baby to a van and he took her back. He should have put the baby back, he said.'

'Did he tell you where the child was left?'

'The toilet block, but I do remember, I did remember, the child was found on the toilet block roof.'

Swifte did not see Carroll again, he says, until after he had been convicted. Carroll was hosing the yard when Swifte approached him. 'I told him, "You've got your right whack, cunt."' According to Swifte, if Carroll heard what he said, he didn't respond. He just kept hosing.

Swifte repeats what he had written in the statement to Cameron Herpich: that he only found out Carroll had been acquitted when he was reading the paper, and a week later, he rang the police. The only person he had told of Carroll's conversation in Boggo Road was prison officer Denzil Creed. But Creed was now dead.

It is now the defence's turn to question Swifte, and Davis immediately goes on the attack. 'By an "old head," what you mean is that you've been in the system, the jail system, for a long time?'

'And boys' homes a long, long time. That's correct.'

'In fact, your criminal history, your adult criminal history, goes back to 1976.'

'That's correct.'

'And of course you've been convicted of literally dozens of offences since that time, haven't you?'

'That's correct.'

Davis outlines his offences through the seventies and eighties and Swifte agrees to them all. Offences of dishonesty? Numerous counts of stealing? Numerous counts of breaking and entering? Convicted of being armed with a gun in 1976? Breaching probation? False pretences? *Yep. Yep. Yep.* 'Consider yourself an honest person, do you?'

'No, not at all.'

It is not the sort of witness testimony the jury expects to hear, but it isn't over yet.

Stealing and false pretences, 1980? Robbery, 1984? Stealing, 1984? Stealing, 1992?

There is sniggering in the public gallery, and Swifte has had enough. 'I'm not denying my criminal history so I don't know why you are going to keep harping on about it, champ; you know what I mean?'

'I shall make it clear in a moment. Stealing again in 1993?'

'Yeah.'

'Break and enter a dwelling house with intent in 1994 –'

'Yeah, my own home.'

'Broke into your own house, did you?'

'Bit of an argument with the missus. No dramas.'

'You did community service for 240 hours for breaking into your own house, did you?'

'Yeah.'

Outright laughter has now erupted from the public gallery, and Justice Muir silences it with a scathing look. 'And you were ordered by the judge to submit to medical psychiatric or psychological treatment, weren't you?'

'That's right.'

Davis is still on his feet. 'And you knew, in 1997, that if you assisted police with their investigation in relation to matters, the fact of your cooperation could be mentioned to a court that's sentencing you . . . You knew that in 1997, didn't you?' An old head knows his way around the system, knows how to manipulate its benefits.

'Known that since day one.' With a 24-year criminal history, grassing to police is just one of the rules of the game.

'As of March 1997, were you facing any charges yourself?'

'Yes, I was, as usual, arrested about every six months and . . . my mother's house burnt down and it was an electrical item found there, and I pleaded.'

Is he, Davis asks, telling the court he pleaded to something he didn't do?

'I left the fish-fingers on the stove; the house burnt down. My brother said to me, "You wear the pinch?" and I said, "No dramas."'

Byrne shoots a nervous sideways glance at his junior, Sharon Loder. This is becoming farcical.

Davis suggests that Swifte contacts police in order to cut himself a deal in relation to this charge, but Swifte shakes his head, furiously. He never asked for nothing, he says. All he did was just mention that he might be in the nick when this come up.

'So the reason you contacted the police in the first place was not to get yourself any benefit in relation to your upcoming sentence; is that right?'

Swifte looks briefly at Faye before he answers. 'I will tell you why I did it. Because I woke up and seen a child sitting at the end of my bed one night and I went into horrors for two days, and I said, "no, no . . ."'

Michael Byrne was thinking the same thing. *Oh, no. This is not going to go down well with the jury.*

Davis has found Swifte's Achilles heel. 'Well, when you say you woke up in the horrors and you saw the child at the end of your bed, you're a chronic alcoholic, aren't you? . . . Has it been the case that, from time to time during your criminal history, psychological reports have been tendered describing you as an alcoholic?'

'Not a chronic alcoholic. I've had a lot of problems.'

'There's a distinction?' Davis can no longer contain his sarcasm. 'Do you often see these sorts of delusions, Mr Swifte? This something that happens to you regularly?'

'It wasn't a delusion. I woke up . . .'

'There was no child at the end of the bed, was there?'

'Yes, there was. I got up and the missus asked me what was wrong and I went in the horrors for two days, thinking I can't believe I seen that.'

Well then, Davis asks, did you contact police in the interests of justice, to be a good citizen?

'Well, if you want to put it like that, no, I didn't put it down to be a good citizen. I am sorry, I would have had the morals of a gutter rat if I hadn't have.'

Davis hooks his fingers into his robe. 'It was in the interests of justice generally, rather than to get yourself some sort of benefits for your upcoming plea of guilty to receiving?'

'No. It was for the parents, OK?'

'The parents? I see.'

'For the family. All right? Not for my sake.'

But didn't he receive a benefit, a suspended sentence? Davis inquires. In his sentencing in August 1997 for receiving stolen goods, didn't the judge indicate that he would have been sent to jail but for the fact he had cooperated with police?

I am not sitting here denying that, Swifte retorts, with a touch of petulance in his answer.

How many times, Davis later asks, did Swifte speak with Carroll in jail? Three, four times, perhaps over different days,' he tells Davis. Time means nothing in jail.

'I put it to you that you did not have conversations with Mr Carroll in the prison where he spoke of the murder of Deidre Kennedy?'

'Well, you're wrong, champ.'

'What you've done is, you've made this up in order to get yourself an advantage in the system. That's so, isn't it?'

'I think I would have gone out of my way *then* – the trouble I was in at the time *then* – to make a story up to get out of trouble *then*. I wouldn't have waited 16 years.'

Byrne rises to rescue his witness. 'Mr Swifte, you've been asked . . . about benefits and advantages in assisting police; that is, giving evidence or offering to give evidence against other prisoners. In your experience in the system, are there any negative or down sides in giving evidence against other prisoners?'

Swifte nods vigorously. 'Bad news if you do. I've seen people being murdered in jail over it.'

'You were aware of that at the time you approached police?'

'That's right.'

'Nothing further, your Honour.'

Peter Davis is dismayed and disgusted at the next day's headlines announcing Trevor Swifte's evidence. 'Baby Killer Confesses to Man in Jail'. *How's that for unbiased reporting?* he thinks.

John Reynolds reads his record of interview with Carroll to the jury and Davis shows him no mercy. His client, Davis rages, had fully cooperated. He had volunteered samples for testing. And it must be evident, must it not, from Reynolds's own searches, that the doorknocks were lost sometime between 1973 and 1984? *Yes.*

Davis has hit the mark. A female juror in her early forties, dimpled cheeks flushed from the warmth of the courtroom, picks at imaginary dust on her shirt and frowns. It is evident what she is thinking. *More stuff lost.*

39

It is time for the prosecution to showcase its new techniques, to use computer-imaging to prove to the jury beyond reasonable doubt that the bite marks were inflicted by Raymond Carroll's teeth. To prove to the jury that the expert witnesses in the first trial got it wrong, that they had the bite marks *upside down*. To prove that the upper row of bruises were made by the lower teeth, and the lower made by the uppers.

His full name, he tells the court in booming voice, is John Frederick Garner. Senior-Sergeant John Garner, with more than 20 years experience in crime scene and forensic photography. Vastly experienced in the field of forensic art – drawing an image description given by a witness; creator of the Comfit Facial Identification system currently in use in four Australian states; lecturer in his field; has studied computer-imaging techniques in America and Scotland Yard. Garner exudes confidence; experienced with the presentation of electronic evidence in court this, finally, is the moment he and his colleagues have worked toward for years. He races through his qualifications with such speed, Justice Muir has to pull him up. 'Senior-Sergeant, could you slow it down a little bit?' Garner smiles, *My apologies, your Honour,* with not a hint that he feels chastened. Let the show begin.

Ladies and gentlemen, presenting . . . the computer operation, displayed on a projector. Photographs scanned live to the jury. Correction of distortions. Demonstrations of layering techniques, one photo on top of another. Photographic terms: negatives, prints, low and high resolution. The jury has the screen right in front of it, following everything as he speaks. The public gallery and the press can also see it.

The original negatives, Garner tells Byrne, were of such excellent quality they were considered gold, by today's standard. So good, they were able to glean an enormous amount of information from them that wasn't visible in 1985. The photographs that were printed then were poor quality and under-exposed, resulting in loss of tonal quality and information contained in the picture.

The jury is leaning forward, intent on the show. What is that information?

The photos, Garner says, were first printed to achieve the best quality reproduction and then scanned. And there it was. The second bite mark, never seen before.

Garner has the jury in his hand, a triumphant showman. He had hoped they would be computer literate, so they could comprehend what he is saying. They do. His preparation has been impeccable. His rehearsals have paid off.

Raymond Carroll is also absorbed in Garner's show. He knows a lot about computers, and, on the whole, would rather spend time with them than with most people he has met.

Garner is explaining the G-scale used in the original photos and some of the problems in the scaling. 'Now,' he says, 'by odd coincidence, I happen to have one for the benefit of the court that I managed to find in an old file somewhere.' The jury smiles – always a good sign for the Crown – and Byrne grins. Garner is a character. All that is missing in this performance is the drum roll and a rabbit out of a hat.

Outlining problems in the scaling, Garner then moves on to show the wax scraping and ink-immersion techniques to the court.

Davis is singularly unimpressed with the theatre. Garner, he pounces, has no experience in matching teeth to dental models? He would agree that was Dr Forrest's domain? *Yes.* Davis continues. These methods were entirely new, developed as they went along. Isn't this the first time the ink-immersion system has been used in an actual case, the first time drag marks have been shown, and, as for this elaborate device for the second bite mark, isn't it the first time he has ever done that?

Garner nods. 'Yes.'

But he does not look the slightest bit crestfallen by the defence's negative response. Davis has wheeled out a book written by the expert witness they intend to call from the United States, forensic odontologist Dr Raymond Bowers. Unbeknown to them, Garner has recently read the book and disagreed with propositions Bowers has made about scaling. It degenerates into light entertainment for the jury. 'Why are you laughing?' Davis asks, gruffly. Garner grins at him. 'I am not laughing. I am most interested in what you are saying.'

Garner knows that the Crown has the back-up of Dr Peter Adams, a mathematical expert the prosecution intends to call. But he doesn't share this with Davis, who goes in hard to discredit Garner's evidence.

It is obvious to the Crown that the defence is going to challenge on the second bite mark, developed through the technology. The US expert Bowers's advice to the defence is that the technology of comparing the bite mark using computer-imaging is total rubbish and would not work. Byrne has called their own expert witness, Dr Peter Adams, into his chambers for a conference and asks Adams what he thinks of the report. 'It's OK,' he says, 'but there's just a few problems with it.' Byrne asks him what they are, and he points to the graph the American had drawn. 'See this? It's a little bit out.'

Byrne quizzes him further. 'What do you call a "little bit out?"'

'Oh, 50 per cent,' Adams says.

He demonstrates what he means and Byrne nearly falls over.

Byrne calls Adams on a Friday, when everyone is preparing to wrap for the week. The likelihood of defence wanting to cross-examine at this end of the week is slim. What he tells the court blows them out of the water. He demonstrates, using mathematical evidence, that Bowers is wrong. Adams is a complete natural on the stand, and as soon as he'd finished, Davis calls Byrne aside and asks, 'Is this bloke fair dinkum?'

'Of course he's fair dinkum!' Byrne tells him.

'Right,' Davis says 'I'll be making a phone call tonight to call off our bloke from America.'

The mathematical and scientific evidence is hard going, and the court adjourns at 11.25 for a 15-minute break. At 11.52, the court resumes. Justice Muir is impatiently tapping his fingers, waiting for Davis to arrive and he is clearly agitated when he does. 'Mr Davis,' Muir reprimands, '15 minutes doesn't mean 20 or something else.'

'I'm sorry, your Honour. I thought I was back in a lot of time. I made a mistake. I very much apologise.'

Red-faced, Davis takes his seat and Michael Byrne chalks one up. Anything that unsettles the defence, works for him.

Alexander Stewart Forrest outlines his credentials: lecturer in Oral Biology at the University of Queensland, employed by the John Tonge Centre as a forensic odontologist. Master of Dental Science with a Graduate Diploma in Education. Worked as a consultant since 1994 and performed cases under his mentor, Dr Kon Romaniuk. He is the same in the witness box as he is socially: an intriguing mix of seriousness and excitability, given to using formal expressions to explain his theories. *One must acknowledge . . . One has a view . . . One needs to postulate . . .*

He tells the court how he makes impressions of teeth, using material that sets like jelly in a representation of their exact shape. Once the model is ready, he scans it on the computer, corrects any distortions and then scans a photograph of a suspect's teeth over the top of the model. Davis is already rolling his eyes. This technology is designed to make teeth fit. Any teeth.

Forrest is describing Carroll's teeth – *the uppers stick out with respect to the lowers* – and explaining to the jury the mechanics of biting, scanning, scaling and wax scrapings. It is sounding like a lecture to dentistry students. *Eight teeth in each quadrant . . . The tooth closest to the centre is known as tooth one, the next tooth two . . . Occlusal is the biting surfaces of back teeth, mesial any tooth closest to the midline . . .* A journalist, bored with listening to odontologists holding forth ad nauseum on dentistry, shifts in his seat and yawns. Forrest is posing a question: in examining a wound, what do odontologists ask? *Is it a bite? Is it human?* The journalist nudges a colleague and passes him a note. *Is it a bird? Is it a plane? Is it nearly over?*

The position of the teeth and the arch, Forrest tells the jury, has left clues behind. The bite was taken slightly from the side, not head-on and the immersion techniques are a guide to how the teeth would have made contact with the tissue: in effect, a contour map. *A contour map*. Davis groans to himself. What next?

In testing their theory, Forrest continues, he and Garner had taken 25 sets of randomly selected teeth of people of similar ages – including sets of teeth from Faye and Barry Kennedy – and had digitally recorded them. It proved their point: it was unlikely that a randomly chosen set of teeth would produce the same mark. There was no match at all.

It is his opinion, he tells the court, that the drag marks seen on Deidre's leg were made by the teeth of the accused and that both arches in bite mark one matched Carroll's teeth. The second bite mark, he says, was also a match. Ragged edges in the wound were consistent with Carroll's fractured teeth in 1973.

Have you, Byrne asks, attempted to reverse the teeth marks in bite mark one – to put the lower set of teeth where the uppers are placed, and vice versa?

'Yes,' Forrest nods. 'We found no correlation.'

They adjourn for the day, spilling out into the bright late-afternoon sunlight. The journalist who had grown increasingly tired of the dental evidence grunts as he checks his watch. He hasn't got long to write his copy for tomorrow's edition, and he's now got the added unpleasant task of trying to explain inconsistencies between dental evidence in the first and second trial *and* the challenge of making it interesting for the average reader. He imagines the headline: 'Odontologists Don't Know Which End is Up'. He grumbles as he thumps along the footpath back to the newsroom. He doubts his editor will find it funny.

Day 10. Barry Kennedy is recalled for cross-examination on his cousin Keith. He looks pitifully uncomfortable, desperate to get out of the witness stand. The exhibit goes up again, and Byrne has a simple question. In 1973, were his cousin Keith's teeth the same as that? Can he say?

'Yes. I think so,' Barry replies. 'As far as I can tell, yes. They don't appear to have changed at any time.'

The Crown's response is to get Keith Kennedy in and have a

look at his teeth, but Byrne is warned that was a bit hard. He is dead. It doesn't faze Colin Bamford; told that Keith is buried in New Zealand, his response is immediate, 'No worries. Dig him up.' Fortunately, it doesn't come to that. The very clear, close-up family photograph that shows Keith smiling, and his teeth in all their glory. There is, Bamford says, no way in the world that those teeth could have made the marks on Deidre's thigh.

Davis also has a couple of questions. 'In that photograph, he is shown to have blond hair. He has always had blond hair?'

'Yes.'

'And how tall does Keith stand?'

'He'd have to be about 5 foot 10. He's slightly shorter than me.'

Justice Muir smiles benignly from the bench. 'Thank you, Mr Kennedy. You're excused.'

Alex Forrest is back the next day, refreshed from rest and keen as a boy scout to continue his evidence. He, too, is shown the photograph of Keith Kennedy. Could his teeth, Byrne asks, have caused the bruise in bite mark one?

'No,' Forrest answers. 'His diastema would exclude him totally.' And he most certainly does not agree that the bruising on the photograph is so diffuse that he would not be able to discount him as having inflicted the bite. It is his opinion, he concludes, that there is sufficient information in these bite marks to allow the implication of the specific individual.

'And that is?'

'That is Raymond John Carroll.'

Davis is ready for Forrest, comparing his experience in bite-mark cases with that of the expert witness Dr Whittaker, who the defence intends to call. Forrest: eight bite mark cases at time of the time of committal, 16 by trial; Whittaker, more than 200. Byrne knows what is going to come next, that wordless moment before the defence pounces.

Did he, Davis asks, take the evidence given at the 1985 murder trial into account? Did he think it relevant?

'I believe very much one has to take that into account, yes.'

Is Forrest aware, he asks, that all three odontologists at the murder trial gave the opinion it was Raymond Carroll who had left the bite mark, but that all of them said, on oath, that the higher bruise mark shown on the photograph was left by the top row of teeth? *Yes*, Forrest says, he is aware of that. And would he agree that all three men are vastly more experienced than him in bite mark analysis? *Sims and Brown, yes. Romaniuk, no.*

'Well, all three of them have, in effect, got the bite upside down?'

'We believe that to be true, yes.'

Davis pours scorn on Forrest's comparison of photographs of the bite marks with other people's casts of teeth. 'So really, aren't they just simply randomly selected people from the public who happened *not* to have killed Deidre Kennedy?'

Davis affects a puzzled look before Forrest answers his question. That is correct, he says, but it is relevant, because it demonstrates the unlikelihood of making a comparison by accident.

The other mark, Forrest reiterates, was made by the suspender-belt clip. On cue, Garner moves the digital imaging over the top of the photograph to show the jury. Byrne affords himself a brief glance at the jury. They understand. They believe. They can see it. If this continues, it *will* be like convincing non-believers of a miracle Resurrection.

Davis won't be won over. It is pure speculation, he asserts. Just pure speculation. 'You are very proud of this computer-imaging, aren't you? . . . And in presenting this technology, you have got to overcome the opinion of Sims, Brown, Romaniuk, Whittaker and indeed the people who did the post-mortem.'

'I accept that completely.'

By day 11, Davis is telling Forrest that his analysis is fundamentally flawed, that it is anatomically impossible to line up the marks as he has done. The so-called drag marks are just bruises. The whole area is just a heap of smudgy bruises. Forrest has simply picked at certain features in order to uphold his hypothesis.

Tempers are starting to fray. Byrne has asked Forrest a question in re-examination and Davis is fed up. 'Your Honour, I ask my learned friend to lead this witness carefully on issues that have arisen in cross-examination, rather than just to invite a lecture. Now I have forgotten what the question was. He has been going on for about 10 minutes . . .'

Overruled.

When Forrest steps down from the witness stand, Garner grins at him. Carroll's eyes follow Forrest as he leaves the court, but his head remains still.

40

Dr Colin Bamford is gravely ill. No longer the robust, solidly built man who dominated the committal hearing, his wafer-thin flesh sags on his 180cm frame and his once thick mane of sandy hair is now just a combover of pitiful wisps. Aged in his late fifties, within months he will be dead from the cancer that is gnawing at him. His doctors advised him against this trip, but he was determined to fly from the United Kingdom, to see this case to its close.

Bamford is well placed to give court evidence. In a Kiwi accent laced with cockney, he outlines his impressive credentials. Degree in dental surgery and Diploma of Forensic Odontology. Bachelor of Laws, with Honours. Membership of numerous dental associations.

Byrne is keen to show that his amiable and brilliant witness is highly experienced in identification using teeth. As ill as Bamford is, his laidback style impresses the jury. He is easy to like. 'In terms of identification by dental means, I've been involved in quite a few mass disasters,' he tells the court. He lists them, a litany of lost lives. The *Herald Free Enterprise*, a car ferry that sank in the English Channel with 150 dead as a result. London's Underground Rail disaster. Identification of the 60 Chinese illegal immigrants who had tried to enter the United Kingdom in the back of a container and in which 58 died in the attempt.

He has given expert dental evidence on various criminal matters. Child abuse. Rape. Murder. Bite marks in inanimate objects such as cheese or apples. A murder case where the killer was identified by teeth marks in a Mars Bar. An armed robbery and murder where the defendant had chewed the plastic butt of a car key, and left his signature in the dental marking.

He reiterates to the court what he told Garner and Herpich when they visited him in London: that there are two clearly evident marks and that it was plain which were made by the upper and which from the lower, by the size and pattern of the marks.

'How,' Byrne asks him, 'would he make identification from the material they had?'

'I would actually do an acetate tracing of the dentition . . . which is very useful in eliminating anybody as a preliminary measure. This new digital technology,' he adds, 'is actually a refinement of this technique.'

He identifies the teeth responsible for upper bite mark one. The biter's upper and lower teeth don't meet, he explains. It is a non-uniform arch, and there is evident crowding in the mouth from some teeth. A normal dentition could bite a tissue paper and tear it apart. This dentition could not. The back teeth would have to be used to bite and chew –

'And how,' Byrne interjects, 'do those bruises match the dentition that you have there?'

'They correlate very nicely with the lower front teeth.'

Bamford scoffs at the idea, raised earlier by the defence, that black-and-white photographs, used in this trial, are of little benefit. 'Colour is more graphic, obviously in terms of bruising and ageing, but, in the identification of individual marks, there is nothing wrong with black and white.' He argues that the photo seems to have been taken at the correct angle, perpendicular to the skin and the mark.

Of the lower bite mark one, Bamford says that the marks match the dentition, including the shape of the arch. He considers the match to be of a very high standard.

He is a perfect witness – fluid, easy to understand and believable – and he has the jury's full attention. For Byrne, he is manna from heaven. 'Now, Doctor, we will see that not all the teeth on that dentition have left bruising. Does that cause you any concern?'

'No. It is well known that you are not going to get a mark if no tooth exists but the same is not true in converse. You can often get a break in the injuries that have been left, even though the tooth does, in fact, exist.'

'Why is that?'

'Possibly the angle from which the dentition struck the skin, or it could be caused by different levels of teeth, which would be an obvious reason for it not to show up. But, nevertheless, you still get wounds where one or other teeth do not actually make an imprint or mark.' He explains that this is the case even if there is an angle in the bite.

The second bite mark, he opines, though not as clear as the first, also matches the dentition. 'I think,' he says, 'this dentition has caused that mark.'

'What do you say to a proposition that the bruise is so diffuse as to not allow an identification to be made?' Byrne asks quietly, gently adjusting his gown as his question tapers off.

'I would disagree.'

'Why is that?'

'I think there is plenty of definition there.'

Byrne pauses momentarily. Could the witness see Exhibit 49, please? Faye registers shock when the photograph appears on the screen. She knows this man. Keith Kennedy. She cringes at the memory, huddling into Barry, desolate with grief. *What does it mean? What does it mean, not guilty on the grounds of insanity?* and his soothing reply: *You've got it all wrong, Faye. Keith would never hurt our child.*

Faye is brought back to the present, Byrne's voice floating through the court. 'See the blond person shown, the blond adult male? What can you comment about his teeth?'

'Well, he has a very prominent gap between his two central incisors (front teeth) known as a diastema . . . It is quite a unique feature.' So unique, he adds, that it would be regarded as a 'forensic odontologist's dream' to get a set of models with a gap like that.

'Would it help in identification of a bite mark left with teeth such as these?'

'This would be wonderful. It is characteristic. If you saw that, you would expect to see a gap between the teeth straight away on the photograph.'

Now. Ask the question now. 'The bite mark we see up there, could the teeth shown in that person have caused that mark?'

Sandra is poised for his answer, hands clasped tightly together. 'No,' Bamford instantly replies. 'It is not possible.'

For the briefest moment, Raymond catches Sandra's eye, then looks away. Bamford is still talking. 'There is no break between the central incisors on this photograph. If this dentition struck the tissue, there would be a definitive mark.'

'It is not possible?'

'Absolutely not possible.'

Byrne resists the urge to grin. 'That's all I have. Thank you, your Honour.'

Davis goes straight in on the attack and Bamford sees it coming as the words leave his adversary's mouth. 'In cases of mass disaster,' Davis says, 'you are matching up teeth on a body with dental records; is that right?'

Bamford agrees that is part of it. But it is not the whole picture. In the Paddington rail disaster, for example, where heads and bodies were in fragments, what they got was a piece of bone with perhaps one tooth on it and another piece of jaw with perhaps three teeth on it. And these fragments were brought in, individually, given a number and slowly pieced back together.

Davis inclines his head slightly to the side. 'Now you've told us that bite mark analysis is about picking patterns; is that right?'

'Well, part of it, yes . . . it's a visual exercise and a comparison of patterns, yes.'

'And that general approach, notwithstanding there's been new technology, hasn't changed for many years, has it?'

'No, it's still valid.'

Davis has turned to look at the jury and now returns his gaze on his witness. 'Well, it's still valid, plus also there's nothing new about this in basic terms, is there, this technology?'

Bamford did not see this one coming. 'This is just a lovely way to graphically show it and certainly for displaying it to the court. It's a lot easier than waving a photograph at the jury in one hand and a tracing in the other.'

'The technique in 1985 was not digital overlay, but acetate etchings? . . . You did an acetate tracing in this case, didn't you? . . . The same procedures that were adopted in 1985?'

'Yes.'

It is a major point, and Davis has won.

Bamford did not review the evidence from 1985?

No, he did not, Bamford says, but he knows the basis of the findings: that the higher arches were caused by the upper, not the lower teeth, and he strenuously disagrees with that orientation. 'Bear in mind,' he tells Davis, 'Sims is my teacher, but there was no reason for me to agree with him just because I know him or simply because he taught me.'

Well, Davis huffs, it seems as though Bamford has dismissed the collective views of the three odontologists without even bothering to view their arguments?

It is now Bamford's turn to look exasperated. He had, he says, given a statement about his opinions long before he even *knew* the other three forensic dentists were involved.

It becomes an exercise in banter. Back and forth, agreeing, disagreeing. Some of the bruising inflicted on Deidre, Bamford agrees, has nothing to do with bites. No, he doesn't agree that to make a cut during a bite would take more force and cause more bruising than seen in the second bite mark. No, the second bite not picked up at post-mortem was not a shadow or other mark that could not be clearly defined in a black-and-white photograph. It was, Bamford says, not unknown for police and pathologists to miss bite marks.

Bamford defends the accuracy of simulating the 1973 condition of Carroll's teeth, but agrees that movement of Deidre's leg after the biting would affect the shape of the bruise. And now Davis is back to suggesting that the bite was made by someone with a diastema, someone with a gap between his front teeth. Bamford, he says, turning again to face the jury, has not seen a cast of Keith Kennedy's teeth. He has discounted him as the author of the bites purely by looking at a photograph. 'I suggest to you that the bruising which is shown on bite mark one and alleged bite mark two is so vague and diffuse that you couldn't possibly exclude him as the biter?'

'Yes, you can. You can expect to find clearer division . . . produced by this dentition . . .'

Davis is finishing his cross-examination. His defence expert Dr

Whittaker has claimed experience in over 200 bite marks cases, and his expert opinion is that the quality of the bites is not of sufficient quality to identify the biter. Does Bamford disagree? *Yes, I do.* He disagrees, but he does not contest Whittaker's expertise? *No, I have no reason to do that at all.*

Barry Kennedy is watching and listening. The odontology evidence is sophisticated and impressive but it's showmanship, too: a battle for supremacy. Herpich, Garner and all the rest want their technique accepted in court. He has seen the evidence. He thinks it's all gobbledygook.

Barry slips outside for another smoke. It is claustrophobic in here.

Michael Byrne is cringing. Swifte had been bad enough with his fanciful tale of a child at the end of his bed, but now one of his expert witnesses is in tears. Despite Dr Pamela Craig's obvious discomfort at the committal hearing, he had still backed her to come through at trial. Blonde, well-presented and professional, she is eminently qualified in her field. A bachelor and master's degree in dentistry. Graduate Diploma in Forensic Odontology. Lecturer in Oral Radiology and Anatomy. She has prepared acetate etchings to help her form her opinion, not relied just on the computer technique, and she starts confidently enough. Carroll, she says, has an unusual bite. He cannot move his jaw forward in the same way as someone with an ordinary bite; instead, he has to bite on the side. The shape and orientation of the bite is consistent with a jaw where the upper and lower teeth don't meet. The dental cast matches this description and shows wear consistent with this dentition. Based on the size and shape of the arch, the second bruise was, in all probability, a bite mark, and broken or missing material of the upper central teeth would probably account for the laceration in it.

Craig identifies points of concordance with the lower dentition and the upper section of the first bite mark. But she is beginning to fumble, not making it clear which teeth she is referring to on the monitor that is displayed to the jury. Davis moves in like a shark. 'I am sorry, your Honour I have got no idea what she is talking about.'

Justice Muir gently reminds the doctor to reference the teeth so that everyone in court can follow what she is saying.

'OK.'

Because Carrol bites at an angle, she explains, the teeth that indent the deepest will cause more of a bruise. But now it is Byrne who needs to rebuke her. 'You have to identify the teeth please, Doctor . . .'

She appears to understand. 'Right . . .'

A family portrait showing Keith Kennedy is up on the screen, again she is asked whether his pronounced diastema could account for the bruise mark. No, she replies firmly. And now she is fighting back in answer to Davis's cross-examination about the pattern of bruises toward the top of bite mark one, a lineal mark running up the thigh with a scalloped edge. 'The other mark may not be a tooth mark?' Davis asks.

'No,' Craig replies, 'it represents a suspender from a corset.'

'Oh?' Davis looks bemused. 'How do you know that?'

'Because I'm old enough to wear these things.'

There is a tittering in the court and Davis doesn't like it. 'You're not going to tell us that you're an expert on the marks that suspender belts leave on 17-month-old babies, are you?'

'No, but I'm an expert on the marks they leave on adult females.' It is the only win she has, but it is resounding.

Davis doesn't take long to come back from the clip mark, trouncing Craig, reminding her of the mistakes she made at committal, when she confused left and right. It is the same trap Dr Ken Brown had fallen into at the first trial, by not insisting that a full explanation be given, and she is trying to explain how it happened. 'As a dentist, the patient's right is on the left and the left's on the right. You look at a bite mark, the right's on the right, the left's on the left. If you look at an upside-down mark, the right's on the left . . . I got absolutely rattled.' At committal, she got it upside down in her mind and Davis is hammering her now and reminding her, when she attempts to assert herself, just who is conducting this cross-examination. She is trying to say she has re-examined the evidence since the committal hearing and has changed her mind and now Davis has reduced her to a crying heap and the judge is calling for a break. Davis is attacking her experience in bite mark forensics, breaking her down and asking her to admit that it would be impossible to mistake the top teeth for the bottom. *I would have thought so. It depends on the quality of the photograph* . . . and she has fallen into his trap. She can't think straight, she is not coping and there is an adjournment until the following morning. It is a humiliating spectacle and the jury shares her discomfort, looking sideways at each other.

It is left to Michael Byrne to tell the court that his witness has admitted that without external clues she has difficulty telling her left from her right. She is ambidextrous. She knows dentistry but she just could not get her knowledge across to the jury the right way around.

Justice Muir kindly offers Craig another break. She declines. 'Your Honour, it is my son's school play tonight and I have got to get back to Victoria to see it. I am sorry, I will have to keep going.'

Davis will not let her off the hook. Isn't the bruise so diffuse, he asks, that she couldn't be sure if it was a bite mark at all, nor confidently say that the laceration was left by any tooth, let alone a particular tooth?

She looks ragged, and Byrne completes Craig's evidence with a series of questions that explain, simply, what she is saying. Or trying to say. 'May the witness be excused?' Byrne asks, with a definite weariness in his tone. 'Thank you, your Honour. That is the case for the Crown.'

Davis is satisfied that all the Crown witnesses, except Forrest, had by their evidence virtually admitted that the computer technique achieved no more than the acetate sketching method. He quietly instructs Liz Wilson to make a note raising the fact that only the 'inventor' of the new technique, Alex Forrest, had formed an opinion based on the computer technology.

41

The Kennedy family's victim impact statements, shown to the jury during this trial but not read aloud to the court, are so harrowing that those who see them bow their heads in tears. If ever there was a moment when the impact of Deidre's murder on the family was defined, this is it. If ever there had been any illusion that time had healed their pain, this is the instant it is dispelled.

Deidre had been abducted from her makeshift cot 27 years before, but she lingers in the minds of her family, as though standing in the shadows off-stage watching their lives play out.

Barry Kennedy, unable to talk about his unendurable heartache, has spilled out his pain and guilt on the page. Here, finally, was what the jury had sensed when he had given evidence: that elusive something in his demeanour that had suggested to them they were witnessing more than an expression of grief – something deeper, more troubling.

'The reality was,' he had written,

> I do and did remember hearing a noise which woke me during the night of Deidre's abduction and murder. I can always remember listening for further noises, but because it had been a long day and I was immobile with my knee operation, I went back to sleep. I will never forgive myself that I did not get out of bed, as this could have prevented a tragedy . . .

He had said from the witness stand he had not heard a noise, had put his head down and rubbed his forehead with a trembling hand when he had made the admission. He could not face that packed court with the truth. But here it was, stark and bleak, the thing that had stalked Barry for years, dogging his every footstep. Guilt.

Barry had further written: 'I would like to say that I grew up in the belief that men didn't show emotions . . . crying, sharing with others, problems of a sensitive nature . . .' Detailing the years from Deidre's murder through to Derek's birth, Barry had written that he believed they had a happy family life until they were contacted at Richmond RAAF Base concerning Carroll. He laid bare his soul. 'After the trial and then acquittal, my life began a downhill run. Because of my inability to communicate, I took to drinking and playing poker machines to numb reality . . .'

Finding it impossible to talk to strangers about his problems, Barry found no comfort in the help offered by the RAAF, meetings with clergy or psychologists. Admitting he could not deal with his own demons was, he believed, tantamount to a flaw in his character. He had grown up in the country, where men were strong and hid their fears. 'My career in the air force suffered and I retired after 21 years,' he had written. Losing his beloved Deidre, followed by his family and finally the structure and support provided by the RAAF, proved catastrophic. Barry's life now spiralled out of control. He hit rock bottom.

> After some time I left and found myself living as a homeless person for approximately 12 months, living out of the car and finding food where I could. Words cannot convey what I went through in this time. I remember when doing late shift at Richmond, I would come home at about 1am, sit in the lounge chair and sob. There was nobody to see me and I was safe.
>
> In all this I deeply regret the anxiety I caused my wife, daughter and son and I still do not fully know the extent of the harm this has done to my relationship with my children . . . Carroll, by his horrific actions, has ruined many lives to this day, and, as far as I am concerned, he will not be put away for long enough.
>
> *'May Justice prevail.'*

Stephanie, haunted by the fact she was in the room with Deidre when she was abducted, has written on behalf of herself and Derek.

It has only been in the past two years of my life that I have begun to try to overcome some of the fears that have consumed my life. My absolute fear of the dark and the noises that haunt me in the darkness. My obsession with ensuring, not once, not twice but three or more times that the doors and windows are securely locked. Derek, at such a young age, has found enormous inner strength to deal with this and provide the emotional support for Mum . . . it has left our strong family emotionally depleted and we will continue to bear the scars for the rest of our days . . .

She has finished her statement: 'To our darling Deidre, you will remain forever in our hearts. May God rest your soul.'

Outlining her loss, Faye has written that, although it was more than 27 years ago, the day of Deidre's murder is as vivid to her as though it happened only yesterday. In her statement, she has poured out her heartache at the breakdown of her marriage, the eight years she has lived on her own, the empty house and the long nights when her mind always meanders back to the past. It has consumed her, usurped any chance of a normal life. She had been raised a Christian, snuggled safely in the loving arms of the Church, nurtured and nourished by an all-seeing God and the teachings of the Scriptures. *The Lord giveth, the Lord taketh away . . .* But this has been no comfort. It is not just that Deidre had been taken, but the monstrous obscenities that had been visited upon her.

As I prepare myself for the final week of the trial, I cast my mind back to the happy times when I had two beautiful little girls . . . Having to accept my loss was always so much more difficult knowing that my baby had suffered so badly at the hands of the monster who took her from us . . .

She has grappled with ways of explaining the loss, how to explain to her grandchildren that their aunt had been killed – not by an act of nature, but by a force of psychopathic evil.

'How I miss that little girl,' she has concluded. 'No one will ever understand the pain in my heart for her. There isn't a day goes by that I don't wonder how different and happy our lives would be if we could erase that day in April from our lives . . .'

'I will always think of Deidre as being busy polishing the stars for us all.'

42

The Crown has called 53 witnesses, and the court now seeks instruction as to the accused's intentions. 'Raymond John Carroll, the prosecution having closed its case against you, I must ask if you intend to adduce evidence in your defence. This means you may give evidence yourself, call witnesses or produce evidence. You may do all or any of these things or none of them.'

Davis rises. 'My client will not give evidence himself,' he announces. 'But he will call two witnesses.'

In anyone's language, it was an uneven ledger. Fifty-three witnesses for the Crown. Two for the defence.

Peter Davis flags his defence in his opening address. He has a lot of ground to cover; this jury is so absorbed in the evidence that the foreperson sent a note to the bar table asking that the lawyers not speak amongst themselves when a witness was on the stand, as they found it distracting. On many occasions, both male and female jurors had noticeably paled when distressing exhibits had been shown. Davis's main challenge is to destroy the prosecution's key platform: the odontology evidence. By the time he has finished, he hopes the jury thinks it is all bunkum.

Experts called by the Crown in 1985 and again at this trial, he says, have made contradictory statements on which teeth had caused which marks, and the 27-year-old black-and-white photograph of bite marks on Deidre Kennedy is so bad it could not possibly be used to identify her killer. The defence, he says, will call Dr David Whittaker, a bite mark expert from Wales. Whittaker will explain that the photographs of the bite marks used by the Crown experts were of such poor quality that they should never have been used and that the bruising shown in the photographs is so diverse it is impossible to match the bites with a cast made of Carroll's teeth. 'The Crown assumption that the teeth marks can be matched to Carroll is flawed,' Davis says. Defence will also call Raymond Carroll's mother, Ilma.

Ilma Carroll, now 70 years old, is bewildered and scared on the stand, her eyes flicking around the court, searching for familiar faces. No one else in her family has been called to give evidence. She avoids looking at Faye Kennedy, torn between the sadness she feels at Faye's loss and the maternal anger that her son has been dragged into a second trial. Over the decades, her own tears have worn creases in her face, sliding down her cheeks like a waterfall on rock. Ilma's answers to questions are often confused, born of extreme nervousness. Being in this witness stand is a hideous ordeal.

After Raymond joined the RAAF, she says, she did not see him again until May 1973 when she was staying with her sister and youngest three children at Casino in New South Wales. He just showed up, out of the blue, and she remembers his visit because it was the Mother's Day weekend. After he married Joy Meyers, the couple lived with her until they were posted to Darwin. She never noticed any abnormal injuries on Kerry-Ann when they were living with her, but she remembers the day Deidre went missing. 'It was such a horrific thing. Everybody knew about it. It's not something that you forget very easily.'

Her health was good, as was the children's, except for normal colds and flus. Certainly nothing significant enough to warrant calling Raymond home from recruit course. Peter had to be hospitalised a month after Deidre disappeared to stop his nose-bleeds, but that was all. Nothing significant. The house was visited by police when they did the doorknock, but she told them there was only one male living there at the time. Peter.

Ilma is cross-examined by Byrne, who dispatches her quickly. Would she agree that after her husband died in 1971 she had told the first trial that Raymond effectively had become the head of the family? *Yes.* Does she recall taking the children, Leanne and Peter, to the doctor's clinic? Well no, she says, but if that's what she said last time, then that must have been what she did.

'Do you remember saying that last time, that you don't remember what you took them there for?'

'Probably for a check-up, they might have had colds; I don't know.'

Byrne is now uncustomarily blunt. 'I'm not interested about probably – can you recall or not?'

'No, I can't.'

'That's all I have; thank you, your Honour.'

The court clerk is asking if Senior-Sergeant Garner could take his position again, please? Garner moves to the computer with light steps. He is ready when the good doctor is.

Whittaker's resume spans 30 years. Doctor of Forensic Dentistry, Oral Biology and Philosophy at the University of Wales. Bachelor of Dental Surgery, University of Manchester. Fellow of the Royal Society of Arts . . . Puffed-up, but pleasant.

Whittaker has been involved in 223 bite mark cases. He has used the computer overlay technique, he says, in more than 100 cases and believes it should simply be an aid to the whole process of bite mark analysis, not used in isolation. Identification cannot be made just from diffuse bruising; there must be marks that identify features of individual teeth, teeth marks, shapes, twists.

Davis looks pleased. This absolutely contradicts the evidence of the Crown's dental experts. And when, later, Davis asks, 'Can you throw any light on whether the top row of bruises was likely to have been caused by a top or bottom set of teeth?', he had even further cause to smile.

'From studying the photographs alone,' Whittaker announces in his thick Welsh accent, 'I concluded that this question was not possible to answer with 100 per cent certainty because there is insufficient information here to be absolutely sure. I concluded the top arch was more likely to have been produced by someone's lower teeth.'

Now it is Garner's turn to smile; the eminent overseas doctor is agreeing with their orientation of the mark. But Whittaker has not finished. 'I concluded it is a rather poor representation of what I do believe is a bite mark.'

Poor enough, Davis hopes, to prevent any definite identification by the jury of who caused the mark.

The court adjourns for the day and everyone appears relieved. It really is becoming heavy weather.

Davis continues his evidence-in-chief of his witness the following day.

'Now, doctor, yesterday we spoke about . . .' Whittaker smiles confidently at Davis, lifts the bottom of his tie and lets it flutter back into position. He is relaxed, as though he is about to attend a gentleman's lunch at an exclusive club instead of being an expert witness at a perjury trial. '. . . The suggestion that the photograph would enable a positive identification of a person. What do you say about that?'

'When I examined this photograph and when I examine it now, I would say that it would be impossible to, with certainty, identify a person making that injury from teeth.' It is to get worse. Romaniuk's replication of Carroll's teeth, in his opinion, was not an accurate representation and there was no way of telling what position the teeth were in before the dentist had started his work.

Whittaker perceives dangers in the immersion layer technique, agreeing with the defence argument that it was subjective, depending on how far the operator decided to tilt the teeth. And, he opines, the bruising also suggests the biter has a gap between his front teeth. Garner knows exactly what he is driving at. Davis will undoubtedly return to this.

And what, Davis asks, does the doctor make of the Crown's hypothesis about how bite mark one was inflicted?

'No one can open their mouth to this extent and swing to that extent physically. It is impossible.' Whittaker lists the points that suggest Carroll is not the biter. He would have to have moved his jaw into an anti-clockwise position to make the mark. The gap in the bruise mark needs to be explained in greater detail. There is not enough detail in the cluster of bruises to separate one tooth from another. There is no apparent gap between the very light bruise at the left of the lower arch and the main bruise. 'I believe,' he says, 'there are so many negatives in this situation that it is unsafe to conclude that Carroll made this bite . . .' He cannot see any drag marks, cannot make any identification from bite mark two.

Davis moves back to Keith Kennedy. 'The Crown witnesses have said that the existence of that diastema excludes him as the biter. What do you say about the proposition?'

'Not in itself, I wouldn't accept that.'

Here it is. Based on his past form and unusual diastema, it is the defence's intention to put Keith Kennedy, now deceased, squarely in the frame for the abduction and murder of his niece Deidre.

Byrne turns slightly in his chair, speaks quietly to his junior, Sharon Loder.

The defence is indicating they have no further questions and Byrne stands, steering straight to an attack on Whittaker's credentials. 'Can we just go back . . . you gave evidence that you were the doctor of both forensic dentistry and oral biology at the University of Wales?' Whittaker agrees. 'And my learned friend asked you how long you had held that position and you said you had held it in various formats for 30 years . . . What you are saying is you have been an academic for 30 years?'

'Yes.'

'You have been a doctor for how long?'

Whittaker now looks abashed. 'I have been a doctor in that department for about three months.'

Byrne lets the statement float in the air for the jury to catch.

He is now reading from a report Whittaker prepared for the defence. 'You say, "It cannot be assumed that the bite mark was perpetrated by the same person who killed the child." What do you mean by that?'

What he means, Whittaker replies, is he has seen cases where a bite mark has been independent of death. And he hadn't been briefed on the details leading up to Deidre's abduction.

'See, Doctor, I don't want to be critical,' Byrne finally says, with a touch of ice in his voice, 'but you seem to be raising new material every time I get you to a point . . .'

Whittaker doesn't know how Deidre was dressed. He doesn't know if a clip made the mark. It seems a reasonable proposition that it did, but, beyond that, he just can't say.

Byrne is struggling to keep the derision from his voice. 'And were you being serious before when you suggested that the mark could be a rogue *freckle?*' He is hoeing into him now. 'Doctor, the point comes down to this: you make no mention in your report of any possibility of a diastema in respect to that mark?' Surely, he demands, if there was such a suggestion, he would have mentioned it? Hadn't he written a book, which he had omitted to tell the court had joint authorship, which read: 'The condition [diastema] is sufficiently striking to be useful as an identification pointer?'

Yes, Whittaker says. He would agree with that.

'See, doctor . . .' Byrne now has the witness so far on the back foot, he is giving him no room to manoeuvre. Up goes the exhibit of Keith Kennedy's teeth, again. 'I suggest, with great respect, that experts in the field have testified that it is impossible for the teeth shown in that photograph to leave that mark, and I suggest, with great respect, you are simply not being objective?'

'I haven't said they could, I don't think. I haven't been asked that question, I don't believe.'

'I thought I had asked you that.'

'I don't believe I have been asked that question. I thought I was asked to describe that the teeth had a space between them.'

'Well, I am suggesting to you those teeth could not make that mark.'

Davis is looking directly at his witness, as Whittaker starts to speak. 'From what I can see here, which is limited . . .' Whittaker flicks at the photograph in front of him, 'I don't think they could. I don't believe I have said they could. I have only just seen this and I haven't really considered it.'

But wasn't he shown the picture last week and given as much time as he needed to form an opinion? Is it now his opinion that they wouldn't?

No, Whittaker retorts, it is his opinion that there just isn't enough information in the mark to form an opinion.

'But it is unlikely they did?'

'It is unlikely.'

Davis's re-examination is relatively brief, and, when he finishes, he inclines toward the bench with a slight tip of his head. 'Your Honour, that is the case for the accused.'

John Garner doesn't think much of Whittaker's performance.

They bring a bloke out from overseas because he's supposedly better than the local guys, he thinks, and his evidence is all over the place about Keith Kennedy, until he finally admits it is unlikely he was the biter. He has also got up with a set of dental models – the ones taken in 1999 – and goes on and on about it. The jury picks up that he had the wrong set, and he continues to waffle on about details that weren't there in 1985. Garner can see what is happening but can't get the message across to the prosecutor. A doctor of dentistry has picked up the wrong set of teeth! How, he thinks, is that possible? How on *earth* is that possible?

43

It is almost over, the last scenes about to be played in a drama no one has wanted to watch. Faye is agitated, withdrawn, reserving her strength for what is to come. Derek is at breaking point, overwhelmed and disgusted by the evidence he has heard. Stephanie has arrived now from her home in Sydney, and Barry stays mostly silent, save for when someone speaks to him. Cameron Herpich has been a presence throughout, a constant buffer for Faye against unwarranted intrusions.

For all of the family, whatever the outcome, there will be no triumph. If the Crown loses, they will be back where they started. If they win, it will be a victory carved hollow by the reality that nothing can bring Deidre back. From now, the press seats will start to fill again, the story picking up pace and dominating newspapers and bulletins as it draws to its inevitable close.

The trial has lasted 19 days and Michael Byrne's closing address is as lethal as his opening. Skipping lightly over the evidence of the controversial witnesses, he has the jury's full attention as he outlines, again, the poignant, tragic story of baby Deidre and the evidence against Raymond Carroll. Direct. Forensic. Circumstantial.

If ever a jury is going to go watery, it is now. Weeks of listening to evidence, to different points of view; tired, possibly unsure ... this is when the real pressure begins. This is the time to rein the jurors in, put the story in a succinct wrapper, reiterate what they have heard. The time to knock out any doubts, replace them with certainties, remind them that the onus of proof rests with the Crown and what the Crown believes is the truth. And what is that truth? That the accused, Raymond John Carroll, is charged before them with one count of perjury and is guilty of that charge. Byrne looks directly at the jury, resting momentarily on each face. The women look exhausted, distressed; the men upright, attentive.

There is so much tension in the court, it is as though he can reach out and touch it.

Byrne picks his moment before continuing in his deep, mellifluous voice. The criminal law, he says, like families and victims, can be patient and relentless. It relies on a jury to assess the evidence. And it is that evidence that will lead them to conclude that no other than Raymond Carroll abducted and murdered Deidre, and that he had lied when he said he did not. A smoking gun and a dead body are not direct evidence. It is circumstantial and the essence of a circumstantial case is fitting the pieces of evidence together, like a jigsaw puzzle. Add opportunity to lies, build it piece by piece, and there it is: an overwhelming case against the accused. And did he lie? To cover up his guilt and fear of the truth coming out.

Byrne wants to remind the jury of an essential fact. 'There is a tendency for people coming into an atmosphere such as this to think this is a special world. It's a world where the players wear wigs and gowns and where the world behaves in a different way and you have to assess people when they give their evidence in some sort of special way. None of that is true. You must use your own common sense and experience of human nature when you assess witnesses. The basic fabric of our criminal justice system depends on that.'

What would anyone have to gain from lying about Carroll's movements or his behaviour? The RAAF recruits were just young men off to their first posting, the start of their career. They had nothing to gain from lying. Memories fade, but photographs don't, Byrne says. Carroll was not in the passing-out parade photo. And this is not just a family snapshot, but an official RAAF photograph. He is nowhere to be seen. Why? Because, the Crown says, he wasn't there. And the women, his ex-wife Joy Meyers and ex-lover, Desley Hill? Are they really just harbouring festering resentments, all those years later? Hardly likely. The jury has heard them, seen them. It is hardly likely.

What of the other pieces of evidence – wanting to call his own daughter Deidre, and biting Kerry-Ann on the thigh? The jury, Byrne says, might think a person would be stupid to behave like that. 'Well, killers aren't necessarily that clever . . .' He dispatches the rest of the evidence from the defence as no more than a red herring.

And Swifte? He had waited years to speak out. 'Swifte is someone who knows that to manipulate the system is a two-edged sword. You can get a reduced sentence. But to be labelled a prison dog or informer can have its own consequences.'

The evidence to date, Byrne continues, is this. The Crown says it could prove the accused left Edinburgh on 12 April; was in Ipswich on 14 April; that he told deliberate, calculated and repeated lies to distance himself from those two events; and that he was within walking distance of where Deidre Kennedy was abducted and her body left . . .

Byrne signifies that his address is finished, sits back in his seat. It's over to the jury, now.

It is the defence's turn to sum up. Davis reminds the jury that during the trial they have heard a lot of contentious evidence and that they must focus on the truth in relation to that evidence. But, he says, one thing was not contentious. 'Although this is a perjury trial, the central issue here is a murder . . . ' He reiterates the bare bones of the Crown case, addressing the jury as though they are well known to him. Old friends, with whom he can share intimate stories. 'Quite often, people come up to me and say, "Oh, gee, you're defending that bloke," and they say, "Oh, he must be a monster." Well, the answer to that, of course, is nothing's been proven against him yet . . . the real issue is whether he did it. In order to come to grips with that, in my submission to you, the first thing you have to do is put aside the horror of it and look dispassionately at the evidence, otherwise you'll just be taken away, swept up in the horror of it all, the emotion of it all. Remember, it is a dreadful thing for young Deidre Kennedy to have been killed, but it's also pretty dreadful for a man, perhaps who is innocent to be accused of it, let alone to be convicted.' This, he says, was the same man who volunteered samples to police – hardly the actions of someone who is acting out of a conscious-ness of guilt.

He slips into easy colloquialism. The description Nugget Carroll gave doesn't come within cooee of matching that of his client. Nugget couldn't identify even one of the photos as being the prowler. And, for that matter, where are those photographs? Is it the case that the police had a suspect as early as a day or so after the murder?

He affords himself a sly chuckle. The Crown, he says, would like the jury to believe that the person Nugget Carroll saw on the veranda was not the same person who abducted Deidre. And, if that was the case, 'Mrs Borchert's underwear must have really been in demand on that night.' The jocularity disappears as suddenly as it came. It is the defence's contention that the man Nugget Carroll saw on the veranda was, in fact, the same person who killed Deidre Kennedy.

The Crown, he scoffs, have dredged up witnesses 27 years after the event. *Twenty-seven years.* His client's neighbour had sat proudly in the witness box and said he didn't know whether Raymond had gone home that weekend. The court hadn't heard boo from Dr Ken Brown. Why not? If the Crown could organise a video-link from London for a witness, surely Adelaide was not too much of a stretch? 'Well,' Davis says, opening his arms in an expansive gesture, 'the reason you haven't had the benefit of hearing from Brown . . . is that he just doesn't fit with what the Crown now wants to say. Because Brown, of course, gave his opinion and he had the bite marks positioned upside down to what the present experts positioned them . . .'

The doorknocks are lost. All gone. 'That evidence, you may think, might have completely exculpated my client; it may very well have been that the doorknocks would have shown my client was not there. It would certainly have shown who was living around my client's address at that time and those witnesses could have been found. But all that evidence is now just gone.' And what of the RAAF records? Funnily enough, he says, those that are still in existence – kit records and course records – seem to suggest that Carroll was in Edinburgh at the time but other RAAF records – travel and general movement – were all gone.

He targets the prison records. Cameron Herpich, he says, was asked a series of questions as to when Carroll was released from Boggo Road and he said the prison records were gone. 'That was his answer.' In effect, he says, frowning, Detective Herpich was quite happy for them to believe the prison records showed Carroll going *into* the prison, but . . . he was bailed the next day and released from the Ipswich Magistrate's Court. So what opportunity did Swifte have to speak to his client?

Where are the missing witnesses, like the canteen lady to back up Ferguson's claims? And why haven't they heard from the man who would have had to consider any application for compassionate leave?

He zeroes in on Keith Kennedy. On his darker side. 'We know that in 1970 he was found not guilty by reason of insanity of . . . biting a three-and-a-half year old girl on the vagina . . .' You might also like to think, he suggests, that the description Nugget Carroll gave more readily fits Keith Kennedy than it did his client. Davis's voice remains smooth, easygoing. 'The Crown has called 30-odd witnesses in order to prove my client wasn't in South Australia and to desperately get him in the right state, let alone in Ipswich, let alone in Limestone Park. We know that Keith Kennedy was in Auchenflower . . .'

He quickly skates over Whittaker's evidence. Doctors Craig, Bamford and Forrest have all said that the gap in Keith's teeth precluded him from being the biter but, while Whittaker said it was *unlikely* – he leaned hard on the word – he had said he could not be excluded. Exoneration of Keith Kennedy is, Davis says, not a matter for the police, but for the jury. 'It's clearly raised here that Keith Kennedy could have perpetrated this offence; the Crown says he didn't do it, that it's Mr Carroll. Well, let them prove it. How was Keith Kennedy exonerated? Was it alibi, was it fingerprints or other scientific evidence? What was it that the police did in order to come to the conclusion that it wasn't Keith Kennedy? Was it that sort of investigation that exonerated Keith Kennedy? We'll never know. They will just simply say to you, don't worry about it, and I say to you, worry about it. You should worry about it.'

He tears apart the Crown's case regarding special leave for RAAF recruits. There is, he says, a whole body of evidence that a recruit had to have a relative on death's door or actually in the coffin in order to get compassionate leave.

He completely discredits Desley Hill's evidence, that it was during her second relationship with Carroll that they saw the Deidre Kennedy story on television. 'It just couldn't have happened the way she said that it did . . .' He reminds the jury of what Desley said at the committal hearing. 'She said she remembered going to the toilet and then having a lay down. It must have been a very memorable trip to the toilet, one would think, to remember it for 27 years.'

Davis crucifies Swifte. He tells the jury that the man is simply an alcoholic with his own agenda: to cut a sentencing deal with authorities. Joy Meyers is an ex-wife with an axe to grind. And the odontology witnesses? The evidence was more like a presentation, a show. 'You've got the very inexperienced Forrest, you've got the quite experienced Craig and you've got the fairly experienced Bamford, and the three experts can't actually agree on which teeth made which marks . . . the forensic evidence really doesn't assist you at all because it is obvious at the end of the day that that photograph and others like it are so bad that the experts can't come to a conclusion.'

This, Davis concludes, is a dreadful case. 'It's a hideous crime, this murder, and all of us would like to be able to say we can solve it, put poor Mrs Kennedy out of her misery, let her close the chapter, but you can't do that by convicting him just because he's there and he's the only one who's there; you really have to look at all the evidence and the vast majority of it is just junk. It's science gone a little bit crazy in a mad attempt to solve this horrible, horrible crime . . . The photographs: how could you possibly identify someone off that photograph of that bite mark? And what is left after that? An ex-wife, an ex-girlfriend and a criminal, Swifte . . .' If the jury approaches its evidence dispassionately and with intellectual honesty, he says, they would realise that the Crown had not gone within cooee of proving anything against his client, and would acquit him.

Justice Muir starts his summing-up to the jury mid-afternoon on 30 October. It would conclude hours later on day 18 of the trial.

'Members of the jury,' he begins. Carroll's family are watching him intently, eyes darting between the judge and Raymond, motionless in the dock. 'It is my duty now to sum up the case before you . . .' The accused, he says, comes before them clothed with the presumption of innocence. They must, Muir warns, disregard anything they may have seen, read or heard in the media, as pieces of evidence looked at in isolation from others can present a distorted and sometimes erroneous view. Their verdict has to be arrived at uninfluenced by external considerations.

With the passage of time, he says, memories fade and documents that may have been able to corroborate or disprove other evidence have been lost or destroyed. Witnesses who gave evidence in the first trial are now dead so their evidence is frozen in time. They should not allow any prejudices to colour their decision, he says, and must not allow the cruel nature of her murder to influence the way in which they approached their task. 'Remember the sole question that you are required to decide is the serious one of whether the accused, on the evidence before you, is guilty beyond reasonable doubt of the charge brought against him . . . If he did kill Deidre Kennedy, you may think it plain that that was something well known to him. If you conclude that this is not established beyond reasonable doubt, it follows that it has not been proved that the accused gave false testimony and the verdict must be not guilty . . .'

Muir deals carefully with Swifte's evidence, as he has advised Byrne and Davis that he would. 'He has been involved in unlawful and dishonest conduct throughout the whole of his adult life . . . For all of those reasons, it would be extremely dangerous to convict in reliance on Swifte's evidence alone and I . . . direct you also that his evidence should be treated with extreme caution.' As to the recruits: '. . . some of the course members do not remember any member being absent at any time, or cannot recall . . .'

The documentary evidence, he continues, is not all in the Crown's favour. 'There are air-force records which support the accused's contention that he was at the course at the time of the graduation. There is his individual kit records which bears the date 17 April 1973 with a signature against it which appears to be his . . . The first leave recorded was between 22 December 1973 and 6 January 1974 . . . There is thus not one official record put in evidence which supports the Crown's case that the accused was absent from the course in about the last week or, at least, from some time on 12 April . . .'

Reiterating the evidence of Meyers and Ferguson, he cautions that Desley Hill's account 'has some obvious difficulties'. Is it possible she is mistaken? Turning to the expert evidence, he notes that at this trial the conclusion was that the marks were made by the lower teeth – the opposite of what was said at the first trial. 'The consequence of the difference of opinion about which teeth caused the marks is that the two sets of experts, in effect, regarded the marks making up bite mark one as having been caused by teeth of markedly different shapes, sizes and characteristics . . . Dr Josephson . . . found only one bite mark as did Romaniuk, Sims and Brown. Bite mark two, as it has been called in this case, was not identified by any of those persons and one may infer that they . . . took considerable care with their observations.' He says that the jury should not put blind faith in the evidence of any expert. While Forrest, Bamford and Whittaker had been confident in their evidence in relation to bite mark identification, Dr Craig had not.

Lost evidence, he concludes, does not help, including 'some prison records . . . missing . . . which show when Mr Swifte left the area at Boggo Road in which he was in with the accused.'

On 2 November 2000, the jury retires just after 1pm. The judge indicates to them that he will not take their verdict after 6 o'clock that night, leaving those left behind in the court with the heightened sense of nervousness that always precedes a verdict. Many stay until 6pm, when it is obvious there will not be a verdict today.

Looking rested and confident, the jury returns to the court-house the next morning. Faye is not rested; neither she nor the rest of her family have managed a wink of sleep.

Near noon, the bailiff knocks. The jury has reached a verdict.

44

The judge's associate addresses the foreman. 'Members of the jury, are you agreed upon your verdict with respect to Raymond John Carroll?'

'Yes, we are.'

Raymond Carroll, his posture immutable, gazes straight ahead. Faye peers down at her lap and kneads a handkerchief between her hands, her mouth parched and her stomach turning somersaults. Ilma Carroll's eyes are fixed on the foreman, in a silent, desperate plea for the jury to let her son walk free.

'Do you find the accused, Raymond John Carroll, guilty or not guilty of perjury?'

It falls from their mouths, each juror in unison, each with the same verdict. 'Guilty.'

Faye, seated next to Cameron Herpich, throws her arms around him before dissolving into a paroxysm of sobs.

'So says your foreman, so say you all?'

'Yes.'

Ilma Carroll's sobs resound throughout the courtroom.

Herpich remains ashen-faced. He doesn't cry; it is unmanly to cry. He is happy for Faye that they'd got a guilty verdict. He feels as if there is an angel in court, the way things have just clicked into place.

Justice Muir pauses before thanking the jury. 'The trial was a long and difficult one and it was plain to me that you followed the evidence with utmost care . . .' Another brief pause. 'I call on the accused.'

'Raymond John Carroll,' the associate intones, 'you have been convicted of the charge, indictment that on the eighth day of March 1985, at Brisbane in the state of Queensland in the judicial proceedings, namely the trial of Raymond John Carroll, you murdered one Deidre Maree Kennedy and knowingly gave false testimony to the effect that you did not kill the said Deidre Kennedy, and the false testimony touched a matter which was material to a question then pending in these proceedings.

'Raymond John Carroll, do you have anything to say as to why sentence should not be passed on you?'

Carroll seems not to hear and Davis responds. 'My client has nothing to say, your Honour.'

Carroll, now 45, stands as his prior convictions are aired to the court. The first in Brisbane, 19 June 1987. Break and enter a dwelling house with intent in the night time and break and enter and doing wilful damage. A further conviction in the New South Wales local court at Leeton on 28 February 1992 for remaining on enclosed lands and offensive behaviour.

The defence objects that the offences have little relevance to this matter, but Michael Byrne outlines the break-in at the WAAF. 'The purpose was stealing of women's underwear and the accused was convicted, his fingerprints having been found on photographs belonging to one of the female service personnel . . . female underwear was taken and the wilful damage relates to the parts of the bras relevant to the nipples being cut from the bras and the parts relating to the vulval area and the underpants being cut from them. It was that matter which, of course, brought him to the attention of police in respect to the present matter.' He agrees that the offence in New South Wales does not bear a great deal of relevance to the present circumstances.

Byrne argues that Carroll should get the maximum term as it is impossible to imagine a worse case. 'What the prisoner has done is to falsely swear under oath on his own trial for murder to avoid a sentence of life imprisonment and, indeed, he has achieved through various means that result. The verdict of the jury makes it clear that they found, as the trial was litigated, that he was guilty of the murder of Deidre Kennedy . . . Of course he cannot be punished for that but the submission is the circumstances of the offence, its result, the effect it has had – part of which is reflected in the victim impact statements your Honour has just read upon the family.'

'Yes,' Justice Muir agrees, 'but of course it hasn't had that effect; the murder has had that effect.'

Davis points out that the victim impact statements effectively concentrated on the damage done by the murder, and, while he agrees that there is no doubt that the Kennedy family has suffered shockingly, that damage has not been caused by the perjury. 'That damage is caused by the death of the child and Carroll does have the benefit of that acquittal.' He submits that a jail term of between seven to 10 years would be appropriate for his client, not the maximum sentence.

It is done; verdict in, submissions over. Justice Muir glances up at Carroll as he delivers sentence. 'Raymond John Carroll, you have been convicted by a jury on the charge that on your trial for the murder of Deidre Kennedy you knowingly gave false testimony to the effect that you did not kill Deidre Kennedy. In short, you perjured yourself in an attempt to secure your acquittal.

'In the event, your perjury achieved no result. The jury disbelieved you and your perjured evidence did not lead to the appellate courts decision to quash that conviction. Perjury offences are regarded as serious offences. Generally, they are hard to detect and to prove and they have an obvious tendency to undermine the whole basis of the administration of justice . . . This is a very serious instance of perjury for two reasons: firstly, because it was committed in a trial for murder, the penalty for which is life imprisonment and for the purpose of attempting to avoid a conviction; secondly, the false evidence concerned the very issue in the murder trial.

'It is necessary to bear in mind that the sentence being imposed is for perjury, not for murder. It is important not to let the horrific nature of the crime perpetrated on Deidre Kennedy, and its profound impact on the lives of her family, divert attention from that fact . . . Although, as I have said, this is a very serious instance of perjury, in my view there are categories which may be regarded as more serious . . . with those considerations in mind, I sentence you to a term of imprisonment for 12 years.'

Faye cries with relief when the sentencing is finished, but part of the judge's statement will echo in her ears forever. *Although, as I have said, this is a very serious instance of perjury, in my view there are categories which may be regarded as more serious . . .* What, she thinks, could be more serious than this?

Carroll is allowed a five-minute audience with his wife, Marilyn, as he stands in the dock. Her face is awash with despair, and she huddles into herself as she walks out past the Kennedy family, after Carroll is led away. They have only been married seven months.

The Kennedys sit in court, hugging Reynolds and Herpich. Faye manages a small smile for the cameras as she walks from court, the first time in many years she can remember feeling a sense of relief. It is, one journalist notes, a smile that replaces the stressed, haunted, sad appearance she has worn as she has run the media gauntlet at Carroll's two long trials.

Desperately shy and private, it has been excruciating for Faye to be in the media limelight. As they lead Carroll away, she thinks, *I damn you to hell.* He is going to jail, where he belongs, and she hopes he never gets out. And for her family, it is now a chance to try and get back to normal, out of the glare of the press.

Faye looks at Herpich. Like John Reynolds before him, he has never given up, worked at it as if he was a man possessed. She will never forget what he and the prosecution team have done and affords herself a quiet smile. She likes to think of Deidre as inspiration to help obtain justice for other little children who have been victims of evil.

Peter Davis goes straight down to the cells to see Carroll after sentencing. He is gutted at the verdict, thought the trial had gone well, that the jury would acquit. He thanks Davis for his hard work.

When he leaves the courthouse, Davis heads to his office. Within two hours, he and Liz Wilson have drawn up the grounds for appeal.

John Reynolds pumps Herpich's hand, tells him that when they were first introduced, he thought he was a pompous little prick. The new style of policeman, who doesn't bend the rules at all. Dots the i's, crosses the t's before he makes his next move. But he shakes his hand and congratulates him, tells him he's done a bloody good job. But Reynolds can't resist adding a cheeky rider. 'We'd have got the same result.'

Barry Kennedy is outside court with Faye, Stephanie, Derek and the police. He declines the opportunity to join them for a celebratory drink, muttering that he would have a drink with his brother instead. It sounds thoughtless, and he is sorry for that. But the truth is he has no interest in sharing this private moment with Cameron Herpich, whom he believes has treated him with utter disdain by not keeping him up to speed on an investigation about his own daughter.

Barry walks along George Street in the opposite direction.

The prison van is leaving the Supreme Court, a grim Carroll hunched in the back cage. The vehicle is heading to the Arthur Gorrie Correctional Centre, where his classification will be assessed in the remand area. Camera crews film the van as it leaves the court precinct, and a handful of people mingle to give him a send-off. 'Filthy bastard! I hope you burn in hell!' a woman screams out.

'Don't worry, hell is where he's headed,' a bloke mutters. 'He'll be bashed senseless as soon as he gets there.'

The *Queensland Times*, in simple language, covers the verdict on its front page. 'LIAR.' Lauded by the popular press as a victory of common sense over the law, one journalist sounds a note of caution.

> Thwarted on the murder charge, the prosecution nailed [Carroll] through the back door charge of perjury. It was a salutary reminder to those of a criminal bent — and their allies – that the justice system has a multitude of weapons in its arsenal. But the perjury option is a weapon of limited value while accused people cannot be compelled to give sworn testimony. Our system, of course, is not always about finding out the truth . . .

The perjury option is good enough for Faye, who speaks gently to Deidre before she goes to sleep that night. 'It's over at last, Dee Dee darling. We're free of it now.'

PART FIVE
Perjury Acquittal: October 2000

'Appeal. In law, to put the dice into the box for another throw.'

(Ambrose Bierce 1842-1914)

45

Peter Davis and Liz Wilson are vigorous in attacking the Crown's evidence and they prepare numerous grounds for appeal. Identification using bite marks was inadmissible and should have been excluded. Forensic odontology had not reached a stage of scientific development that enabled identification of an offender by comparison of a cast of the suspect's teeth with a photograph showing diffuse bruising. The evidence of the witnesses Hill, Ferguson, Grinter, Gnezdihoff and Swifte was inadmissible, unsafe and unsatisfactory. It was an abuse of process based on the double jeopardy principles. Much of the evidence was circumstantial. The judge should have stayed the prosecution as no fair trial could be achieved due to time delay and lost evidence.

Davis knows from the outset his case is strong. A jury will hang a man on emotion; the Appeals Court only sees fact and logic.

Carroll has been in Wacol for nine months. Liz Wilson has now opted out of the case and Carroll's new defence barrister, Milton Griffin, with Peter Davis as his junior, is arguing it before the Queensland Court of Appeal. Griffin, admitted to the Bar in 1975, is known as a fine legal intellectual with extensive experience in criminal law. He took silk in December 1999, 10 months before his appearance for Carroll, funded by Legal Aid.

His client's conviction, he tells the court, may not be legal because it was predicated on the Crown effectively running a second murder trial. He had been acquitted of murder, was immune from other trials on that charge and should be released from prison immediately. Michael Byrne rises to argue the contrary. Carroll, he says, had given false testimony. The perjury conviction should stand and Carroll's sentence increased on the grounds that it is manifestly inadequate.

Justice Glen Williams errs on the side of the defence. He writes in his judgment:

It really was a retrial for murder rather than a perjury trial . . . the indictment identifies the lie as being that he hadn't killed her, and that seems to me the very thing a jury wasn't entitled to do – to retry on that particular issue.

The only real issue is whether Carroll had told a lie when in that trial he said he did not kill Deidre Kennedy.

And what was the prosecution's case? Opportunity. Hill's evidence. The appellant's propensity – supported by canteen worker Diane Ferguson – for biting small children. Odontological evidence. The jail confession to Swifte.

In his written judgment, Justice Williams launches straight into an attack on the witnesses' 'new evidence'. Hill's and Ferguson's statements, he notes, did not amount to proof that Carroll had perjured himself at his murder trial. At best, he concedes, it might 'strengthen a circumstantial case . . . that he was responsible for the death, but that was not the main issue at this trial'.

He tears Swifte's evidence apart; critically, his claim that he had spoken to Carroll at Boggo Road over a couple of days, the time when he said he had cautioned him he was a 'shot duck' because bite marks were as good as fingerprints. He questions, also, Swifte's failure to reveal the confession between February 1984 and the trial in February 1985. Swifte's decision to ignore the advice of the prison officer who had told him to speak to someone else about Carroll's confession comes under fire. By the time of the perjury trial, the officer to whom he had allegedly spoken was dead. And Swifte's reason for ignoring the advice – because he did not want to get involved – was not, according to Williams, a satisfactory explanation.

The vision of the child at the end of the bed was quickly dispatched; whether caused by delirium tremors or a true apparition, it had earned him a reduction in his prison sentence. Williams criticises the trial judge for not referring to some of Swifte's assertions in his summing-up, including his claim that his conversations with Carroll had taken place over a number of days.

While the judge had warned that Swifte's evidence should be treated with 'extreme caution', Williams has gone further:

What the jury were not told . . . was that [it] was highly unlikely to be true (perhaps more likely to be untrue) because the appellant had been in Boggo Road for no more than approximately 24 hours. There was clearly no time for Swifte to have had the series of conversations he swore to over a 'couple of days'. The underlying premise in Swifte's evidence is that it was not on the first occasion they met in Boggo Road that the alleged confession to murder was made. That came at a later date . . .

Williams then delivers his coup de grâce.

[Swifte's] evidence should have been excluded. It could not meet the test of being substantial new evidence . . . Not only was it not excluded at trial, but it went to the jury on that basis that they could, subject to a mild warning, accept it as direct evidence of a confession . . .

The jury decision, he writes, was 'unsafe and unsatisfactory' – sufficient, in his view, to set the conviction aside.

He then turns to opportunity. The evidence at the perjury trial, he notes, was substantially the same as that at the murder trial, save for Desley Hill's assertions. Her parents – the two people she said were at the house when Carroll visited on 14 April 1973 – were dead and her story could not be checked. Hill, he continues, had been approached by a police officer in March 2000 and she had admitted he had jogged her memory. 'It seems clear that some input from the police officer was necessary in order for the witness Hill to be able to place the events in question in point of time.' The judge criticises her placing of the date in context with her pregnancy. 'Her evidence immediately runs into problems because there is no doubt [Carroll] . . . was on the Edinburgh base . . .' Hill, he notes, was able to pinpoint the date she saw Carroll by the news item of Deidre Kennedy's murder, but was unclear about other events around that time. Her evidence, he concludes, did not positively place Carroll in Ipswich, was not new and significant, and did not substantially point to perjury.

The time lapse between April 1973 and November 2000, Williams writes, clouded clear recollections of RAAF witnesses. Relevant RAAF documents had been lost. And the photograph?

> It is correct that on the murder trial, [Carroll] gave evidence of where he was standing at the material time. True that [it] shows some part of the general area referred to by the appellant. But that does not prove he was not there; he could have been just outside the area shown . . .

After making a logical, objective assessment of the entire evidence, on 21 September 2001 the three justices of the Court of Criminal Appeal – President Margaret McMurdo and Justices Williams and Holmes – deliver their unanimous decision. Appeal allowed. Conviction set aside and accused acquitted. Appeal by Attorney-General against sentence dismissed.

Carroll knows the decision is going to be handed down today, goes around to the blokes in the yard with a cocky jaunt, and says, 'See you later.' A short time after, he is called up to the office, told, 'You're outta here. Go and pack.' He goes up to the visiting area, yells out 'Yes!' and throws all his gear together.

Raymond has been in jail for his first wedding anniversary. All the time he was inside, Marilyn cried. He had gone down for 12 years, a long time to be without him. The solicitors ring her at their home in Ipswich and tell her he's been acquitted. Her first question is, 'Can I go get him?' She rings the prison and they say no, because they haven't got the paperwork. After phone calls back and forth, it is nearly five o'clock, but finally she gets a call that says she can go and pick him up now. She gets in the car and drives as fast as she can get there.

Garner and Forrest are poised for the appeal decision, and decimated by it. Their new evidence had not passed the scrutiny of the appeal court, but they stand by it. 'There is no question in my mind who produced those bite marks,' Forrest comments. 'I can't say that Raymond Carroll is the person who *murdered* Deidre but the odds are so high that he was the *biter* as to make no difference from certainty. Because circulation was still occurring to produce bruising, I am confident she was alive when these marks were inflicted. Also, there was no evidence of bite marks on her before she went missing, which led us to this conclusion.'

They subjected the second bite, he says, to the same analysis as the first and again reached the same conclusions. 'The balance of probability was that they were Carroll's teeth. Two bite marks, analysed separately and independently, with the same patterns. Add the number of similarities and the case is very strong.'

Davis is pleased at the outcome. It speaks for itself. The basis of the Court of Criminal Appeal's decision was that there was insufficient evidence in the Crown case to identify his client as Deidre Kennedy's killer. He believes there were aspects of the evidence that had gaping holes. For example, he says, Cameron Herpich understandably wanted to bolster Swifte's evidence by proving that Swifte and Carroll had been in jail together. That was obviously why the gate book was put into evidence. But, the book showed the day on which Carroll went *into* custody but not the date he came out and prison files apparently didn't show when he came out. But, he says, everyone knew that Carroll had bail during the first trial so he would have thought that it was a simple task – which the defence actually did – to search the Supreme Court files and obtain a release date. The defence never produced documents substantiating the bail situation, because they were shown to Byrne who then made an admission to the jury about Carroll's release. Swifte said the confession occurred after he and Carroll had been together for five days, but the Crown admitted they were only in jail together for about 24 hours. Davis has another thought. Isn't it rather odd, that evidence was right under their nose in the legal centre of Brisbane – George St – but not looked at for the release date from Boggo Road? Yet, they can go halfway around the world, to London, to find incriminating evidence against Carroll? The bottom line, he ruminates, is this case should never have been re-opened. Right from the start, with those newspaper articles that were popping up like mushrooms about new witnesses, etc – it should have stayed closed. It only served to gut Faye and her family and was doomed to failure. In his opinion the evidence, quite simply, did not stack up.

When Faye hears the news of Carroll's successful appeal and acquittal, she doesn't go anywhere; instead sits in the gathering dark and stares into space. She does not move until daylight. In Longreach, Barry wanders about, stunned. This has become a nightmare, from which there now seems no escape.

PART SIX
High Court Appeal: 2002

'We've lost, Faye. It's all over.'

Detective-Sergeant Cameron Herpich

46

Prosecutors immediately flag a High Court challenge, and John Reynolds demands one. 'How can two juries be wrong . . . what the hell is happening to our judicial system?' he fumes when he hears the decision. 'I don't think anyone can believe it, and it is just devastating for the family.'

In October 2001, Faye sends a letter to the Hon. Ron Welford, the Attorney-General of Queensland and the Minister for Justice. She calls it 'A Mother's Plea'. Setting out the details of Deidre's story, she writes:

> It seems to me that the Justice system has failed in every aspect. How can this person be found guilty by two separate juries and be allowed to walk free? It is my under-standing that the reason we have juries in our Justice system is to make the decision as to guilty or not. How can a judge overrule this decision . . . Why do we bother with a jury? What is wrong with our Justice system or do we have one at all? . . . The Justice system most certainly needs to be revisited and a better system put into practice, or our laws need to be changed. I hereby beg you, Mr Welford, to grant us the opportunity for the Crown to take this case to the High Court so that justice can be served.

It is a big ask. Notoriously difficult to receive an audience with judges who sit on the Full Bench, the highest court in the land is riddled with stiff convention and concerned only with the minute detail of legal principles. Lawyers call it the toughest gig in town, where even the slightest blemish in their argument will send them packing. Make a mistake in front of those justices, they say, and lawyers are hosed, wigs and all out of court.

In March 2002, two judges failed to make a decision on

whether the Crown should have special leave to appeal and refer to a full High Court. Faye's wish is granted.

As homage to Deidre, the High Court is filled to capacity when it convenes three months later to hear legal submissions. Faye, Stephanie and Derek are flanked by Reynolds, Herpich, Forrest and Garner. Barry is in Longreach. Derek turns to see if Carroll is in court. He is not.

Michael Byrne addresses Chief Justice Gleeson and his four fellow justices. It is, as always, dressed in legalese. Byrne has two main grounds: that the Court of Appeal was wrong in its findings on the new evidence presented at trial and that it was wrong in finding the trial was an abuse of process.

Senior Counsel Milton Griffin and Peter Davis again appear for Carroll and argue that the question of whether he murdered Deidre has already been resolved by the Court of Appeal. The perjury trial, Griffin says, had simply added an extra ingredient – that he had told a lie – and was essentially no more than a re-litigation of the central issue.

The High Court invites further submissions on aspects of Queensland's Criminal Code and reserves its decision on whether the principle of double jeopardy has been breached.

The story is receiving blanket media coverage. Peter Davis sighs: here is yet another request from a television outlet to talk about the case. They seem to think that because Raymond Carroll and his family won't talk, his lawyers are the next best chance. Davis won't come to the party.

'I am in receipt of various communications from you wherein you have advised that you are preparing to air a story on Mr Carroll's case and inviting comment from those representing him,' he replies to a journalist. 'It is obvious from media reports since Mr Carroll's acquittal in the Court of Appeal that some of those involved as witnesses for the prosecution of Mr Carroll are willing to discuss the case. That, of course, is a matter for those persons. Those defending Mr Carroll (myself included) take the view that it is inappropriate to ventilate, in detail, aspects of the case until all litigation is concluded. Unfortunately, if you do not share this view then, given some of the Crown witnesses' eagerness to speak about the matter, any report of yours will necessarily only tell one side of the story . . .'

The same people who attended the High Court hearing are waiting at Brisbane's Federal Court building for the decision. Saying little, mute with tension, their hope is that if the outcome goes in their favour then Carroll could possibly be tried for a third time.

It is three weeks before Christmas, 29 years after Deidre's death. The Full Bench of the High Court is handing down its judgment in Canberra and Byrne nervously keeps checking his watch. It shouldn't be too much longer. Herpich's hands are thrust deep into his pockets, his hands clenched into anxious fists.

A television journalist is walking toward Faye, a camera crew trailing in her wake. 'I'm so sorry about the decision, Mrs Kennedy. It's tragic.'

'What decision? Has it come in?'

'Oh. Haven't you heard?' The reporter is visibly embarrassed, whips her head around to stare at Michael Byrne. 'You haven't heard yet?' She is trying to back away. 'Look, it hasn't been confirmed. I'm sorry. Really sorry.'

Cameron Herpich feels it like a kick deep in his guts. Faye is looking at him, her face haunted with despair. 'What does she mean, Cameron? What does she mean?'

He swallows hard. 'We've lost, Faye. It's all over.'

He reaches out to catch her as she collapses.

The written judgment has been presented in the stiff language of the judiciary. No jury here to cringe when they see the exhibits. No witnesses to cast doubts. No family members to weep as they hear the evidence. Five justices, examining points of law.

In a joint judgment, Chief Justice Gleeson and Justice Hayne say the Court of Appeal was right in staying the indictment for perjury. The issues at both trials, they argue, had the same focus: did Raymond Carroll kill Deidre Kennedy? Justices Mary Gaudron and William Gummow find the laying of the indictment constituted an abuse of process and was, simply, an attempt to re-litigate the earlier prosecution. The Court of Appeal was correct as a matter of law. Justice Michael McHugh finds that the Crown's appeal should be dismissed because the charge of perjury against Carroll undermined his acquittal of murder. The Crown's appeal based on the new evidence has not been analysed by the High Court; its finding on the abuse of process, it says, did not make that necessary.

It is a judgment Carroll celebrates at his Ipswich home by punching the air and hugging Marilyn. They can never take his freedom away again.

For Faye Kennedy and her family, the findings mean only one thing: there are no avenues left.

Cameron Herpich wants to get Faye away from the media that has now surrounded them at the Federal Court building. Peter Davis is shocked when he sees Faye's reaction. He thinks she is going to die, has never seen anyone that distraught, before or since. He feels terrible for her, but angry too that it had come to this in the first place.

Granite-jawed and distressed, Herpich holds on to her as they walk out through a side building. Weeping uncontrollably, a hand covering her mouth, Faye is bent over, crippled with emotional pain. The press is following them, and Herpich shepherds Faye into a restaurant, the only place they can seek refuge. He speaks to the journalists as he bars their entrance at the door. 'Listen, enough is enough. You can see the state Mrs Kennedy is in. She has endured so much. Please leave her alone.' The media retreats back down the street, already formulating their stories in their heads.

The press releases the story under headline banners and the letters to the editor pour in. No one understands the decision.

Devastated at the outcome, Michael Byrne is, at the same time, pragmatic. The Crown had done the best it could. It had a second go at Carroll. It had failed.

No one, he says, will ever know if Deidre's sexual assault descended to rape, because the technology just wasn't available to determine that at the time of her murder. At the first trial, evidence was led that the hairs found were similar to Carroll's — that was the extent of the technology. By the time the second trial was being worked up, mitochondrial DNA testing had become widely used. It hadn't been done in Queensland before, and the John Tonge Centre attempted to do it. Sadly, Byrne says, the hair was destroyed. There is absolutely no doubt in his mind that that evidence would have secured the truth of the killer's involvement. But he recognises the irony that even if that had been proven to be Carroll's pubic hair, the double jeopardy ruling would still have overturned that.

On the law, he says, it was found prior to trial that this was not double jeopardy. Carroll was tried and convicted for the murder and later acquitted, and the Crown didn't go behind that. Eight years later he was tried for having told a lie in the witness box at his murder trial. Carroll didn't, he says, have to get in the witness box; he didn't have to tell a lie; but he did. If he hadn't got in the witness stand, there wouldn't have been a perjury prosecution. And that to Byrne is the greatest irony of all. What the High Court has said is that anyone has immunity from perjury. A person can take an oath, or an affirmation, to tell the truth and can do so without any sanction apart from biblical. And that doesn't make any sense to him at all.

A comment by journalist Tony Koch in Brisbane's *Courier Mail* encapsulates the public's feeling:

> The British legal system has served our type of democracy well for centuries. There is no argument that the appeal process is necessary and myriad examples exist where appeal judges have overturned injustices. But in the case of baby Deidre, the question will forever be asked how it came about that two separate juries — decades apart — could

find a person was guilty in regard to her murder, but the verdicts never stood. Justice, in its most intricate exactness, might have been afforded Raymond John Carroll. But what justice has Deidre Kennedy – aged 17 months – ravaged and murdered and then thrown lifeless on to a toilet block, received?

PART SEVEN
Double Jeopardy

Nemo debet bis puniri pro uno delicto

(No man ought to be punished twice
for one offence)

Courtesy William Nicholson

47

Following the High Court decision, in 2003 the *Australian* newspaper, under the stewardship of its editor-in-chief, Chris Mitchell, explores the legal option of bringing Carroll before a civil court. Unlike the legal system in the United States, which successfully – and spectacularly – re-tried OJ Simpson in a civil case, such a move is unprecedented in Australia. The legal fraternity is divided between the opinion that justice has not been served, and those who claim that bringing a civil action would be tantamount to persecution, not prosecution.

Mitchell, a former editor-in-chief of Brisbane's *Courier Mail*, is well aware of the emotion generated in Queensland at the mere mention of the Kennedy story. A feeling of frustration, even resentment in that state, that two jury decisions were overturned. People, he muses, do not necessarily understand the technicalities of the law; all they want to know is, has justice been served, and, if not, is it going to be served?

The *Australian* looks to a British campaign by the *Daily Mail* newspaper that ultimately led to changes to the protection afforded by double jeopardy rules. It was a story all too familiar in a Britain riven by racial tensions. In 1993, 18-year-old black student Stephen Lawrence was stabbed to death by five white youths, all of whom were arrested. Whilst charges against two were dropped, three proceeded to trial where the jury was ordered to acquit. Under the terms of the double jeopardy principle, this ruled out any further charges being brought against them. The *Daily Mail*'s 'Justice for Stephen Lawrence' campaign was designed to lure the youths into suing for libel, which would entice them back into court. Bold headlines above their photographs carried a simple message. 'Murderers.'

In February 1997, the Coroner's Court ruled Stephen Lawrence's death an unlawful killing and, five months later, the government established the McPherson Inquiry into the investigation and the culture of racism in the police force. By early 1998, the Blair government agreed to recommendations of the McPherson Inquiry; three years later, the Law Commission recommended that the rule against double jeopardy be changed with regard to murder, which it has been since.

Mitchell has little patience with civil libertarians who publicly denounce further legal options against Carroll as harassment or who claim an offer to fund any action is no more than a publicity stunt. Newspapers, he says, have an important role to play in exposing injustice and campaigning against it, whether that be at a personal or systemic level. The concept of double jeopardy does not apply in civil cases. The burden of proof is also markedly different: where the test in a Supreme Court is 'beyond reasonable doubt', a civil case turns on the balance of probability. Could a civil action be successful? It would first have to get to court, and their advice is that this case is right on the outer limits. But if it was given the green light, the *Australian* has been told that the chances with a civil jury are positive.

On behalf of the *Australian*, Queensland's then Crime Commissioner, Tim Carmody, looks at the options to back a civil action. There are obvious problems. One was the time constraint, Mitchell says. In Queensland, the statutory limitation to bring such an action is between three and six years. Deidre Kennedy was murdered in 1973 – 31 years ago – so that would need to be addressed. In effect, the Supreme Court would have to grant a time extension and that is by no means a given. The goal would also need to be realistic: what outcome is Faye Kennedy hoping for? It is not money – Carroll has none and this is not about money for Faye – so the basis of the action would likely be on the grounds of emotional distress. Because Carroll has been acquitted of both murder and perjury, then the best option may be to push the civil case on the grounds of the baby's abduction.

Carmody finds that despite many obstacles, Faye Kennedy has grounds to take Carroll before a civil court and that if he could get it to a civil jury, he is optimistic about the possible outcome. He recognises that the High Court does not need to consider the strength of the evidence against Carroll on perjury, having already decided that to even bring the perjury charge into a criminal court amounted to a relevant abuse of process. That is the end of it; the strength of evidence is irrelevant. But civilly, Faye could take action for the delayed onset of nervous shock, which could override Queensland's usual statutory period of limitation for a civil prosecution.

The office of Raymond Carroll's solicitor, Peter Russo, is a short block from police headquarters: handy, as he spends half his working life there trying to keep his clients out of the nick.

Russo has a big voice, honed from years of snapping at police heels. He is a character, passionate to the point of obsession. You put two and two together, he says of the Carroll case, and what do you come up with? A mess.

The tensions against the defence, he says, were palpable in the Carroll case. Hysteria and media hype didn't help. He admits people have ice in their veins if they aren't moved by the story but would warn that one must look at the facts, not gut feeling.

Russo describes the evidence against Carroll as a whole heap of hocus-pocus. In his opinion, the teeth evidence was no better at the second trial than it was at the first, even with the advanced technology. He has his suspicions about why the police and the Crown pushed so hard: he thinks promises had been made to Faye Kennedy and they followed it through from there. The police, he says, always believe that they've got their man, but the reality is, they don't always have. It's just the way the system works.

Russo says the problem was the length of time between when the offence was first committed and when they ultimately charged Carroll. It added up, he believes, to a lost opportunity to solve something, making it more difficult to piece it all together.

Just because Carroll is a loner, he says, does not qualify him as a psychopath. And there is a quantum leap between mutilating female underwear, however distasteful that might be, to doing what they reckon Carroll did. He admits his advice to Carroll is to ignore the stories written over the years, insisting on his guilt despite two acquittals.

The media, he believes, have set traps for him, taunting him, *go on, sue us for defamation*. But the minute he sues, the shoe is on the other foot, and he then has to prove the case again, that what they said was not true. He doesn't have the resources to take anyone on. It's expensive to run a civil challenge and he can't get Legal Aid for that.

Russo can't understand why the police did not follow the description given by Nugget Carroll and says the other point police always want to gloss over is that it was total bedlam the day after it happened. This was not an inner city, densely populated area where it is easy for someone to hide. Everybody knows everybody else; you go into town, people know if there's a stranger around and they know the kid who's gone away to join the RAAF and come back for the weekend.

Props, make-believe, the law as theatre. The magician pulls a rabbit out of his hat. Sim-sala-bim. Smoke and mirrors. But there was no magic in Carroll's appeal win. It's not every day, Russo says, that the appeal courts interfere with a jury verdict. By his reckoning there was no magic in that, no trickery. The evidence was simply not sustainable.

The day we meet, I tell Russo I would like to inverview Carroll.

He laughs. Course I would. People have wanted to interview him for more than 20 years. But there is nothing to be achieved by him talking to me, he says. That's just the sad reality of the situation.

Will Russo at least ask him on my behalf?

He will do that. But he knows what the answer will be.

No.

Barry Kennedy is no crusader. A reserved, quiet man, he returned to his roots after the breakdown of his marriage to Faye, back to hot and dusty outback Longreach. Far from big-city legal decisions, scientific argument and police investigations. He has not much time for the circus that rolled on through convictions, appeals and High Courts and even less for the double jeopardy laws. Laws are all very fine, he thinks, but try understanding them when it is *your* daughter who has been murdered. Law-makers, Barry believes, should walk in the shoes of the victims and their families when they make weighty decisions.

Of all the murder cases in Australian legal history, it is the Deidre Kennedy story that has pushed for changes to the double jeopardy law, the one story that has inflamed and outraged public opinion. Festering through two appeals, the issue comes to a head following the High Court's ruling. Across the country, talk-back radio is jammed with callers demanding answers, television airs the public's disgust and disquiet, and newspapers afford the story columns of space. Double jeopardy is a hotly debated, emotive subject. In November 2002, an editorial published in the Adelaide *Advertiser* had seethed with indignation.

> Let's imagine, for a moment, that a person was acquitted of a murder 20 years ago. Evidence about blood samples was largely circumstantial and inconclusive and the jury had its doubts. The verdict must be not guilty. Today, DNA testing of those blood samples would prove beyond doubt what science could not prove 20 years ago. If police reopened the case they might be able to prosecute successfully. Under the present law they can't.

The debate continues for months. The jury system, an editorial in the *Queensland Times* states in April 2003, is not perfect, but dumping its decisions on the basis of legal interpretations in no way enhances the delivery of justice.

The message from the punters and from the fourth estate is clear. The rights of the accused have usurped those of the victim. The law is truly an ass. With the chorus of protest pushing for change, the barricades have to fall.

Enter a politician.

Six weeks before the February 2003 State election, New South Wales Premier Bob Carr declares that, if re-elected, his government will overturn the double jeopardy rule. We owe it, he says, to the victims of these crimes to make sure the guilty are brought to justice. His sentiments echo that of British Prime Minister Tony

Blair, when he had argued in favour of substantially reducing the double jeopardy rule in his country. We will, he says, rebalance the system emphatically in favour of the victims of crime, for offenders get away too easily.

On the back of Carr's announcement, the Standing Committee of Attorneys-General of Australia, with the cautious support of the Federal Government, announces it will review the double jeopardy principle.

Carr keeps his promise. Returned to office in April, he reiterates plans for abolition of the ancient rule. But problems are already looming. Lawyers warn that New South Wales should not stand alone as a rogue state. It would be far preferable that there is a national approach from all states. Queensland and Western Australia support review, but Victoria drags its feet on fundamental change. Watching from the wings, Prime Minister John Howard indicates he will back changes to allow for retrials in exceptional circumstances.

The mooted changes to double jeopardy follow the British lead, arguing for a re-trial for serious offences such as murder, manslaughter, rape and firearm offences if compelling new evidence subsequently emerges indicating that the acquitted person is guilty. In Britain, the law operates retrospectively; defendants already acquitted will still be able to be re-tried. Many advocates for change hope Australia will also enact retrospective laws.

However, change to the law, no matter how minimal, is not going to be straightforward.

A letter to the editor of the *Queensland Times* in February 2003 made this point:

> This archaic English law now works against the person on the street by allowing murderers, rapists and drug barons to remain at large. But with scientific advances of recent years, which can prove the guilt of an individual, it is unacceptable such new evidence cannot be used in a later trial . . .

In the first week of April 2003, the ABC television program 'Australian Story' airs an episode titled 'Double Bind'. Introduced by Bob Carr, it proves to be one of the higher-rating programs for the year. Across five states, 1.14 million viewers tune in.

> Tonight's *Australian Story* is about a notorious murder case unsolved for 30 years, back in the news because of moves to change the law itself. At issue is the legal principle of double jeopardy . . . Late this week, Attorneys-General from around Australia will meet to look at this very question. But behind all the legal arguments is a human tragedy, the death of a baby called Deidre Kennedy.

The program does not pull any punches. With the main players from both trials – bar anyone from the Carroll family who declined to be interviewed – interviewed, the message is blunt. Raymond Carroll had been acquitted because the law was over-technical. It concludes with stark words on the screen: 'Faye Kennedy is now hoping to take civil action against Raymond John Carroll . . . Mrs Kennedy says she doesn't want compensation but hopes for an acknowledgment from the justice system that Mr Carroll is responsible for Deidre's death.'

Viewer comments pour in to the on-line forum after the show, overwhelmingly supporting change. '*Double jeopardy is an anachronism.*' '*This law must be changed to keep pace with changes in forensics and medicine.*' '*I often wonder if our Appeal and High Court Judges have become techno-judges – worried more about the technical points of law rather than the law itself.*'

Many messages, like the letters and cards sent to Faye's home, are personal. '*Our hearts, prayers and support go to Faye and her family.*' '*My deepest compassion to the Kennedy family. I salute their bravery.*' '*For Faye to have gone through two trials with such outcomes is outrageous.*' '*As an Australian, I would like to apologise to the Kennedys for the unimaginable pain that they must carry with them.*'

Angelo Vasta, who entered the double jeopardy debate afer the High Court decision, says that whilst our law states that a person shall not be twice convicted for the same offence, Carroll wasn't. The issue in the second case was, did he swear falsely that he did not kill the baby? The double jeopardy concept, he says, stems from the fact that if a person is tried by a jury of their peers and found not guilty, they ought not be re-tried by a jury in an identical matter. But when a not guilty verdict is entered by a court on appeal, the same constitutional sanctity does not apply. The High Court has made that plain in a number of cases but, in this case, it was not reminded of that. The term 'miscarriage of justice', he adds, generally applies to a person who has done a long stint in jail for murder, which it is ultimately found he didn't commit. But, he asks, is this also a miscarriage of justice?

But Vasta believes that even if changes in the law are made retrospective, and if new evidence was to emerge, Raymond Carroll should not face court again. He thinks if that happened, the feeling would be that it was more persecution than prosecution. Fair is fair. Enough is enough.

In April 2003 former policeman and Federal Member for Dickson in Queensland, Peter Dutton and Faye Kennedy circulate a petition asking Queenslanders to sign for an overhaul of the double jeopardy rules. The petition is called 'Deidre's Law' and their expectations are modest. They hope for 10,000 signatures in 12 weeks.

'Deidre's Law' petition is distributed predominantly in Brisbane and south-east Queensland. It reaches way beyond its target: beyond all their expectations, more than 33,000 people put their signatures on the petition. It is the second-largest petition ever tabled in the Queensland Legislative Assembly.

The support for her petition has given Faye Kennedy confidence that the justice she wants might one day be served.

Late in the afternoon of 8 September 2003, Dutton delivers his grievance debate on double jeopardy to the Queensland Legislative Assembly. It is not the first time Dutton has spoken in the House on the issue and the need for reform. Referring directly to the Kennedy case, he says: 'The presence of this law in our states' legal systems in its current form has resulted in at least one grave injustice and certainly has the potential to create many more . . . My message today to the Queensland Premier, Peter Beattie, and his Attorney-General, Rod Welford, is that you need to have the courage to make a commitment and a decision, just as New South

Wales has . . . that double jeopardy will be reformed . . . I can tell you that there is no doubt in the mind of Mrs Kennedy or anybody with knowledge of this case that the evidence proves the suspect's guilt – no doubt at all. Yet, 30 years after the crime, this killer is allowed to walk free . . . In my view it is a travesty that advances in forensic technology mean nothing in this case because double jeopardy prevents a retrial to prove the suspect's guilt . . . I share a view with Mrs Kennedy that there is something basically and fundamentally wrong with a legal system that allows a child killer and rapist to walk free . . .'

Outlining the petition, he says it is not about challenging the rights of the defendants or the finality of the justice system; it is about providing justice to those who have had the most horrific circumstances inflicted upon them. About creating a system to put serious offenders in jail when the evidence proves they committed the crime.

Political media advisers keep track of public opinion on double jeopardy laws, which is, on the whole, scathing. A *Queensland Times* editorial rages:

> It's about time that the general public woke up to the corrupt and out-of-date Common Law system, imported from England when Australia was first settled. The whole edifice is rotten from the top to the bottom. Probably a daunting task, though long overdue, for an overhauling commission without replacing the whole system which the Law Society feeds off like seagulls following fishing boats or vultures seeking out carrion . . . People power and citizens rights are now on the move with the Deidre's Law petition which will overthrow lawyers – in democracy, not a totalitarian regime – giving them the message that the 800-year-old law has no relevance today and to stop trying to hoodwink the public taxpayers.
>
> The terms of sentencing whittled down by Machiavellian lawyers is another area of vociferous public disquiet and disgust . . .

In early September 2003, the Model Criminal Code Officers' Committee – a national body of criminal law experts – raises concerns that the pressure to secure a conviction in the Deidre Kennedy case had precipitated a number of Premiers and former Chief Justices to support the partial abolition of the double jeopardy principle. 'What this would seem to indicate,' they write, 'is that in a high-profile case the pressure to push for a re-trial after an unsuccessful prosecution would be enormous. It also seems unlikely that the presumption of innocence could be retained at a re-trial. Though we clearly do not want criminals set free, we surely do not want innocent people incarcerated. Removing the double jeopardy provisions could well result in this.'

Some commentators suggest that Australia could learn much from the Scottish judicial system. That country has three verdicts: guilty, not guilty and not proven. The latter makes provisions for a case to be re-opened if new evidence is found.

The Hon. Justice Michael Kirby writes a lengthy paper on the subject, in which he concludes:

> As to the rule against double jeopardy in Australia, we can truly say, with Churchill, that we are not at the end of the story; nor, even at the beginning of the end. We are simply at the end of the beginning.

48

It is a brisk late July morning as the bus pulls into Ipswich station. It had cruised along the River Bremer and past Limestone Park, virtually deserted this time of day. Sandra has met me, and we are heading to her unit.

Raymond Carroll's 74-year-old mother, Ilma, is tall, grey and fretful. Her family has asked her to meet me, but not to stay around as it is too distressing for her. Carroll's third wife, Marilyn, smiles and says hello, a little shyly. She will tell me, later, that she, too, was nervous and that she is permanently on anti-depressants to quieten her trembling nerves.

Sandra's ex-husband and Raymond's best mate, Roger, a knockabout bloke with an easygoing disposition, is here for a show of support. Carroll is sitting, his long legs spread-eagled under the kitchen table. Tall, but unprepossessing when he stands to greet me. Body firm in jeans and a casual shirt but starting to show just a hint of thickening, compliments of middle age. He is 47 now.

The Carrolls appear a close, affectionate family. Painfully normal.

Sandra takes a seat and the family jostles into position for the duration of the interview, ashtrays for the cigarettes they will chain-smoke at the ready. It is, they know, going to be a long day.

Ilma Carroll is emotionally frail, but angry, too. It is her family's support that has given her the strength to keep going, what stops her from lashing out at her son's accusers. 'I believe that every-thing happens for a reason. But I will never be able to explain how I feel, the heartache I have gone through.' She rubs her fingers behind large gold-rimmed glasses, dollops of tears wet on their tips. 'I'm 74 years old, and this has hung over me for more than 20 years of my life, like a dark shadow. I feel such sadness for Mrs Kennedy, but . . .' She falters to find the word. '. . . But the cost to our family has been so high.' Ilma is an emotional wreck, trapped by circumstances beyond her control. She has had little sleep the night before, she says, fretting about the interview, worrying she will say too much. She stands to leave and shakes my hand. Her grip is firm and her gaze steady. 'Thank you for coming,' she tells me. 'I'm very glad I met you, and I am sure you will be fair.' She hugs Raymond farewell, a warm bonding of mother and son against the world, and I turn away, feeling like a voyeur. Ilma turns at the door. 'He didn't do it, Debi,' she says. 'He didn't do it. My son is innocent.'

Carroll's life reads like a drover's travelogue. Crisscrossing from Queensland, New South Wales and the Northern Territory four times, disgruntled at the lack of purpose in his life, he is now a farmhand, a long fall from his job in the air force as an aircraft electrical fitter. 'I riz to the rank of corporal,' he says, 'and after that I became a licensed household electrician in New South Wales.' He counts the jobs he has had on his fingers. Factory work. Food processing. Farm work. Contract harvesting. But he needs more than two hands to count the jobs that he's lost when his employers or co-workers have recognised him. *Pack your bag, sport,* they tell him. *We don't need your type 'round here.* He needs more than two hands to tally how often he has slammed a door behind him and jumped into his car, his face scarlet with fury. Seems like everywhere he goes, he has to drink from his own poisoned well. He is never sacked because his work isn't up to scratch, and he doesn't tell them about his past when he applies for positions. But they find out soon enough. He can't hold down a job: his notoriety follows him like a frightening shadow.

There is so much to get through, we launch straight in. 'With all the adverse publicity, why do you stay in Ipswich?'

'People often wonder about that. I've had to change me life twice, right? I had a perfectly normal life up until 1985. I'd been 12 years in the air force; another eight years to go and I could have retired on a full pension. Everything set up the way I want it, at the age of 37. Right? Then I'm arrested in 1985; I'm automatically discharged. I was strongly advised to move out of Queensland by me lawyers, otherwise I'd just be hounded by the media. I went to

New South Wales, stayed down there for quite a while, had to start all over again and try to find work. But the weather wasn't beneficial to me health. I moved back to Queensland to be with me family.'

'I mean to say,' Marilyn says, 'like, he's been saying that he's not guilty all along, and that, and then these people are trying to put it onto him that he did do it, so whenever he gets jobs or that, they don't actually say that he's fired, but . . .' She has run out of words. Now it's Sandra's turn.

'Everyone in the family has been to hell and back over this,' she says. 'We were warned when Raymond was convicted that he could expect at least three good bashings in the first week in jail, because of the type of crime. If he survived them, he would be all right until he was transferred to a new jail where it would start all over again. But it didn't happen.'

'Why not?' Raymond has asked her the question, but he surely knows what her answer will be?

She must have said this before. 'Because they knew you were innocent.'

Raymond Carroll often bumbles through sentences, clumsily joining words together. But he seems street-smart, well able to handle himself. 'Look, it's a very horrendous crime,' he says. 'I know that. Any crime against a child is wrong and horrendous. I sympathise with Mrs Kennedy; I empathise with her. I can't imagine what she's been going through.'

It's obvious already that the interview is going to take its own path. I may as well follow its twists and turns.

I ask was he aware, after the first acquittal, that the police stopped Barry Kennedy from taking the law into his own hands?

'Nup, but I have no doubt about that at all. I'd do the same thing.' He recounts a story from his time at Boggo Road. 'Swifte said to me, "You're guilty, gotcha," and I said, "So you think I'm guilty too?" I took him to my cell, showed him the photos of me daughters through the window. "Any bastard," I told him, "and I mean anybody, touches them and they're dead."'

'So you *did* have a conversation with Swifte?'

'Yeah, but it was after I was convicted. He claimed it was when I went in on remand, just after I was arrested.'

'Did you ever ask him what happens with bite marks – '

'No . . .' His answer is whispered.

'. . . and he said, you're a shot duck?' A long, uncomfortable pause follows the question. 'OK,' I say. I am treading a fine line between asking questions and being inquisitorial. They can pull the switch on this interview at any time. 'Had you ever been in Short Street, in Ipswich?'

Carroll shakes his head, repeats the name as if he is hearing it for the first time. 'Short Street? Nup. Never went there. I lived in Quarry Lane.'

'But didn't you know Ipswich well? You spent time there as a child.'

Sandra is clearly annoyed. 'We lived in every side of Ipswich possible, but it doesn't mean we knew every street.'

'That's right. It's like me saying to you, "You come from Tasmania – that's a small place; you must know Joe Blow",' Carroll counters. 'But of course you don't.' He says he has never been to the Borchert house next door, or the units where the Kennedy family lived. 'The only time I have seen them was when the jury went out for a viewing. Just because I was in the RAAF doesn't mean I knew about all the married quarters.'

Sandra is at pains to point out that their childhood was normal. No sexual or physical abuse. A normal, close, loving family. 'Raymond was examined by a psychiatrist after his first conviction and he was found to have normal patterns. The CAT scan they gave him was normal.'

'I asked Copley, my defence lawyer for hypnosis,' Raymond counters. 'I asked for a lie-detector test. He said that after all the accusations that had been put to me, that under hypnosis it might come out that I admit to it, subconsciously or however he put it. He said that would be detrimental to me so he advised against it. Same thing with the lie-detector test, but I'll still go through with one. Bloody oath I will.'

Good. Saves me asking that question.

He wants to talk about the photograph, about why the police

pushed so hard to prove his mother had taken his brother and sister to the doctor. 'OK, if the kids are sick, it gives them an excuse to get me out of Edinburgh on compassionate grounds. Right?'

'But a lot of people said you weren't there.'

'That was because I wasn't in the course photo. I told Reynolds I wasn't in the course photo.'

'Yes, but you said you were standing off to the side and then they proved you weren't there by showing someone else's photograph in which you were clearly nowhere to be seen.'

He seems exasperated with the verbal ping-pong, looks at Sandra who starts pacing. 'They couldn't remember him being there. They remember someone leaving. They assumed it was Raymond. My ex-husband was in the army. He can't remember who he was on course with, or who he travelled with, either. OK? It's a big space of time. The cops have got all their notes to refer to. Nobody told us to do that.'

The morning light has caught her face, and, for the briefest of moments, there it is: all the years of defending her brother from the enemy – media, public, police; all the years of being the family guardian; all the years of playing mother ingrained in dark hollows under her eyes and in heavy creases around her mouth. For the briefest of moments, it looks as though her frustration, her exhaustion, will tumble out in tears. But she has turned away, taken stock. She is the eldest. The head of the family. The one they all lean on.

Raymond comes back into the conversation. 'I said I was standing to the right of the parade ground, this bloody massive rectangle area. Not every square inch of that area is photographed. So they produced evidence to say, right, if I wasn't on the pass-out parade, they assume I'd be standing at a particular spot. I was off in a line of trees at the edge of the parade ground.'

He doesn't know who he was standing with, can only make assumptions. 'The person who was back-coursed.' Murmuring to himself. 'Bloody hell, who was he?'

'So what happened to your paperwork?'

'You tell me,' he challenges. 'There were three visits to Canberra records. On the first visit, the clerk can remember me records for course 1203 being pulled. All the records were there. *All* the records were there. On the second visit, two people went down to peruse the records of 1203. At that time they were all there as well, including the course roll. On the third visit, by me lawyers, the course roll was not there. You tell me where they've gone. Casper the ghost has come along and destroyed things?'

He runs through the litany of evidence built against him. 'OK, they say I wasn't at Edinburgh. Why? Because I wasn't in the pass-out photo. They ask, was I in Edinburgh at the time? Dunno, they answer, but if I was, I'd have been in the pass-out parade. Did I march on that? Well, if I had, I'd have been in the photo. Why wouldn't I march? Because I wasn't there. OK, they say, we've got evidence to say I did something in Ipswich; is there any reason why I'd go there? "Ah," they say, "Stephenson went on compassionate leave; maybe Carroll went on compassionate leave, too?" Somebody who hasn't got a direct memory can be led into thinking another way. Especially under pressure.'

'Can we get this clear?' I ask. 'Your line is that Rowley didn't like you; he picked you up for some speeding offences on the base; the women's quarters are broken into, he's looked at you and thinks, your teeth fit, you must be good for that and also for the Kennedy girl's murder. Is that it?'

'I dunno what my line is . . .'

He queries the evidence of the witnesses. Why didn't his first wife tell anyone that he had bitten his own daughter? Swifte's time frame is out of whack, the conversation didn't happen and he manufactured the story to get a deal on his sentence. Stephenson, one of the course members, had a vague recollection of introducing Raymond to his parents after the pass-out parade. 'They had two witnesses on a video link-up from England, and they were both sitting at a table discussing what was going on. The judge came in and said, "I hope those men aren't the two witnesses." They separated them and they gave their evidence, which matched with what they were discussing previously . . .'

'People only hear what they want to hear,' Sandra says. 'Our system works on "beyond reasonable doubt" and that's why Raymond was acquitted. There were too many doubts.'

They are in full swing. I don't have to ask a thing. 'At the first trial,' Raymond says, 'three expert witnesses had the bite mark upside down. But then in the second trial they say, "Now we've got it right." Now, if that's not reasonable doubt, what is? Honestly! Teeth are supposed to be similar to fingerprints, but if three people say it's the same bite mark but use different points of reference, how can it be the same? The technicalities that I'm supposed to be gotten off on aren't technicalities. They've taken the emotion out of it and looked wholly and solely at the physical evidence that's been presented, and they've come to their conclusions from that. Now it hasn't been a conclusion where they have said, "We'll re-try him," or "It's a bit dubious," or "It's a two-thirds majority". It's been a unanimous decision of outright acquittal. Unsafe and unsound.'

Everyone in the room is nodding. 'You don't just leave the base, particularly rookies. There has got to be documentation, travel orders, leave granted, whatever. In the service, your whole life is documented.' He sighs again. 'I could make allegations about conspiracy and everything else . . .'

'But to what end?'

'For closure. To make it fit me. And, even with the computer presentation, they were still identifying different teeth with different points. It's also anatomically impossible for anybody to bite in the pattern they said I did. I've got an overbite, but so do a lot of other people. Going on this so-called "uniqueness" of my bite, they say it's like a fingerprint – only one match. How can you have six people saying different teeth match? Even in the second trial, they had different teeth lining up with different bruises.'

It is the most animated he has been all morning. 'The so-called second bite mark has never been proved to be a bite mark to start with. If you go through the original autopsy report, there's no mention of a second bite mark. Romaniuk doesn't mention that second bite mark and neither did any of the panel of 10 dentists. The Queensland law system is a play. Whoever acts the best at the time wins. Nugget Carroll assumed the person taking the clothes off the line was Paul Borchert. The description he gave – how could he mistake that with someone who had just been in the

RAAF, with very short black hair? He said the prowler was five foot six to five-eight. I was six-two. It was a big case.'

And a big sentence he has just spoken. He stretches out his long legs. 'The justice system in Queensland needs a huge revamp.'

'It had one. They called it the Fitzgerald Inquiry.'

'It needs a better one! In Queensland, if a person's in the dock, they're perceived to be guilty. End of story. Particularly if it's a high-profile case . . .'

Raymond Carroll's freedom, so hard won, haunts him. He dismisses calls for an overhaul of the double jeopardy laws as little more than a 'political move' and plans for any civil action against him a rerun of OJ Simpson. But fear that he may one day face a civil court gnaws at the edge of his consciousness, scraping like bony fingers. 'During the committals and trials, I knew I was innocent and that the system would prove that, so I didn't really have a great worry. So when the guilty decisions came down, I felt numb, nothing. "How could this be?" I thought. "This can't happen." But now they're changing the double jeopardy laws and, while they say they can't touch me again, there's still the possibility of something going wrong, that it will all start up again. So I have to prepare myself in a fashion for that.'

It is his turn to ask a question. 'Have you actually seen photographs of the bite marks?'

Flashback. Plump, dimpled thigh. Faye had called Deidre 'a little porker'. Plump, dimpled baby flesh covered in obscene bruises. 'Yes, I have. They are hideous. Upsetting.'

'I know it's hideous. But take away that emotion, right . . . ?'

Take away that emotion. I stare at him, confounded by what he has said. 'That's a bit hard to do. She was only a tiny girl.'

'Yeah, but I seriously believe I was convicted on emotion, not fact. That's why the Criminal Court of Appeal and the High Court looked at the facts, without the emotion, and said, "It doesn't stand up." Cigarette smoke is curling around his moustache. 'I honestly hope that Faye Kennedy gets closure, but not at my expense, because I didn't do it. But, I tell you, the way the police have handled this case, it will never be closed. Now, if they wanted to charge someone else with the murder, any first-year defence lawyer is gonna say, "Hang on, you've put Raymond Carroll through two trials, you definitely said it was him, so how can it be my client?" Somebody could come up and confess to this crime, and a lawyer would get him off. They would say, "If Carroll's dentition was so unique, how can it fit two people?"'

Sandra is striding again, nodding. 'The legal team told us that after the first trial. They said they'll never get anybody for this.'

I move on to another topic. 'Why *did* you go into the super-market where Faye worked?' I ask him. The question slides quietly between the smokers' coughs and the clattering of coffee spoons. 'You know that it was perceived as a very sinister thing to do. Why did you go in there?'

When Queenslanders had read the newspaper story about this, they found it beyond comprehension. Raymond Carroll – the name they had come to know over almost three decades, the man accused and then acquitted of murdering Faye Kennedy's daughter – had casually strolled into the supermarket where Faye worked. Strolled in, put his food on the counter and waited to be served.

But she would not serve him. Ever.

She saw him heading toward her and wanted to scream out, instead stood riveted to the spot, her stomach turned to liquid. His family had been in before, but it was the first time she had seen him in there, and the first time she had seen him up close. So close she could reach out and swipe him.

His hair was longer than it was when she last saw him at the perjury trial, longer and peppered with grey. He stepped up to the register and put his groceries on the conveyor belt. For Faye, it was as if the world had stopped and there were only two people in it. Herself and Carroll.

He doesn't blink in response to my questions. 'I had no idea she worked there. I went in and got a couple of things and went to the quick checkout. I was looking at things on the stands, the checkout became vacant, I looked up and thought, "Oh shit, it's Faye."'

'But surely you knew she worked there. Ipswich is not that big a city.'

'No, I didn't know. Anyway, I didn't make a scene, I just put me stuff on the counter and she refused to serve me. I just stood there and waited until someone else came to serve, said thank you very much and walked out.'

A cool customer, I thought. But it wasn't that easy for Faye. She fell apart, just managed to splutter out her outrage before she staggered away from the counter. 'There is no way in hell I'm serving you,' she had hissed. In the lunch room, she shook violently, her body racked with sobs.

Given the lynch-mob emotion, I ask Carroll why he didn't go to another checkout, or just leave his stuff and walk out of the shop.

He is suddenly belligerent, defensive. 'Why should I? I've done nothing wrong, right? I am a member of the public. I am innocent. Why should I have to change my lifestyle because of something that has gone horribly wrong? I was already in front of her, put me stuff on the counter, looked up and saw it was Faye Kennedy. Before I could do anything else, she had just stormed off.'

He went in another time, later to buy cigarettes. 'I wasn't trying to be antagonistic. I had a look around before I walked in the door.' He shrugs. 'She wasn't there.'

Sandra takes up the story. 'Raymond has been made to look like so much of a monster, he realises some things are going to have to change. But he has as much right in this community as anyone else. Whether people believe he's innocent or not, he has been acquitted. He's a free man. There was a story in a newspaper that sort of made out he went in there stalking her. We don't even know where she lives, don't want to know. He didn't deliberately go into that supermarket.'

It's a Mexican standoff.

'We were living in a housing commission house in an Ipswich suburb,' Marilyn adds. 'We weren't hidin'. But we've never been back into that supermarket since. We go further to do our shopping now.'

Little wonder. The newspaper story that exposed Carroll going to the supermarket generated huge public sympathy for Faye. Though legally entitled to shop there, Carroll risked encountering ugly scenes from an outraged public if he upset Faye Kennedy again. In small communities, they protect their own.

Raymond says it is he who should be upset. 'The crap people come out with!' He is shaking his head. 'The *Sunday Mail* started running articles – I was supposed to be living in Mackay and all sorts of stuff. I wasn't there; I was living in Ipswich. They were just trying to bait me, to find out where I was. Then it started all over again. After the second trial, I had to re-build me life all over again.'

'It's hopeless,' Marilyn says. 'He gets a job and next minute he's finished. Once, he worked just one day at a factory and then the media was there out the front to greet him when he come out. It's hopeless.'

Raymond tells me he has a good relationship with his daughter Kerry-Ann, whom he refers to, sarcastically, as 'the *supposed* bite mark victim'. 'I've told her there is a book coming out on the story. Her response was, "What's the name of it so I can go buy it?"'

'Ray's mum said that even when Kerry-Ann had a snotty nose, Joy would rush her straight to the doctor,' Marilyn says. 'So why would she ignore somebody abusing her child?'

They say Kerry-Ann, now 31, has no memory of being bitten. 'She wanted to go on the stand but they wouldn't let her. She couldn't believe that her father would do that. They are very close. We went to her wedding last November.'

The family laugh at Joy Meyers's version of events about why their marriage broke down. It is bitter laughter, laced with scorn, but they don't share the joke with me. 'The fact of the matter is, Raymond was the good guy,' Sandra says. 'He gave her a divorce hassle-free, so it didn't restrict his already limited access to Kerry-Ann. And he paid the price for it. All that other stuff never came up until *after* Raymond was put on trial.' She is stridently loud, half shouting.

Raymond interrupts her, his voice soothing and quiet in comparison. He traces a finger around the bottom of his moustache as he speaks, following the contours of his mouth. 'I don't sling mud. I will not go down to the dirt, smut, in-the-gutter-fighting crap. I have done nothing wrong. I've been brought up to respect the law.

If something goes wrong, you go to see the police. I still respect the police. I haven't got much *time* for 'em, but it's the system that I have absolutely no respect for. Right? Herpich, Reynolds, all the others; they had a job to do. And they did it. But the problem is, a lot of stuff I've got no physical proof about and, if I haven't got that, what's the point in making the allegation?'

'What about the business with Kerry-Ann, in the bedroom, screaming? Why would Joy have said that?'

'Have you met Joy? She likes shock value. She'll say anything to get a reaction.'

Desley Hill wasn't truthful, either, by his account.

'She said you turned up at her place the night they found Deidre's body.'

'Nuh.'

'Why would she say that? Why are so many people out to "fit you up"?'

For the notoriety, he says. And Desley is impressionable.

'Impressionable? But if she loved you, why would she do that to you?'

His voice becomes higher. 'But that's just it! What makes you think she loved me?'

'Well, did she?'

'I don't know!' He is curiously defensive now, refusing to deny outright how she felt about him. 'After my divorce from Joy, I saw her again. She was living by herself then.'

'So you didn't see her at all during your marriage?'

'No.'

'What about the letters, the engagement ring, the letter Desley wrote to Joy in Darwin?'

'I don't know. I never saw the letters. I was never confronted by Joy, either.'

'Yes, you were. It came up at trial.'

'I confronted her, not the other way around.'

It is a quick response and it takes a while to sink in.

'OK, answer this,' he says. 'If I was in Ipswich at the time Deidre was murdered, why wasn't I contacted by the police in 1973?' He seems to be daring me to speculate. 'Well?'

'Presumably because you weren't at the house. Let's assume for a moment that you were in Ipswich; you're not going to answer a police doorknock, are you?'

'If I was in Ipswich, where else would I be staying?' His voice rises. 'I'm 17 years old, I've supposedly just been dragged out of my course on compassionate grounds because my mother is gravely ill; they do a doorknock, my mother answers when they ask, "Who's here?" and there's no record of me. If there had been, why wasn't I contacted back then?'

'Perhaps it was your mother's instinct – a natural maternal instinct – to hide you?' As I say it, I am remembering what a lawyer told me, years before: that a mother could see her own adult child, smoking gun in hand, standing over a dead body, and still declare it was a fit-up. Blind loyalty and a mother's love: the two most immutable instincts.

Sandra's voice has a cold edge I haven't heard before. 'That would infer,' she says with a withering look, 'that he came up here to kill the baby.'

I sense I should probably back off, but I don't. 'No, it doesn't automatically imply intent. But isn't it possible Raymond came to Ipswich, killed the baby and that your mother protected him?'

'If she thought he did it, she'd hang him,' Marilyn says. 'She would be the first to march him into the cops if she thought he was guilty.'

'We've been brought up to abide by the law,' Sandra adds. 'Our mother would fight until hell froze over for us, but if it was protecting criminal behaviour – she'd make us front up.'

I turn to Raymond again.

'Raymond, has your mother ever looked you in the eye and asked if you killed Deidre Kennedy?' This is hallowed ground, and it's starting to feel a bit shaky.

'Yes, she has.' It is Sandra who has answered but Raymond seems bamboozled, surprised.

'Has she?' he asks.

'Yeah, she did. She said, "Did you do it, Son?"'

What despair, I wonder, must Ilma have felt to be driven to ask her son such a question? Haunted by the fact she was unable to afford dental surgery that would have altered his appearance, did she ever wonder if, in a symbolic act of revenge against constant baiting, taunting and teasing, he had used those teeth as a weapon? She *must* have wondered, to ask that question. *Did you do it, Son?*

Raymond shrugs non-committally. He doesn't remember it happening.

Sandra offers the explanation. 'Like there haven't been heaps of other important things happening in the last 20 years.'

'Look, I've got a shocking memory,' he offers. 'And it's my memory that has got me into a lot of trouble. I can't give you times or dates.' It is a recurring theme, the reason Justice Vasta asked the jury: is a bad memory a convenient refuge?

'There are lots of things you've said that don't look good,' I venture. 'Like when you said to John Reynolds, "Oh, that shit about the baby again?" It sounds flippant, doesn't it?'

'Yeah it does. But if somebody comes hounding you over something that you know you haven't done, and they keep going and going and going, what are you going to do?'

'I don't think he ever meant to be flippant about the death of that baby.' Sandra is on the move again.

'I'm not, no! I try and help the police and this is what I get for it! If I go in there and shut me mouth, what's it look like? Oh, he's guilty. If I go in and try and help the best I can –'

'He doesn't show any emotion on the stand and they go, "He's a cold-hearted killer",' Sandra interrupts. 'But what people don't know is that his legal team told him not to show any emotion.'

'Is that why you've been described as coldly detached?' I ask Raymond.

'Yeah, and I am. After all this has been going on, the only way I can survive is to detach meself from the whole lot of it. People ask me how have I handled it so well, and my answer is, "In a way, it hasn't happened to me." It's a part of me life that's there, but it's that bricked up it's worse than Fort Knox.'

'Do you think it's possible to murder a baby and block it out?'

'Do I? Nuh. I don't think I could totally block it out. Like I say, I detach meself from all that's happened to me, it's the only way I can survive. But it's still there. My memory is bad in dates, times, birthdays: stuff that I'm not totally engrossed in.' He's an introvert, he says. A flippant, blasé introvert, more interested in computers than people. A truthful, average Joe Blow just trying to go about his business and thwarted at every turn. 'Like I say, I don't have to worry about all this because my whole family is worrying enough for me. They're worrying, so I don't have to.'

We break for lunch, fish and chips and a cool drink. It is a welcome diversion from the intense questions.

There are so many people out to get him, he says when we resume, and Reynolds is one. 'He comes to see me about the Deidre Kennedy murder . . .' He lights a smoke. 'After me conviction, Reynolds become Senior Detective-Sergeant Reynolds.' He steps on the word, hard and sarcastic. *Senior.* 'He was only a Detective-Sergeant at the start of it. Then, after me acquittal, he was demoted . . .'

It doesn't square with Reynolds's version. 'My understanding is that he blew the whistle on a senior cop,' I venture. 'They demoted him; he deliberately stayed in the police force like a thorn in their side until he got out. I don't think it had anything to do with you.'

He doesn't miss a heartbeat. 'Oh? All right. Anyway, I give him as much help as I could, even where to find information. I voluntarily give him dental impressions and hair samples.'

It was not quite like that in the police record of the interview.

'Sorry, but what you actually asked him was, "Do I have to?"'

'And what did he say?'

'He said, "No, you don't have to."'

'Right, well, I did.' He is leaning back now, arms folded.

'Yes, but if you hadn't they could have arrested you,' I remind him. 'And then you would have had to. So . . .'

'Oh well, anyway.' He is impatient with the to-ing and fro-ing. 'Even if I did query it, I still voluntarily give it. Right? Um, even with Herpich, to a point, yeah admittedly, OK no, I did not give a record of interview, I did not say anything. He asked me to go over to Forrest; I did that, but I wasn't made to or escorted.'

He says he believes he went through Sydney when he left Edinburgh. 'We left on a truck, went to a rail station, got on a train, changed at a station and transferred to Wagga.'

Hang on, I think to myself, back up. Didn't he tell Reynolds he left Edinburgh by service air?

'We then got onto another vehicle and went to the base. They asked me a question – how did I get to Wagga? – and I gave them an answer. My memory has got me into a lot of trouble. I was carrying travel documents from Edinburgh to Wagga, I had to hand them in, and from memory I was also carrying me medical documents, clothing card and a trunk.'

He would like some answers, too. 'Whose fingerprints are on the Kennedys' front and back door that match those found on the toilet block? They have never been matched with anybody. They are identifiable, but not identified. And how is it that all the recruits' memories miraculously got better over 20 years? They get a police officer come to them and say, "We know Raymond Carroll wasn't in the course photo, and we've got evidence to say that he was in Ipswich at the time. Can you agree to this? Is that true?" And they say, "Yeah, it's quite possible." And where has all the evidence gone? Why can't someone tell me that? Has it just disappeared into bloody thin air?' He is shaking his head. 'It's a bit convenient, isn't it?'

His teeth, the crowning exhibit in both trials, still need work, though some was done when he was a young man. 'Why haven't you had them fixed?' I ask. 'Surely, with all the publicity, they must bother you?'

He bristles again. 'Why? Why? I've got nothing to hide. It's me, it's the way I am and, knowing in me heart that I've done nothing wrong, why should I change? It's what I know about meself to be true is what I worry about.'

'He's an excellent family man,' Marilyn adds. 'I can't fault him. The kids adore him, and the grandkids.'

'What about your sex life?' It's a gamble: they will either answer, or tell me to mind my own business and take a hike.

Raymond answers. 'My sex drive is low, even though psychiatric reports done after the WAAF break-in reckoned it's normal.

I've decided myself that it's low.' He turns to Marilyn. 'We could both go for, how long?' he asks her.

She smiles, shrugs and I don't think I want to go there. 'Don't worry,' I say, airbrushing the question away. 'That's not important. Bit personal.'

But Raymond wants to tell me. 'I'm not into anything kinky,' he volunteers. 'Definitely not.'

'What about women's underwear – are you interested in that?'

Marilyn giggles. 'No, he doesn't even buy me any. I've gotta go and buy me own. No, he's not into that sort of thing. I can verify that, after being with him 12 years.'

It is getting late in the afternoon, shadows lengthening in the lounge room of Sandra's unit.

'You've had years to consider this, Raymond. Who do you think murdered Deidre?'

He doesn't miss a beat. 'That Borchert kid.'

'Do you mean Paul Borchert? He was only 12 years old when Deidre died.'

'So? Meaning?'

'What happened with Paul? Why did he suicide?'

'I don't know. All I know is what I've been told, right. All through me trial he's sittin' there watchin' the news, saying about me, "he didn't do it, he didn't do it, it's not him."'

'Who is he saying this to?'

'I don't know. I can't give you specifics, I can't give you proof; all I know is what I've been told.'

'Well, who told you?'

He repeats the question in a whisper. 'God, who told me that?'

'Surely you would know *that*?' I press, a little exasperated. 'Was it your lawyer?'

'No, it wasn't me lawyer.'

'How did he commit suicide?'

'I don't know. And apparently he left no note.'

'These sorts of allegations can just be rumour and hearsay, and it's very dangerous.'

'That's why I don't bring things like this up. I can't prove it, and, if I can't prove it, I won't bring it up. But you keep asking these questions; I can only tell you what I've heard, and, if it's rumour and hearsay, I don't know. But it's just very coincidental that it happened at that time. Also, Nugget Carroll assumed at first that the person taking the clothes off the line was Paul Borchert. The description he gave of a bloke with collar-length blond hair, how could he mistake that with someone who had just been in the RAAF, with very short black hair? Nugget's statement was taken just after the incident.'

'So, Paul Borchert. Anyone else?'

'Well, Keith Kennedy had an overbite and a gap between his teeth which would, if you look at the photos the way they've done all the enhancements, match better than mine. If you look at it, between the two bruises there is a gap. But they say that gap is caused by the way my teeth have been chipped.'

'So you think either Paul Borchert or Keith Kennedy. Both men are dead and dead men can't speak.' I look him in the eye. 'What do you think should happen to the person who killed Deidre Kennedy?'

The whole room erupts in shouted answers to my question. Carroll's answer is drowned out.

I study his face when the commotion dies down. 'I can't see your teeth.' The sentence has fallen abruptly from my mouth before I can catch it. It sounds more of an accusation than a state-ment, and I shift uncomfortably in the silence.

Raymond inhales the last of the cigarette smoke and grinds the butt into the ashtray. He pins me with a look, and it seems to take an eternity for him to answer. 'No,' he finally says. 'You can't, can you?'

It is like someone has let the dogs loose in the conversation.

'What do you think happened to the pubic hair?'

'The pubic hair?' He has repeated it softly, as though the question is a surprise. 'From what I understand from the commit-tal hearing of the perjury trial, they tried to do DNA sampling on the hair found on the child, and they stuffed it up. Accidentally. Well, that's what they told us. Either that, or they couldn't get a c-c-c. . . .' he stammers, clears his throat, 'a conclusive match so they made an excuse. So there is actually no DNA evidence.'

'In the months leading up to the perjury trial, all the media releases were, "We've got him now on DNA evidence, new DNA technology, there's no doubt, blah blah blah",' Sandra says. 'Trouble was, there was no DNA.'

'Never has been,' Carroll adds.

'You tell me how my brother had a fair trial with that! Anything that would damn Raymond to hell, absolute, or clear him, absolute, is missing.'

'But it doesn't make sense,' I say. 'Why would they want to fit somebody up and let the real killer walk free?'

'After the ball was rolling, I don't see how they thought they could stop it. Mrs Kennedy had already been told that they had found the baby's killer.'

'She had been told this pre-trial,' Carroll says. '*Pre-trial*. And I think Faye Kennedy has been brainwashed. Do you want to know why?' He is leaning back in the chair, on sure ground. 'For years and years, she's had all these detectives and so-called experts sitting in her head going, *he's the one, he's the one, he's the one*. That's all she's ever heard.'

Marilyn joins in. 'Look how much it would cost 'em, darlin', if they proved that you were innocent. If somebody come up and said, "I'm the one who did it; you've chosen the wrong guy," how red-faced would they be?'

'Yeah,' Raymond adds, looking at me. 'If someone fronted up and said, "I'm the one who did it," a bloody first-year lawyer would get 'em off.'

'The frustrations with all of this are incredible,' Sandra says. 'We know how bad it looks and we just have to accept that we have to live with that. We just have to accept it . . .' Her voice trails off. A weariness has descended, the family's frustration and sadness colliding with rage and impotence. The interview has extended over six hours and it's close to ending.

'What would you do if Raymond made a death-bed confession?'

They snap their heads up, jolted from their reverie. 'He wouldn't get the chance to die of natural causes,' Sandra's ex-husband, Roger, immediately answers, virtually the only thing he has said all day. 'I'd shoot him.'

'I wouldn't just shoot him,' Marilyn snorts. 'He'd be barb-wired.'

'I'd cut his nuts out and shoot him,' Roger repeats.

'Yeah, and I'd hang him by 'em,' rejoins Marilyn. 'Believe me, if anything happened for us to suspect that Raymond was guilty, I don't know what I'd do, but it would be gruesome.'

Carroll remains silent, save for the guttural noise that escapes from his throat.

49

'**R**ight. Now it's my turn to ask *you* a question.' Raymond John Carroll has moved closer toward me. Close enough so that I can smell his cigarette breath and notice the tendrils of grey hairs that snake through the moustache covering his lips and teeth. Those teeth: Exhibit A in two Supreme Court trials, two appeals and a High Court hearing. He has fixed me with a penetrating stare. 'Well? *Now* do you think I did it?'

50

The bus pulls out of Ipswich station, cruising alongside the River Bremer and past Limestone Park again. The city looks tawdry, drab in the late-afternoon light. Too small to hide in, with its pockets of clustered suburbia filled with RAAF housing. Small enough for people to remember, to stop and point. *That's Faye Kennedy. The woman whose baby was murdered.*

I am gazing out the window, mentally running through the interview. Hearing Carroll's mother's voice, anguished but determined. *He didn't do it, Debi. He didn't do it. My son is innocent.* The way they hugged when she was leaving, the bond between a mother and her eldest son.

Two juries had believed Carroll had left Edinburgh on compassionate leave. What do psychiatrists say? That emotional stress can trigger unconscious conflicts, that people are more likely to behave differently when they are aroused or frightened about loss. Do things they may not normally do. If his mother *was* sick, that would have placed Carroll – the oldest boy, the male head of the family just 17 years old – under considerable emotional stress. But if two juries believed he went home, two Appeals Courts had found there was not enough evidence to prove it. And a High Court decision has backed that up. It had not been my job to put him on trial again, simply to ask some questions.

Some of his answers had seemed contradictory to me, unconvincing, but he had admitted his memory is terrible: *I can't give you times or exact dates.* Angelo Vasta's voice echoes in my head: *is a poor memory a convenient refuge?*

His composure never altered throughout the long day. What did that say about his personality? I can't answer my own questions: I am not a psychologist. But it was obvious he was self-assured in the bosom of his family. They appeared to give him strength. Boosted him.

I am now on the train that links up with the bus service to Brisbane. It's clickety-clack is rhythmically in tune with my thoughts. Why would he have told me, 'It's the first I've heard of it?' when I asked if his mother had ever questioned him if he was guilty. The family must have been over this territory a thousand times. Why didn't they challenge him?

Sandra obviously looks out for him. Is he dominated by women?

I don't have to worry about all this because my whole family is worrying enough for me.

His lawyer, he told me, advised against a lie-detector test. I have no way of checking this. Kerry Copley is dead. So many people are, including Nugget Carroll – the one person who actually saw the intruder on the night that Deidre Kennedy was abducted. Police doorknock evidence has vanished. *Any males over the age of 12 . . .?* RAAF leave records: all missing. *Forget the paperwork. Get him on a plane.* Air travel records. *Sorry, Sir, the records are thrown out after seven years.* Medical records, stamped only. Prison records missing. Any records that would show opportunity for Swifte to speak to Carroll, gone. The pubic hair, ruined: that one, precious piece of DNA that could have held the key, bungled in the John Tonge laboratory before it was sent to the FBI in the United States. And when it got there, already ruined, they could not use it. What had Sandra said? *Anything that would damn him to hell, absolute, or clear him, absolute . . .*

The train is moving through the leafy suburbs of Brisbane. Past Auchenflower, where Keith Kennedy had lived. Clickety-clack, clickety-clack.

What happened that night, I wonder? Why would a man be lurking around where the Kennedys lived? Did he live nearby, or was he visiting the area for a purpose? Or both? What was the most likely thing that would entice a man to wander around alone, late at night?

Sex.

Had he targeted an adult or child who lived near the Kennedy unit, but was thwarted? Was he visiting, or intending to visit a house of ill-repute nearby? And, if so, what went wrong? Was he turned away, *no one available tonight*, standing at the closed door consumed with rage and frustrated desire? Take the next best thing. There is underwear hanging on a veranda. Stolen underwear, the thrill of illicit sex. And there is a chink in the curtain of the flat next door to where the underwear is hanging. He can see a baby fast asleep in the bedroom. Vulnerable. Easy prey. Perfect.

But if the man had knocked on the door of a house of ill-repute, wouldn't police have been told? *Unless* . . . unless the residents of the house hadn't mentioned their late-night caller to police, didn't want their backyard operation closed down. Best to shut up, say nothing. There is no way of checking the doorknocks: *any visitors on those days who have since left Ipswich?* But a city as small as Ipswich in 1973, when everyone knew everyone else's business – was it possible no one mentioned it?

And is it possible that Nugget Carroll, a hard-drinking Totally Permanently Incapacitated pensioner with a penchant for minding other people's business, deliberately gave a false ID to police of the prowler? Did he know the person and was protecting him?

What happened that night? *Someone* knows.

The train has pulled into Central Station. I am no more enlightened than I was when I left Ipswich. The best I can come up with is conjecture.

51

There are so many questions that still need answers. I decide to go over things with people already interviewed, tie up some loose ends, re-check some facts.

Dr Ken Brown has agreed to meet me at the old medical school in Adelaide where he still occasionally consults. I have entered the twilight zone of different scientific opinions: teeth supposedly upside down and back to front; mirror images, graphs and scales; mathematical concepts way beyond my understanding. Clearly, one set of dentists got the bite mark *upside down*. But which one?

Dr Brown is cagey about his age, but his slightly rheumy eyes are a giveaway that he is now, as he describes himself, 'as old as the Queen'. Occasionally crusty, he is still, nonetheless, sharp as a tack. There are concepts I need clarification on. 'Dr Brown,' I start, 'Cameron Herpich told me that while he and John Garner were in London, Bernard Sims expressed the view that the bruising caused by the teeth marks could have been made either way. That the top teeth could fit the bottom, and the bottom fit the top.'

'What?' His head has shot up, his expression incredulous. 'He told you that?' It is undisguised anger, contempt that a colleague of international standing could be portrayed in such a way. 'Bernard Sims is now retired, ill with diabetes, but the man has all his faculties. He knows odontology. Are you seriously telling me he would make a claim such as that?'

Brown has never changed his opinion that it was the odontologists called to the second trial that got the bite mark upside down. He bites his own arm to show how the mark occurred, 'I've done this before many juries,' he smiles, his flesh now showing definite marks. 'You can see when my teeth close, they draw up a fold of the skin. In Carroll's case, as he closed his mouth, the lower teeth pushed that fold against the surface of his upper teeth, which accounts for the unusual-shaped bruise. Our job was to make the jury understand the mechanics of the bite, which is unique, like a rubber stamp. Bernard Sims said the same thing as we did, though he didn't mark out the same number of teeth, because there was enough evidence in the mark for him to draw his conclusion. It was impossible for Carroll to bite with the tip of his teeth because of the size of his overjet. And this,' he says, 'is where the second odontologists made their mistakes, by considering each as a separate mark. They didn't consider the nature of the baby's tissue: very flabby, very elastic, and, when teeth approach that, they push in and the fold of the skin is sucked up into the mouth. That is why there were no impressions in the skin. If there had been, they would have disappeared in about 20 minutes when the skin reverted to normal again.'

Brown has packed up his notes. 'The problems started in the first appeal,' he says, as we walk out of the old medical school into a blazing hot Adelaide afternoon. 'A golden rule of any lawyer is "Never ask a question unless you know the answer." And so with the appeal judges – they had no idea what they were commenting on. No idea at all.'

I ask him again, 'What happened to the original casts? How could they be lost?'

Brown had initially thought the police had thrown them out, a cardinal sin because evidence should be kept. Kon Romaniuk had the originals and had made some copies, preserving the originals that had remained untouched. The casts were submitted as evidence at the first trial; after, Brown picked up two copies and took them back to Adelaide.

Now, he stands on the footpath and relates a story about his colleague. 'After Kon's accident, he never really returned to work full time and someone else – a former student of his – took over his forensic lab. I knew that Kon hadn't taken all of Carroll's casts into the court and it was out of character for him to throw anything away. Maybe they were just simply thrown out because it was believed he would not be coming back again, or maybe they are still around, somewhere. Who knows what happened to them? It is a mystery.'

Another mystery.

Alex Forrest – Kon's former student – sighs when I raise the question of the original casts with him. He and John Garner mounted a huge search for them, he says, certain they would turn up. Perhaps they were in a police evidence room somewhere, perhaps stored and forgotten in Romaniuk's collection? They contacted Adrian Gundelach to see if he knew where they were, but to no avail. They never materialised.

'What to do with old records is an issue within government departments,' Garner ventures. 'This was a dead case. Maybe they ended up somewhere within the DPP. I don't have a clue where they went, but we weren't very happy either. Evidence should never be lost.'

Now to Paul Borchert. I want to find out what happened, but first I have to find his family.

There are quite a few Borcherts in the Ipswich area, and I start at the first name in the phone book, hitting pay dirt straight away. Paul's brother Doug answers the phone.

'Hel-lo?'

'Is this the Borchert household?'

'Yes.' And yes, Doug says, he had a brother called Paul. He is friendly, happy to chat. 'How old are you, Doug?' I ask him.

'Don't know.'

'You would have to be in your thirties. When is your birthday?'

'June 9.'

'What year?'

'Don't know.'

'What happened to your brother?'

'Don't know. I think he was murdered.'

'Pardon?' I am taken aback. 'I thought he had committed suicide.'

'I don't have a clue about how he died, but they reckon he was murdered. Shot outside the picture theatre in Ipswich, they said. And me other brother, David? He's dead too. Someone punched his nose right up to his brain. Blood everywhere.'

'Oh.' I don't quite know what to say.

'Mum hasn't got the phone on but I'll get a message to her to ring you. OK?'

'OK.' I thank him and hang up. His mother, Kathleen, never calls.

Doug's father, Arthur, separated from his de facto wife Kathleen years ago, married and moved to New South Wales. When I call, his wife answers the telephone. 'May I speak to Arthur Borchert, please?'

'Yep. Hang on.' She doesn't cup her hand over the mouthpiece. 'It's a lady on the phone for you, Arthur,' she screams. 'I dunno who she is or what she wants.'

'Yes?' His voice has a tinny rasp, and he is yelling. 'What do you want?'

I introduce myself, explain I would like to find out what happened to Paul. 'I've already been in court over this baby case,' he shouts. 'What do you want? Eh? Eh?'

'I am sorry to bother you, but I would like to find out the details of your son's suicide,' I venture. 'Could you tell me what year it happened?'

'What suicide? He didn't commit suicide!' He is so loud, I have to hold the phone away from my ear. 'He was murdered! You didn't know that, did you? Eh? Eh?'

Assuming Arthur is yelling because he is deaf, I raise my voice so he can hear me. 'NO, I DIDN'T KNOW THAT. WHY WAS HE MURDERED?'

'Stop yelling at me!' he roars. 'What do you really want?'

I lower my voice. 'Arthur, if Paul was murdered, could you tell me what happened?'

'There's no need to whisper at me! He had my gun, a Winchester that only takes long bullets. But he was shot with a short bullet, fair through the head. Game of Russian roulette. I know the bloke who done it but they protect their own; they'll never admit it. Do you know who done it?'

'No, it's the first I've even heard of this,' I admit. 'Who are you talking about? Who protects their own?'

'Well, if you have to ask that, you're not as smart as you think then, eh? Eh? I'm not going to talk to you.'

'Why not?'

'Because you're a journalist.'

I try to steer him back to the topic. 'Arthur, was there ever any question that Paul may have been involved in the death of Deidre Kennedy? I have heard that he possibly committed suicide because he couldn't live with his guilt. I'm just trying to check the facts. Can you help me?'

'My son didn't kill that baby!' He is shouting fit to burst. 'My son didn't kill that baby! He was only a boy, still doing paper rounds. You want to know who I reckon murdered her?'

'Yes, I would like to know that.'

He is cackling. 'Course I know who done it! Well, you think you're so clever – you work it out! You can't, can you? Eh?'

He hangs up.

John Reynolds is surprised that Paul Borchert may have been murdered. 'No, I've never heard that one,' he tells me. 'Far as I knew, he cheated the hangman. I'll get back to you. Leave it with me.'

He calls the next morning, early. Old habits die hard: he has been up before dawn, on the phone networking, hassling old contacts for information. 'Nup, Arthur's got it wrong,' he says. 'Paul Borchert wasn't murdered. He committed suicide. Drugs. Maybe it was accidental, maybe not. But he definitely wasn't murdered.'

'Was this around the same time that Raymond Carroll was convicted?

'No, don't think so. It was later.'

'What year?'

'Don't know,' he says. 'I'll get back to you. Leave it with me.' He is never able to give me the date.

The grim set of Herpich's face betrays more than he says. A career policeman, he does not put a foot wrong. He picks his way through his sentences with exquisite care, following the beaten path to the letter of the law.

'As far as the service is concerned,' he says, 'Raymond Carroll has been acquitted. That's the system.' He swallows and indicates, with a flinty look, that he will not say any more. 'We get paid to do a job, and that's to investigate crimes. Carroll has been acquitted. That's the system.'

Faye regards him as her saviour, a fact he accepts. 'It's hard to turn someone's life upside down and not become attached to them. They depend so much on the copper that they're dealing with and everything that they know about the justice system gets funnelled through that person. So it invariably comes to a situation where the victims depend a lot on the police.'

In mid July 2004, I forward some questions to Cameron Herpich, via the normal channel of the QPS Media Service. Reiterating what defence lawyer Peter Davis had said regarding Keith Kennedy – how was he exonerated? – I ask for Herpich's comments. And what of Carroll's entrance and exit into Boggo Road Jail? I query the truth or otherwise of statements made from the Bar table. Were the prison records lost? Were the bail documents found? Quoting the defence line in the second trial: 'It shows a general incompetence in the investigation by Herpich . . .', I ask if he has a copy of this section showing both the prosecution and defence line? Can he respond to Davis's assertions? I conclude by advising him that I hope to catch up with Faye in Sydney the following weekend – three days' time – and to meet her daughter, Stephanie.

The QPS response arrives Friday morning, answering my questions and expressing concern about the direction of the book, particularly if defence comments that clouded the issues were taken seriously and created possible damage to Herpich's policing career. Would this material, they want to know, be included in the book? They would take issue with any reference to 'incompetence'.

My return email makes it clear that my role is to look at the entire case, flawed or otherwise; that I cannot be expected to toe a line that suits and that I must work independently to maintain balance. Faye, I assure them, was well aware of the extent of my questions and research.

I had first met Faye in February 2004, on a miserable, stinking hot Ipswich day when the thermometer reached 44 degrees. She remained composed, serene, took the heat and the questions in her stride, but I didn't. Too hot for me to bear, we decamped to a five-star hotel in Brisbane, with air-conditioning that worked. And that's where it happened, when Faye's inscrutable mask broke, where she sobbed uncontrollably about her daughter's loss and the emptiness she can't fill. I watched, a hopeless onlooker to her pain. Nothing – *nothing* I said – could ever help.

We had met again earlier this month at her spotless, comfortable home, where she met me at the door and started crying, immediately. Tense, wound up, nervous, she was glad I was there, so we could start the interview. Talking was cathartic.

We talked for almost two days.

Faye had cried often during that interview, breaking down when she looked at photos of Deidre, when she recalled a small memory, when she spoke of her daughter's funeral.

Then, without warning, following my email to the QPS, Faye does not respond to my numerous phone calls that weekend in Sydney, nor do I meet Stephanie in person. Bewildered and saddened by Faye's sudden and unexpected silence, I receive a text message from Stephanie – with whom I had spoken several times by phone but not met – apologising for the mix-up. Stephanie had not been aware, she explains, of any plans for us to meet.

I do not hear from Faye again until after I contact her in May 2005.

I had kept all the papers she had given me at our interview, countless newspaper reports on Deidre's death and letters from journalists wanting to tell her story. *Dear Mrs Kennedy . . . I am a reporter with Channel 7. Now that Carroll has been convicted, I would again respectfully request an interview with you and your family . . . I appreciate it is still very difficult for the family to deal with the incident . . .*

Dear Faye, I am a producer with the Nine Network . . . I am interested in airing a story on the police investigation and subsequent perjury trial . . . While the court cases, verdicts, media stories and public reaction come and go, what you feel will never change . . .

Dear Mr Byrne . . . My colleagues have previously contacted your office and put in a request to speak with you and the Kennedy family . . . If it is suitable, I would propose doing something with you all today . . .

Sometimes Faye responded, sometimes she didn't. It depended on how strong she was feeling.

Letters and card from strangers had poured in after each trial and appeal. *Dear Faye, Our hearts break for you . . .*

Dear Mrs Kennedy, May God give you peace . . .
To the Kennedy family, We are thinking of you . . .

I pack the papers up to return to Faye, as I promised I would. Thousands of words. They haven't brought Deidre back, but they give her strength.

On Monday 19 July, I receive a response to my last email to Cameron Herpich, answering some further questions.

At the end of July, I send the following message to the QPS:

Could you please pass this to the appropriate person for comment, (probably Cameron [Herpich])?

1. Can you please confirm whether a gentleman made a verbal or written statement to police re finding Deidre's body in a rubbish bin inside the park? If so, when was it made, what was the nature of the allegation and how, according to this person did Deidre end up on the roof? Did police take this seriously? If this person does not exist, is it simply rumour that is repeated by various sources?

2. Who made the final decision to clear early suspects? (Did it move through chain of command or was it made as it individually came up?)

3. Are statements from the early suspects available? I can't see that they were tendered (in court) but are they still around?

4. Was there any resolution on the origin of the grass seed? (John Reynolds did not know.)

5. Was there a theory re the pilchers on the roof of the units?

Many weeks later, I send a second request asking if I could expect a response to the questions. My queries have been forwarded to DS Herpich, I am assured.

I do not receive a reply from him.

52

In 2004, Adrian Gundelach defends serial killer Lenny Frazer – originally accused of murdering teenager Natasha Ryan who emerged from hiding in a cupboard at her boyfriend's house years after she disappeared. Truth, Gundelach says wryly of that story, is stranger than fiction. And he has another story, equally bizarre, perplexing.

During Lenny Frazer's trial, Gundelach was approached by Homicide Detective Senior-Sergeant Dave Hickey. Nine months before, Hickey said, an 84-year-old man had come to see him, told him he wanted to get something off his chest. He was dying of cancer and scared he would take the secret to his grave. It was about that baby who was found in Limestone Park 31 years ago.

It had been the man's habit to walk through the park early in the morning. And he had done so on 14 April 1973, just before dawn. There were dogs hanging around a rubbish bin deep inside the park, barking, excited, their front legs extended and pawing the bin. Something inside it had caught their attention, something they were desperately trying to retrieve. Curious, the man approached the bin and looked inside, reeled when he saw what it was.

A baby. Dressed up like a woman in underwear that swamped her tiny body. Her thigh bruised with hideous marks. The sight defied description.

The man panicked. He was scared. So scared. This child had obviously been murdered and dumped and soon it would be light enough for other people to come into the park. He didn't know what to do. If he went to the police, they would think he was responsible. If he left her in the bin, the dogs would attack.

He cried as he lifted her out of the rubbish bin and looked for a place to put her. It had to be high off the ground, away from the dogs. There was a building nearby. A toilet block. He would put her on top of the toilet block.

He wanted her to be seen, wanted her rescued from this lonely place. He climbed up with her in his arms and arranged her so that her head and arm hung over the guttering. Anointed her with his tears and scrambled back down, running, running to get away from there. By the time news breaks of the discovery of little Deidre Kennedy's body later that afternoon, he had hunkered down with his secret. But the memory never left him, stayed in his conscience through three long decades. Haunted him, how he was too cowardly to go to the police in case they thought he was the person who did it.

The police checked the veracity of his story. Verified where he lived. Spoke to his doctor. Chatted with people who knew him. And, in the end, they agreed the personal details he had given them all added up. The man was kosher.

Dying of cancer, and wanting to get it off his chest. And, when he died a short time later, he was satisfied he was going to his grave with a clear conscience.

53

So much has happened in three decades. Journalists return to the Deidre Kennedy story when something new breaks but there is always competition for copy space, every day a new story breaking somewhere in the world.

Lawyers involved in the case have long ago moved on to new trials and challenges, but the defence in a high-profile case like this can cop a hard time of it. Peter Davis, still working in private practice, grew to dread going to dinner parties and the inevitable, whining question: 'But how *could* you defend him?' He has a theory about how this case got so big, a juggernaut out of control. 'The RAAF is little different to the legal profession,' he says. 'People just can't stop talking about each other. And from the time Carroll's name was thrown in the ring, the legend grew bigger and bigger.'

Faye Kennedy made a lasting impression on Davis. Four years after the trial, he still remembers her with great sympathy. 'Faye was a very sad case. You will see from the answers which she gave to my cross-examination of her that she was very defensive and thought that she was under some sort of attack. Nothing of course could be further from the truth. Because I was defending, it became an "us" vs "them" scenario, which is the problem with the adversarial system. The jury just had so much sympathy for her, and I wouldn't have wanted to be a juror who found against her. They got caught up in the horror of it all. They could not be objective.' He ruminates about Faye's strength. 'I thought she was bigger than human. Anyone who can turn up to court every day and listen to evidence about how her daughter had been butchered is pretty special. She is extremely brave. She is totally convinced that Carroll murdered Deidre, though I believe that must be because people keep telling her that. I have certainly never seen proof that would convince me beyond reasonable doubt that he did it and I have never formed an opinion one way or the other. People often ask me, "what would you do if he confessed, would you still defend him?" and my answer is always the same. Yes, I would, though I may change the tack of my questioning to witnesses. Our system of justice operates on a jury trial, and it's not about truth. It's about proof.'

Carroll's defence teams remain scathing about what he has had to endure, pointing to two jury trials, two appeals, a High Court judgment and intense media coverage as proof that he is one of Australia's most vilified men. Finality, they point out, is a vital element of any system of justice. Peter Russo admits he was treated by some in the community as a pariah, a leper for defending him. 'It's my job to defend people. I think this was trial by an hysterical media, like the Chamberlain case.'

Adrian Gundelach is now in private practice, and maintains the Kennedy case is the saddest he has ever prosecuted. Philip Nase and Milton Griffin are now Queensland District Court justices. Peter Barron is Assistant-Commissioner of Police in far north Queensland.

After the Carroll case, Michael Byrne left the DPP office in late 2001 to work in private practice, a resignation that was greeted with controversy. Widely tipped to take over as Director, the position was instead given to Leanne Clare, who later came to national attention for her controversial handling of swimming coach Scott Volker's sex scandal case. Byrne's departure was regarded as defection by those concerned at the loss to the department of his considerable experience and by others as reflective of the extremely low morale in the DPP. His passion for criminal law has not diminished.

In the years since he presided over Carroll's murder trial, Angelo Vasta has never been swayed to believe the jury was wrong. 'The way to right a wrong is by having a series of people coming out and saying it's wrong,' he says. 'The Appeals Court hears no evidence, and does not seek witnesses.' Now 66 and with Bell's Palsy, Vasta was never found to have done anything in the discharge of his duties that hinted at impropriety. He has been exonerated every step of the way, including vindication by the International Commission of Jurists. Over the years, he has lost great champions of his cause, cheated of their support by their sudden deaths. 'I finally had to think that the good Lord was trying to tell me something,' he says. 'I am still fighting to clear my name, but I had to step back, lest I became consumed by it.'

He admits he has been hurt at the betrayal against him, dismayed that the mud has stuck. But he remembers the words of Sir Thomas More, who confronted an accuser at his own trial. 'I pity you, Sir, for your perjury.'

Vasta outlines to me what he regards as the two great tragedies of the Kennedy case. 'The pubic hair should have been preserved. It was the one piece of evidence that would have irrefutably proved who killed that little girl.' The other is the quirky nature of the law, so often misunderstood by those who rely on it most – the victims of crime. 'If nothing happens except that Deidre's murder acts a conduit to change the double jeopardy laws, then it is some small consolation that her suffering has not been in vain.'

John Rowley's accent hasn't softened after more than 35 years in Australia, though at 62 he admits his hair now enjoys a close relationship with Brylcreem and is streaked with silver. Try as he might, he can't seem to escape the fall-out from the Kennedy story. 'To be honest, I'll be glad when it's all over,' he says. 'I just can't seem to leave it behind me.'

I check some assertions Carroll made to me. 'Did you suspend him for driving on the base and deliberately hand him the photographs so that his fingerprints would be on the picture?'

'That's ridiculous, I didn't even know the man!' Rowley snorts. 'This is the first I've heard of this rubbish. The first time I got to hear of him was when there was the break-in at the airwomen's block at Amberley. And he wasn't suspended for driving, not by me and, as far as I know, not by anybody. And Carroll didn't see the photographs – that's not the way we worked. We wouldn't have handed him the photograph so that he could leave his fingerprints on it. The RAAF police is not the same as civvies where ambition can push you to chase a conviction that will further your career.'

Rowley ended his 21-year career in the RAAF as a warrant officer, the highest senior non-commissioned rank one can achieve. During his career, he had hundreds of successful investigations, but he is still intensely irritated at press reports that followed his involvement in the Kennedy case. 'Some articles made out that I'm a paragon of virtue – a hero. I was a good policeman, but I was not a cross between James Bond and a knight errant. I'm just a dogged sort of a bloke, that's all.'

It was, he says, just another job. 'I can't describe a man; I can only describe the impressions I get. There were times when I was interviewing Raymond Carroll for the break and enter at the women's base that I got the distinct impression he was there but not there. Like I was talking to him but he was looking, like, through me. He can say all he likes that it was a fit-up, but the fingerprints on that photograph and his car in the area were not circumstantial. And the jury proved that.'

Peter Davis agrees with what Rowley has told me about this. 'No question,' he says when asked. 'No question at all that he did that one.'

John Reynolds made a recommendation that Rowley be given the $10,000 reward, posted by the State Government in 1973, for his key role in re-opening the Kennedy case. Neither Rowley, nor anyone else, received a reward.

John Reynolds is now director of his own water-analysis company, but he will never forget Deidre. 'Anything to do with kids hits a copper hard. A lot of people did a lot of work trying to solve this case.' He occasionally keeps in contact with Faye, and still feels gutted at the lack of resolution. 'This is one of the greatest injustices ever seen in Australian criminal history. Where is the justice for that little girl?'

Demoted from Detective-Sergeant, CIB, back into uniform, Reynolds says he was effectively hustled out of the force in 1993 after he investigated and exposed the corrupt practices of a senior officer and was openly critical of the judicial inquiry into Angelo

Vasta. Passed over for position of Inspector by a policeman 13 years his junior, he opted for early retirement after his appeal against that failed. He applied for retirement on a Wednesday. 'By Friday,' he recalls, 'I got a call from the Commissioner's office, basically telling me to clear my desk.' From that moment, he was persona non grata. In police parlance, he says, 'There is no one so ex as an ex-copper.'

All the odontologists in both trials are unequivocal in their opinion that the evidence they gave – however it was later construed by the appeal's courts – was right. 'No one – *no one* – has ever changed their mind about whose teeth made those bite marks,' John Garner says. He defends their digital computing system. 'There were very few forensic odontologists in the world actually doing bite mark identifications at that time because it was looked on as a subjective science that had very little credibility. It was the dark ages. Trying to trace something conjured up all sorts of problems, and people saw that. It was only through Alex and computers that identification has gone ahead in leaps and bounds.'

I remind him that not everyone shares his opinion, and he sighs. He knows that. He sure as hell knows that.

He admits to unease about some aspects of the original investigation, theories he had that he tried to check but where he came up against a brick wall. Theories: join the dots and follow the trail. But he wasn't an authorised investigator. No one was much interested in his theories.

Storage of case material has improved since the original trial. 'In the past, cases were managed by the lead detective and occasionally coppers would compare notes. It was an ad hoc situation; if a cop was sloppy in management of data, then it often simply got lost. People were at cross-purposes with no holistic approach. These days, officers are very conscious of doing everything by the book.' And it is precisely this, Garner says, that can create problems. 'Good policing involves a mix of discipline and experience, following the direction set by the co-ordinator, countless hours of foot slogging, 10 per cent inspiration and 90 per cent perspiration. It's about listening to what is being said, and what is not. It is too easy these days to overlook gut feeling.'

Some forensic odontologists involved in the committals and trials have been called on to use their expertise in helping to identify victims from terrorist attacks, such as the Bali bombings, or natural disasters, such as Asia's tsunami tragedy on Boxing Day 2004. 'It is then,' Alex Forrest says, 'that our job gets to the human level, which is really, after all, what it is about.'

Forrest equates forensic dentists as resembling a loose confederation of warring states and believes that government departments, police and lawyers became bigger than the case they were representing. Somewhere along the way, in the quest to try and prove who murdered a tiny child, egos and personalities fudged the purpose, and paranoia and ambition poisoned common sense and reason. 'The real test of any evidence is when it goes in front of a jury. The trick is to behave like a politician, and not take it personally. But,' he cautions, 'this case has been a misery from start to finish. I don't know one person who hasn't been affected by it, one way or another, who isn't sick to the stomach by the whole thing. Not one.'

Dr Kenneth Brown has now retired but still consults on some cases. Dr Bernard Sims is ill with diabetes and has also retired.

Dr Kon Romaniuk, debilitated with brain damage after his accident in Sydney, suffered further deterioration from a stroke in late 2004 and is now in permanent high-dependency care. His wife, Leona, graciously has given me background information on her husband, and, though I have Kon's number, she warns it may not be worth the call. 'He moves in and out of lucidity,' she says. An hour later, I call her back to check a date, but Kon answers the phone. I have called his number in error. And so we speak, as he looks out to a garden of beautiful bougainvillea and describes their colours to me. 'Do I know you?' he asks.

'No, but I have just spoken to your wife and I am writing a book on the Deidre Kennedy case. You are an important part of that story.'

'Oh, thank you. I'm embarrassed now.' He does have a melodious voice, just as Leona had said. Lyrical.

'Do you recall the case?' I am mindful of what his wife has told me, upset I have called the wrong number. 'Yes, I remember. It was one of the biggest of my career. The little baby. There was a court case, and I was in the witness stand an awfully long time. It was terrible.'

'Kon, the dentists at the second trial said that you, Dr Brown and Dr Sims got the bite mark upside down. What do you say to that?'

He chuckles. 'They're wrong. We got it right.'

Now it's my turn to chuckle. 'That's what the other odontologists say, too.'

We chat about the case, about how power and politics sometimes clouded issues. Of those long-ago days when he worked closely with John Reynolds and, later, John Garner. Have his opinions changed, I ask?

Never, he says.

It is time to hang up. 'Thank you, Kon. It was lovely to talk to you.'

'And to you. I met your father the other day. He is a fine man.'

This is an unexpected digression, and I gently explain my father passed away many years ago. He accepts that. We talk some more about his own family, and now I must go. 'Goodbye, Kon. Thank you again.'

'Goodbye. And don't forget to give my regards to your father. He is a fine man.'

The *Australian*'s Chris Mitchell concedes there have been unforeseen impediments to the mooted civil case. Tim Carmody is now a Queensland Family Court judge, which means he is no longer at liberty to speak on legal issues and can no longer offer advice to the *Australian*. The *Australian*'s lawyer, Brian Gallagher, was forced to withdraw after suffering a stroke. On legal advice, Mitchell is now taking a wait-and-see approach, pending the outcome of the Attorneys-General decision on possible changes to the double jeopardy laws.

'We will turn our attention to the civil action when those decisions are made,' he says. 'But one thing is for sure: this story is not going to go away in a hurry. It is not just about a murdered baby and a mother's grief: it strikes at the heart of justice.'

To date, changes to Australia's double jeopardy laws are still on the table. Public opinion has not changed; overwhelmingly, the majority of Australians want the current laws overturned.

In the early stages of research, I waded, bewildered, through the vagaries of different government departments. Finally advised to place a request for specific information to a specific area, I was confronted by a taciturn and imposing senior public servant who materialised from nowhere and stridently demanded I tell her what I wanted. Stunned at her rudeness, I said I was searching for particular documents that pertained to the Deidre Kennedy case. The answer clearly displeased her. The department she represented, she snarled, could be of no assistance. Was I in the wrong place? I could only guess: the sermon was delivered in a hallway and, with a glacial stare that indicated I was dismissed, she executed a three-point turn and stomped away. I never saw the exhibits I requested, exhibits that had been used at trial and were on public records.

So many people related to or involved in the case have died in the years since the story first broke. Kerry Copley, QC. Keith Kennedy. Dr O'Neill who did the autopsy. Paul Borchert. Prison officer Denzil Creed. RAAF officer Lesley Meacham.

Colin Bamford succumbed to cancer in 2001. John Garner was able to honour his memory in a small way. 'I got a call around midnight from one of his sons in the UK, telling me his father had passed away. His brother was holidaying in Cairns and he needed to urgently contact him to tell him the bad news. He had come up against red-tape problems; the official channels had told him it could take up to two weeks to locate him. I called Police Operations Centre, explained who Colin Bamford was and what he had done to help in the Deidre Kennedy case. I asked if they could relay a death message to his son.

'He was located in 20 minutes.'

Deidre's older sister, Stephanie, was in Year 12 during the murder trial, and was 31 years old by the time of the perjury trial. On her wedding day, she cried for the sister she no longer had who should have been her bridesmaid. 'It has had an enormous impact on all our lives,' she says. 'You can't live with something like this and not be affected. How Mum has come through it as she has – with so much dignity and courage – amazes me. She is an extraordinary woman.'

Stephanie, formerly a nurse at a Sydney medical centre, tried hypnosis to see if she had locked any memories of the intruder's face in her subconscious. It failed. 'I thought that maybe I could have woken up and seen something, but I was scared and blocked it out. It spooks me still, knowing that someone was in that room where we both slept. I hoped hypnosis would return some childhood memories of Deidre and me, but they are all gone.'

Until Stephanie started high school, Faye walked her to school every day. Still obsessive about security and terrified of the dark, Stephanie locks the house like a fortress and keeps a close eye on her children. Even when she is home alone, she keeps the doors locked and rarely opens the windows. 'My ritual is to kiss the kids goodnight, lock the house and then check the front door again.' If she ever had to put washing on the line at night, she made her husband, Shane, stand at the back door.

Stephanie now has to call on her own courage. In early 2005, aged just 42, her husband, Shane, suffered a sudden heart attack at work. He called out to his mate for help, but, by the time he got to him, it was too late. Stephanie called Faye as soon as she heard what had happened. 'Mummy,' she said in a whimpering voice breaking with grief. 'Oh, Mummy. Shane is dead.' Faye's screams reverberated around the room. Faye contacted Barry to tell him she had bad news. 'Oh, God,' he remembers saying to her. 'Please don't tell me something's happened to one of the kids?' Barry flew to Sydney for the funeral. He hadn't seen Stephanie since the perjury acquittal, but he was heartbroken for her and the children. 'Shane was a terrific bloke,' he says. 'They are bereft. How much more do they have to suffer?'

Derek Kennedy won't let his children out of his sight. He watches them all the time, even in the house. All the time. Faye, he says, bordered on obsession when he was growing up, not resting until he was home, but she tried to keep it in check. In early 2005, Derek and his wife had another son. He watches him all the time too.

The smell of roses reminds him of Deidre. Roses, from the times in his childhood when he went with his family to the memorial wall where Deidre's ashes were originally held. He was too young to know why they went there, but he remembers the scent and the feelings. Roses, tears and a terrible anguish that he couldn't quite understand.

Now 58, Barry Kennedy has been in a happy relationship with his partner, Jenny, for 10 years. He doesn't have much hair left and his beard is grey, but he has cleaned up his act, no longer drinking or gambling to excess.

He discovered his weaknesses, he says, after Deidre's murder, and he didn't like them. Demonised and haunted by guilt that he didn't get out of bed the night she was abducted, he self-flagellated for years. He was weak. Useless. He had failed as a father, a husband and a man. Self-forgiveness was a long, painful process, but one he has finally reached. What happened wasn't his fault.

And it wasn't his way to crusade for Deidre. Easygoing, placid, he doesn't like attention and hates confrontation. The trials, the media made him nervous as hell. It was bad enough the first time, but the second? He sensed it was doomed from the start, that double jeopardy laws would be a stumbling block. He wants to see the law changed, but he will leave that to others to do. 'I'm not obsessed about any of it,' he says, quietly. 'It's happened. I have no control over events and so I just have to live with them.' Everyone, he thinks, had a point to prove in the second trial and he wasn't going to get on that band-wagon. It's not his way.

He thinks about Deidre every day, the lovely little girl who scooted along the floor on her bottom and smiled up at him when she hugged his knees. That's enough for him. That's his way.

Faye had not seen her father since she was pregnant with Stephanie. He died of pneumonia in the early nineties and she went to his funeral, to get some closure. Her attendance caused an irreconcilable rift between her mother, Frieda, and herself. She has not seen her mother since.

Faye has long accepted that nothing can fill the void left by Deidre's death. In 2004, she visited a clairvoyant to try to calm the nagging ache, and find out if her daughter is safe.

'My parents had such a bitter separation, and Dad didn't ever contact me after we lost Deidre. I could never understand his silence, but he always asked other people how I was coping. The clairvoyant told me she could see a little girl with my father. She said, "Tell Mum I'm doing OK." That's what I always worried about – that she is OK.'

Faye's voice is soft and light. Never loud, nor jagged with bitterness or anger. Often, choked with tears and caught in a purgatory of grief, her words are inaudible.

In May 2005 Faye and I again make contact. Her prolonged silence – 10 months – was, she explains, because of her grief. The memories were too hard to bear. Her grief contributed to the silence, and another reason we only lightly explore. We both know what it is, but best not to dwell on this. The most important thing is that I now again have Faye's full trust and support. Deidre's story, I tell her, is now complete. I have done what I said I would do, I assure her; I researched the nooks and crannies of the police investigation, the court cases, the characters. And it is done. Faye weeps, quietly, as we talk. Thank you, she says.

She is more media savvy now, stronger than the woman thrust into the limelight who shied from camera flashbulbs. Every time there was a turn in the investigation, police wondered how much more she could cope with, how many more hurdles she could jump. But, underneath, she is the same woman: emotionally fragile, amused and touched by simple things. Still the shy country girl who does not trust easily, who has a steely inner strength but is warm, loving with those she allows under her guard.

Those who know her – police, lawyers, friends – describe her as an inspiration. She understands pain, the gnawing, inconsolable emptiness reserved especially for those who have lost a child. She once worked with a woman whose 23-year-old daughter jumped off a bridge in Ipswich. They found her body the next morning, sprawled carelessly in death; no suicide note, no reason offered. Her mother turned to Faye to find a meaning for her loss, to help her understand the incomprehensible.

Faye once attended a victims of homicide meeting, where she found the pain in the room overwhelming. When she had to introduce herself, she wanted to run. It was the first time she had ever uttered that her daughter had been murdered.

She listened to a man speak about his murdered brother. 'Things that are inconsequential to other people can become huge to those who have lost someone in sudden death. It concerned the man that he was wearing his brother's shoes,' Faye remembers. 'I told him, if it feels right, wear them. Who are we to judge?' So much pain in that room, she never went to another meeting.

So many things bring back memories. Derek's young daughter bears a striking resemblance to Deidre, and she points at photographs in the family album. 'Is that me, Grandma?' she asks Faye. 'Is that me?'

'No, it's not you. It's your Daddy's sister.'

'I haven't seen her. Where is she?'

And Faye has to explain. 'I have to tell her that Deidre is dead. It shouldn't be like this. She is only three years old.'

Faye has not been to church in years, but she calls quietly on her old faith for comfort. 'Our children are only on loan to us. I remember an old lady once said to me, it is obscene for a mother to have to bury her child. I believe we all meet again in time and that there is somewhere safe where people go. I guess it's what we know as Heaven. And the person who did this to Deidre – he's yet to meet his maker.'

Faye's faith in God has been severely tested. 'I have to believe Deidre was put here for a reason and that we have had to suffer like this for a reason. I refuse to believe that her little life was in vain. Perhaps the purpose of her being was that the laws of double jeopardy could be changed so that other families would never have to endure what we have.'

The victim, Faye says, deserves as much finality as the accused. 'Families of murder victims are left with nowhere to turn when

Appeals Courts overturn a jury's decision. If we can change this law, other people won't have to suffer. What is the point in juries if their verdicts are ignored? It is hard to understand the legal system.'

Deidre's cremation negated any opportunity of a later exhumation that may, possibly have helped identify her killer. Graciously, Faye says that authorities didn't know then what they know now.

They didn't know then what they know now. And would it have made any difference if they had? What information was contained in those lost doorknocks? Would the RAAF records have yielded decisive clues? And the pubic hair; if the testing protocols had been applied correctly, would a DNA match have been found?

Faye never questioned the police, never demanded answers. They treated her gently, kindly, included her in everything they did. They never gave up fighting to find Deidre's killer. Cameron Herpich warned her on the first day of the perjury trial that, if she ever asked a question, to be sure she wanted to hear the answer because he would only ever tell her the truth. And, when the jury returned a guilty verdict, he thanked her for allowing him to turn her world upside down. But still, there were so many unanswered questions, things the family had been shielded from. The police had shouldered her burdens, become her saviours. It would be 29 years before Faye could summon the courage to finally ask details of what had happened to her baby.

She wished she hadn't asked.

When doubts niggle, which they frequently do, her instinct is to offer clemency. It was a long time ago. Things were done differently in those days. They didn't know then, what they know now.

She thinks about the day John Reynolds told her police were re-opening the investigation, and the call from Cameron Herpich that followed years later. Knowing what she knows now – that her marriage would end, the ongoing trauma her family would suffer, the obsession that people would bring to the case and their final, futile outcomes – she knows exactly what she would have done.

Under no circumstances would she have answered those calls.

Plagued with insomnia, Faye often wakes at night, padding quietly into the room where she keeps Deidre's special belongings, and the soft pink chest that holds her ashes. Sitting on the edge of the bed in the darkness, talking tenderly to her daughter.

Happy birthday, darling. You would be 36 today.

It's Christmas Day, bubby. I wish you were here with us.

And the anniversary of that terrible, bleak morning when Stephanie had roused her. 'Mummy, wake up! Dee Dee is not in her bed.'

Sitting in the darkness, sobbing.

She is driven to keep fighting. 'When my mind casts back to my last memories of Deidre, I know why I continue to do this. For a stranger to come into my home, where he wasn't supposed to be, take my child that wasn't his to take and do the things he did, is truly evil. If the double jeopardy laws are changed, they will always be known in my heart as Deidre's Law.

Faye now has a partner, a gentle, caring man whom she adores, someone she can talk to and cry without shame. Love, she says, has helped her restore some balance in her life. In 2004 she made the decision, finally, to leave Ipswich and move in with him. They will marry one day, but not yet.

Faye drives out of her street, glancing through the rear-view mirror at the council sign erected on the corner. 'We love our children. Please drive carefully.'

It has taken years to decide to leave Ipswich, to sell the home she fought so hard to keep. She closes the front door for the last time, stifles her urge to cry. She will drive out the long way, as she has always done, avoiding Limestone Park.

No matter where Faye goes, her daughter's memory is with her.

'Deidre was too little to form sentences, but, if she was awake, she would have been crying. She was so shy, so very scared of strangers. This monster had no compunction about what he did. If he had a conscience, surely it would have kicked in, either at the time or in the years following. I know my little girl would have cried. Couldn't he hear her?'

Couldn't he hear her?

of that evidence into simple language was invaluable. For this

Acknowledgments

Thanks are due to the many people who were wonderfully generous with their time and knowledge and who trusted I would do this story justice.

In Queensland: warmest thanks to Faye Kennedy, Barry Kennedy, their daughter, Stephanie, and son, Derek, who are at the heart of this story. Former judge Angelo Vasta, QC, for his dignified wisdom and help, and his staff, Rose Mather and Ellise Van Dam. Michael Byrne, QC, for his exceptional support, and his PA, Rhonda Lewis. John Reynolds, who was fabulous with his help and always got back to me when he said he would. Kon and Leona Romaniuk for a poignant interview. Defense lawyer Peter Russo, who gave an insightful and lengthy interview. Barrister Peter Davis for his time and for trusting me with precious appeal books. Barrister Adrian Gundelach for his knowledge and photographs. John Rowley for his memories. John Garner for mapping out this complex story and never losing patience with me in trying to understand it. Alex Forrest for his painstaking deconstruction of difficult scientific concepts. Criminologist Dr Paul Wilson for his insights into criminal behaviour. Former policeman-turned-lawyer Gordon Harris for sharing his overall knowledge of Queensland and its politics. Thanks to the Carroll family for allowing me the first interview they have ever given, the staff at Brisbane's State Reporting Bureau – Scott Braidwood, Ben Russo and Ian McEwan for their help with transcripts and Florence and Jimmy Lee for accommodation in Brisbane.

In Hobart, special thanks to forensic odontologist Dr Paul Taylor who spent weeks of his own time checking that the dental evidence in the book is correct. David Peberdy, whose translation of that evidence into simple language was invaluable. Dr Maree Wilson, who gave evidence at the perjury committal and entrusted me with transcripts. Forensic psychiatrist Dr Saxby Pridmore, who threw light on the darkness of human behaviour and helped me understand the psychopathic mind. Dr David Basser, for his kindness.

In Adelaide, Dr Kenneth Brown for his help in explaining the wonders of forensic odontology. Carmel Vowles, Daniel Vowles and Leonie and Mitch Williams, who opened their home for me to share for two months during the final edit. And the crew at SAS 7 for their fantastic support in allowing me to juggle the manuscript in tandem with a television project.

Thanks also to Janette Hughes, Ipswich Library and Ben Bartl, researcher at the Tasmanian Law Reform Institute, for helping me make sense of double jeopardy laws, Joseph Bondin for his continual battle with my jinxed computer and my brother, Wayne Marshall, for his terrific help checking the final manuscript.

Copyright of court transcripts belongs to the State of Queensland and the material is reproduced with permission.

Thanks to the many journalists who have gone before me, whose brains I have picked whilst researching this story. Particular thanks to David Nason, former Queensland Bureau Chief at the *Australian* newspaper who, ironically, gave me my start in journalism in Darwin in 1986. Also to Jamie Walker, Paula Donaman, Peter Hansen and the *Australian's* editor-in-chief, Chris Mitchell.

Huge thanks to the team at Random House publishing who nursed this story through to publication. Executive publisher, Jane Palfreyman, who backed my idea, again, and whose faith in this project made it possible. Former publishing assistant, Renée Senogles for her unending patience. Associate publisher Meredith Curnow for her buoyant enthusiasm despite some nail-biting setbacks, editor Brandon VanOver for reading and re-reading the manuscript and rights manager, Nerrilee Weir. Thanks also to freelance editor Jo Butler, who didn't miss a trick and lawyer Richard Potter, a font of legal wisdom.

Faye Kennedy requested that I thank, on her family's behalf, MP Peter Dutton who keeps snapping at the heels of the Queensland government to change the double jeopardy laws; the Queensland Police Service; the RAAF; the University of Queensland and the John Tonge Centre, who have all, over the years, played an enormous part in this story. Barry Kennedy wishes to pay particular thanks to 3AD section at RAAF, Amberley, for their help.

For their unwavering support through good times and bad, my wonderful friends: Traceelea and David Peberdy, Jenny Robinson, Joanna Thyer, Glen Pears, Heather and Geoff Hocking, Kate Hansford, Mick Titley, Kevin Hunt. Thanks also to my family; Ralph Richardson Esq. for the crime books he gave me; Margaret Hawkins and Deb Martin for their awesome help in preparing the book launch and to Eilleen and John Breadon and Lyn Kelly for helping with my daughter when I was interstate researching. To my other friends and colleagues around Australia who helped me through some dark days and believe in me: you know who you are. Thank you.

Finally, special thanks to the two women to whom this book is dedicated. My mother, Monica: a fabulous travelling companion and an invaluable help with research in Queensland, who never complained about sore feet, long hours and no pay. And my own precious daughter, Louise, who had a lot to endure through my obsession with this story and for whose life and love I am truly blessed.

Bibliography

Brown, Dr Kenneth. 'New Evidence in the Carroll Case'. Forensic Odontology Consultant, The University of Adelaide

Diagnostic and Statistical Manual of Mental Disorders, (DSM IV) ed. 4, American Psychiatric Association, Washington, 1994

Gundelach, Adrian. 'Lawyer's Reasoning and Scientific Proof: A Cautionary Tale in Forensic Odontology', *Journal of Forensic Odonto-Stomatology*, Vol. 7, No. 2, December 1989

The Hon Justice Michael Kirby. 'Carroll, Double Jeopardy and International Human Rights Law', *Australian Law Reports*, 27 Crim LJ 231, Law Book Co., 2003

Nordby, J.J. 'Can We Believe What We See, If We See What We Believe? Expert Disagreement', *Journal Forensic Sciences*, JFSCA, Vol. 37, No. 4, July 1992

Queensland Parliament, Extracts from *Hansard*, Speech of the Honourable Mr Justice Vasta, 7 June 1989

ABC: 'Australian Story', *Double Bind*, 7/4/2003

Legal Transcripts
Queen v Raymond John Carroll, 1985

Court of Criminal Appeal, Supreme Court, Queensland, 27 November 1985

Indictment No. 662 of 1999 Q v Raymond John Carroll, Brisbane

Court of Appeal, Supreme Court, Queensland, CA No. 330 OF 2000 and CA No. 315 of 2000, Appellant's Outline of Argument – Conviction Appeal

High Court of Australia, No. B82 of 2001, Application for special leave to appeal

The Queen v Carroll [2002] High Court of Australia 55